SPECIAL EDUCATION'S FAILED SYSTEM

A Question of Eligibility

cs

JOEL MACHT

BERGIN & GARVEY
Westport, Connecticut • London

Library of Congress Cataloging-in-Publication Data

Macht, Joel, 1938–
    Special education's failed system : a question of eligibility /
Joel Macht.
        p.   cm.
    Includes bibliographical references and index.
    ISBN 0–89789–589–4 (alk. paper)
    1. Handicapped children—Education—United States—Evaluation.
    2. Handicapped children—Education—Ability testing—United States.
    3. Special education—United States—Finance.   4. Federal aid to
    education—United States.   I. Title.
    LC4031.M22   1998
    371.9—dc21   98–9535

British Library Cataloguing in Publication Data is available.

Library of Congress Catalog Card Number: 98–9535
ISBN: 0–89789–589–4

First published in 1998

Bergin & Garvey, 88 Post Road West, Westport, CT 06881
An imprint of Greenwood Publishing Group, Inc.

Printed in the United States of America

The paper used in this book complies with the
Permanent Paper Standard issued by the National
Information Standards Organization (Z39.48–1984).

10 9 8 7 6 5 4 3 2 1

For Suz, my kids, and Norton, Ralph, and Spoofers

Contents

x   Contents

Acknowledgments

Many thanks to my friends and colleagues at the University of Denver; at TUSD and Rosemont Service Center; and particularly to the staff, parents, and children at SEMBCS. Thanks to the children at the Valley for teaching me so much. Great appreciation to Cyndi Casey and to Chester Stacy. Additional thanks to Jane Garry, Nadia Blahut, and Julie Cullen, to Susan Henderson who had the courage to try, and to my Susan who puts up with me when I fall in love with my projects.

1

Special Education Eligibility: Introductory Problems

This book takes the easy stance that all children are exceptional, special, and re-markably unique. It acknowledges that some youngsters are clearly more excep-tional than others, a fact made abundantly clear after a visit to a school, zoo, restaurant, or shopping mall. It affirms that some exceptional children will re-quire more professional support than others to experience scholastic success in school. It advises that the eligibility system used by our public schools to pro-vide these exceptional children with classroom support is very time consuming and expensive. It shares the worry that, given the present and stubbornly persis-tent growth in the number of children identified for special education, there won't be enough money or general resources available to assist all schoolchildren in need of help. It believes there is an immediate need to review the present con-cept of school-based disabilities and the assessment methods used to validate their presence. It argues that, once scrutinized, special education's eligibility system will be seen as thoroughly ineffective, no longer serving children who are struggling with their schoolwork. It offers a solution to special education's flawed eligibility system that effectively will provide educational assistance to all schoolchildren who would benefit by it.

ELIGIBILITY LEADS TO ASSISTANCE, ANSWERS, AND DOLLARS

The federal government's and the public schools' view of exceptionality is not as simple or generous as mine. Both institutions require proof, no matter how elusive, that exceptionality exists before it can be awarded. Students and parents must proceed through a complex and often frustrating eligibility maze before exceptionality is affirmed or denied by school personnel. Because federal standards governing eligibility are open to interpretation, and a school's recognition or denial of eligibility can be disputed, school hearings and staffings can become unpleasantly adversarial. Why do parents put themselves (and their children) through such an ordeal? Through word of mouth or direct experience, parents have learned that if they want to obtain additional school-related assistance for their children, they most often must suffer the eligibility process.

Assistance without Guarantees

A school system's official recognition of a student's exceptionality results in several outcomes. Most noticeably, the award brings new professional people into contact with the student. A change of teachers, a tutor, or a full-time aide might be provided once a child has been designated exceptional. Perhaps the youngster will moved into a new classroom with decidedly new assignments. Almost certainly the youngster will experience new classmates. An alternate schedule of school-related activities is a possibility, as are different books or electronic communication devices. Some exceptional children are sent to new schools, with extremes ranging from a segregated, barbed-wired enclosed school for "disturbed" students to a stimulating, ivy-clad college with few or no containments. The appointed adults, locations, classmates and equipment are intended to help the student succeed in school. Intentions aside, a student designated as exceptional and eligible for special education enhancement might not benefit from any of the newly provided assistance.

Answers without Information

Identification of exceptionality is nearly always accompanied by a special label or name such as "learning disability." For many parents and general educators, labels appear to clarify why a child's actions are different. A label becomes an answer, one capable of either easing or increasing anxiety. The resignation, "At least I know why," may provide momentary comfort to the distraught and confused mom or dad whose child is experiencing so many problems. Unfortunately, the label assigned to the child and passed on to the parent may be counterfeit. It may not answer anything correctly. It may provide no usable information. It may cloak the true reason why the youngster is struggling with his schoolwork and himself.

Dollars without Integrity

Once a student meets federal eligibility criteria and is labeled exceptional, the U.S. government occasionally forwards money to the student's parents. In 1993, for example, a 13-year-old student met eligibility requirements for an exceptionality referred to as "attention deficit disorder." Shortly afterwards, the boy's mother began receiving monthly federal checks for $458. She also received a retroactive check for $23,000 from the federal treasury because her son's apparent disability had gone unrecognized by his school; the government reasoned the boy had been denied earlier professional services due him. Another parent received a $458 check for each of her seven children, ages 13 to 22, all of whom were deemed officially exceptional because they "lagged behind in school [and] scored poorly on psychological tests," and failed to demonstrate "age-appropriate behavior."[1] Collectively, the youngsters (and their mother) received more than $38,000 yearly from the federal government.

Most probably, the government's intent decades ago was to assist financially only those schoolchildren who were severely, and multiply disabled. The money that Congress set aside was to help parents defray the costs of their exceptional youngsters' extensive or unusual therapeutic needs. Unfortunately, the yardstick used to measure exceptionality has changed over the past 30 years. Monthly mailings of federal dollars presently find their way to parents whose children fail to exhibit anything remotely resembling severe, multiple disabilities. The federal carrot simply is too tantalizing for some folks to play straight. The 13-year-old boy's mother, for example, used the money "for...summer camp, karate lessons, computer, fish tank, stereo and television—and a 5-year-old family car for [the boy's] transportation."[2] The system that provides the alluring carrot to the parent, as much as the parent who takes unfair advantage of it, is at fault.

ELIGIBILITY: A CAPRICIOUS DETERMINATION

The eligibility process used by schools to determine exceptionality and to finance special education assistance is inconsistent and often inaccurate. Some children, who are said by school personnel to be significantly exceptional, quite frankly aren't. Other youngsters, who are said not to be exceptional, are. As a result, some children are placed in special education programs unnecessarily, while others are wrongly denied placement. Standards used to make judgments regarding exceptionality differ considerably from state to state,[3] accounting for some of the confusion experienced by parents and decision errors made by educational staffs. Merely taking a child across state lines can impact the child's chances of being labeled exceptional. Worse still, standards differ widely within each state.[4] Enrolling a child in a school district whose boundary begins across the street can dramatically influence the chances that the child will be labeled exceptional. If that weren't enough, let me share a piece of information that's not much of a secret. The aforementioned absence of uniformity occurs not just between districts, but between schools in the very same district. Further, this inconsistency can take place within the same school: Two teachers or school psychologists can interpret observations differently and influence any number of decisions made by a school's eligibility team. Finally, special education eligibility may be granted or denied not because of any particular trait or difficulty associated with the child, but because a school district's current pocketbook is flush:

> [T]he subjective nature of the definitions and criteria used in deciding eligibility make classification an arbitrary process. The particular criteria used by any one school district are a function of what school personnel believe

and of how much money society is willing to pay for the education of handicapped students. When there is plenty of money available, school personnel tend to use relatively lenient criteria, criteria by which many students are eligible for service. When funds get tight, school personnel use more rigid criteria.[5]

LEGAL ACTION

Not surprisingly, some parents seeking assistance have taken issue with the outcome of their child's eligibility hearing. This evaluation process does not engender much confidence in parents who are aware of its whimsies. The unsuspecting or inexperienced parent usually learns the ropes after the first round of psycho-educational evaluations and eligibility meetings. Given our present propensity toward suing anything that breathes, the results are predictable.

Suits filed to obtain special education have been brought primarily by parents whose children are unquestionably disabled and are being denied any education at all or being given very meager special services. The parents who file these suits believe that the advantages of their child's identification for special education services clearly outweigh the disadvantages. Suits filed to avoid special education have been brought primarily by parents of students who have mild or questionable disabilities and who are already attending school. These parents believe that their children are being stigmatized and discriminated against rather than helped by special education.[6]

The professional literature is filled with instances in which parents, schools, and courts have battled over wide-ranging quarrels centering around who is officially and legitimately exceptional, who should receive special education services, what services will be needed, where the services will be provided, and lastly, who will and who will not pay for the services rendered. As of this writing, a local school system's special education department is embroiled in a dispute as to where a particularly child should receive special education services. The school contends the child is doing well within the public school's educational program. The child's mother and her lawyer see things differently. The legal cost to the school district of the many irritatingly extended meetings is more than $60,000 (and climbing) and none of the participants has yet to set foot inside a courtroom!

FEDERAL GOVERNMENT'S INVOLVEMENT

Hotly contested is the question of whether the federal government should continue to be involved in the "eligibility for exceptionality" debate. In 1975, the federal government, with guidance from an assemblage of respected experts, denoted ten exceptionality categories encompassing a wide range of school-related academic, social, and physical difficulties. Those ten categories were described as:

Learning disabled

Mentally retarded

Hard of hearing and deaf

Orthopedically impaired

Visually handicapped

Speech impaired

Emotionally disturbed

Multiply handicapped

Other health impaired

Deaf-blind

Fifteen years later during the 101st Congress, the federal government added two new categories to the previous list of eligible exceptionalities: traumatic brain injury and autism. As a direct result of combined efforts from governmental agencies, parent advocacy groups, clinicians, and academicians, many exceptional children have received much-needed assistance through our public schools. Understandably, government personnel are proud of their accomplishments. Madeline Will, former U.S. assistant secretary of Special Education, commented:

> The past decade has produced results for students with disabilities that were considered unobtainable and unthinkable only a few years earlier. Little more than a decade ago [early to mid-1970s], many children were left completely out of the nation's school systems. When Congress passed legislation creating an entitlement to education [Public Law 94-142], severely and multiply handicapped children entered the schools across the nation....The passage of this legislation ushered in the most creative period in the history of special education.[7]

Progress Seen Differently

Not everyone, of course, sees progress in the same light. While government personnel have judged much of their involvement in special education positively, others have expressed a different view. Notice the language of the following excerpt, opinioned by Eileen Gardner, policy analyst at The Heritage Foundation:

During the past two decades, control of education has been centralized in Washington, D.C., where unelected and unaccountable special interest groups have skillfully maneuvered Congress into creating for them federal programs from which stunningly successful lobby efforts have been launched....Laws for the education of the handicapped...have drained resources from the normal school population, probably weakened the quality of teaching, and falsely labeled normal children. In a misguided effort to help a few, the many have been injured. Yet, the handicapped constituency displays a strange lack of concern for the effect of their regulations upon the welfare of the general population—the very population upon whom the well-being of these children ultimately depends.[8]

Ms. Gardner's criticisms are accurate across the board. Evidence will support that education's resources are being drained, general education's teaching quality has weakened, and children by the thousands have been falsely labeled. Her laying blame on "stunningly successful lobby efforts" would appear to have merit as well. A step back, however, might suggest that those denigrated lobbying efforts referred to by Ms. Gardner were a function of a preceding set of variables that will gain our attention shortly. One deserves quick mention now.

The vast majority of multiply disabled children during the early 1970s were consigned to residential institutions, basements of churches, and living rooms of private homes. Public school buildings, their rooms colored with promise, were mostly inaccessible to these exceptional youngsters. Many of us working directly with these children believed that had various parent support groups and their legal council not coerced the federal government into action, schools throughout the country would never have opened their doors to most school-aged, multiply handicapped children. These lobbyists (mostly parents) produced the keys to those doors, and a fair, fighting chance for their children. Every coin has two sides, and both are often right.

FOCUS: THE NEW SPECIAL EDUCATION STUDENTS

In 1975, arguably more from external pressure than altruism, the federal government established the ten categories of exceptionality to ensure that no exceptional child would be neglected by a public school system receiving federal monies. In part to appease a growing number of child advocacy groups, Congress passed laws mandating that public schools provide all exceptional children with free and appropriate public education. Unfortunately, several of the categories of exceptionality were developed without the benefit of clear definitions or guidelines. Errors made by trained professionals while judging which children warranted being labeled exceptional were therefore inevitable. This was particularly the case with a new group of very capable schoolchildren, which school psychologists and special education teachers unexpectedly were asked to serve. These newly designated exceptional children were quite different from those youngsters previously supported by most special education personnel. Identifying the new children's disabilities was nearly impossible. In fact, the public schools' suggestions that the children were disabled to any degree was confusing to many of us who received them.

Today, some 30 years after the passage of Public Law 94-142, public school officials continue to identify and mark busloads of children sufficiently disabled to require a special education beyond what is offered in the regular classroom. Where once their numbers were small, they now are about to topple the flawed system that is producing them. At fault is special education's eligibility system.

NOTES

1. "America's Most Wanted Welfare plan," (1995, January 22-25). *Baltimore Sun*, p. 1-10.

2. "America's Most Wanted Welfare Plan."

3. Mercer, C. D., Forgnone, C., & Wolking, W. D. (1976). Definitions of learning disabilities used in the United States. *Journal of Learning Disabilities, 9*, 376-386.

4. Ysseldyke, J. E., Algozzine, B., & Thurlow, M. L. (1992). *Critical issues in special education.* Boston: Houghton Mifflin Company.

5. Ysseldyke, J. E. & Algozzine, B. (1990). *Introduction to special education.* Boston: Houghton Mifflin Company.

6. Hallahan, D. P. & Kauffman, J. M. (1994). *Exceptional children: Introduction to special education.* Needham, Mass.: Allyn and Bacon, p. 34.

7. Will, M. (1984). Let us pause and reflect—but not too long. *Exceptional Children, 51*, 11-16.

8. Gardner, E. (1984). The federal role in education. *Backgrounder.* Washington, DC: The Heritage Foundation.

2

Changing Faces:
The New Children

The rivulet of new "exceptional" children, its first trickle appearing during the late fall of 1974, was seen but hardly noticed. The handful of children appearing at the door of our exclusively special education school were certainly different from the children already enrolled, but it was precisely those differences that gave us no cause to do more than offer the newcomers a friendly glance and smile. We did wonder why the local public schools had sent us these children. Their academic skills and physical strengths, real and relative, were spectacular. They walked and talked, smiled and laughed. They could read, write, and solve math problems. If asked, they could stand comfortably in front of a small gathering of peers and adults, and with voices clear and unhalting, tell a lucid story or crack a youthful joke. These new children owned no surgically implanted narrow snake-like tubes visibly protruding from under their thin stretched skin, which drained excessive cerebral fluid from their skulls and emptied it harmlessly into their stomachs. They didn't cry out sharply as though overcome by searing pain, didn't isolate themselves in a corner of a darkened room while hunched in a fetal ball, afraid of every sight and sound, didn't attack a teacher or unsuspecting neighbor with flailing arms, never with an intent to hurt, but only to communicate that an infection was ravaging a middle ear. They didn't, without warning, fall harshly to the hard tiled floor and wriggle violently in reaction to the sudden surge of electrical energy charging through an anomalous brain.

The new children, on the contrary, had good control over their minds and bodies. Playing softball or flying a kite offered barely a challenge. A walk across the school's play area occurred without incident. A conversation in the hallway was more than possible, it was successful. The children rode the bus home after school to take walks, ride bikes, go to movies, or play with friends under a tree. They seemed a fairly happy bunch of nice kids with many skills. They were indeed different from their new schoolmates.

SPECIAL EDUCATION SCHOOL

These designated exceptional youngsters from the public schools, in the beginning less than a dozen or so, presented no problems. When alerted to their coming, our school's administration simply hired a new teacher and aide to assist the children. An unused classroom in the single-story, aging building was identified and quickly renovated with a fresh coat of paint to the walls and a thin layer of wax to the floor. Ours was a "cooperative school," established by surrounding school districts to provide the best services possible to a relatively small, but select group of severely involved, multiply handicapped youngsters. We did not choose which students came to our school; that decision was made by the school districts and their respective special education directors. Initially, we served the most exceptional children officially enrolled within several school districts located throughout the central and eastern parts of the metropolitan area. Now, for reasons that escaped us, the school districts had decided to ferry *capable* children from their regular classrooms and bus them an extended distance to our facility. It seemed not to matter to school officials that these new children, by most any reasonable barometer, were fine.

Developing Programs for Exceptional Children

We rarely had a problem satisfying a district's or special education director's request to provide a unique program for any youngster who was sent to our special facility, particularly a youngster who was severely, and multiply involved. In the early 1970's, we had buckets of money. (Using a formula and process understood by only a select number of state and local officials, a school district would be reimbursed twice for expenses that accompanied each of their identified exceptional students. The requesting school district paid a portion of our school's services and salaries, then placed the unused portion of their state reimbursement into, presumably, their general school fund or operating budget.) This money allowed us to hire whatever staff we needed. Our staff-to-student ratio made us the envy of most school districts. Before the rivulet of highly able children began to widen, we supported our fifty to sixty multiply handicapped special needs children with a principal, a full-time nurse, a part-time consulting school psychologist from the university, several full-time speech therapists, a full-time physical therapist, a part-time social worker, a slew of teachers, countless volunteers from local organizations, an unending supply of excited graduate students from the university, and continual parental support. Most of our classes contained a maximum of six to eight children. Several classes had as few as three children. Each class had at least one teacher and an aide. A small class of severely language impaired, hearing youngsters was taught by a speech and language pathologist and her aide. Our classrooms were spacious and bright, and the children's playground was grass-covered and dotted with all manner of equipment. We had a polished gym/auditorium that would have served the needs of a good-sized high school.

Because we provided a full range of therapies for our students, district special education directors knew their most challenging children would be well served. We were not bound by any particular educational or psychological theory, current wave, or panacea. We focused and built on each child's strength. Rarely were we interested in how one child compared with any other child. Most of our attention was directed toward each child's individual growth. Our interventions were based on careful assessments that relied more on direct observation than standardized test numbers. All the children mingled comfortably with each other, learned from each other, and benefited from each other.

We were always prepared to develop a new program for a child almost on a moment's notice. I remember a call from one of the more admired local special education directors. "I have this child," he announced, his tone and subsequent sigh suggesting the youngster would require considerable accommodation. "He's 5 years old, nonverbal, and has little interaction with much of anything outside himself; he has severe seizures—unfortunately uncontrolled and quite frequent, and needs lots of medications; his parents are new to the district; they are nice folks; they are hurting and need help. Put something together for the child," he would say, knowing it would happen. Then quickly he would remind us: "Cost is not an issue." In this particular case, a carefully constructed program was made available to the child and his parents within days. That the new child was the only student in the class did not matter. Before too many weeks had passed, word of the available format reached other districts in the metro area. Soon the class was filled with equally unique, multiply involved children from all over the city.

The Death of the Golden Goose

Ironically, it was that same special education director who sounded the death knell a few years later. Shortly after he and I had finished lunch at a local haunt, he leaned close and quietly voiced with discernible disappointment, "The day of the golden goose is gone." There would be no more double reimbursements to school districts from the state, he explained. Because the stream of new children said to be disabled had increased exponentially, dollar demands to serve them had increased to a point where money was becoming scarce. Several of the cooperative districts sharing our special school's expenses had decided to bring all their children back to their neighborhood schools. They argued they could serve the children more effectively at a lower cost at their home schools. Cost, indeed, had become an issue for them.

Each passing month saw more capable schoolchildren identified as special or disabled or disordered or exceptional. More and more children, quite similar to those few who were unexpectedly bused to our special education facility, children who walked and talked, who could read and do math, were said to be sufficiently different from classmates to need special assessing, labeling, and placing in special, isolated classes. The natural student diversity that general education had chosen to disregard for so long was now quite suddenly upon them like a stampeding herd of buffaloes. To deal with children who were performing academically below expectations, school districts developed their own standards for qualifying and placing children into special education programs. In truth, the districts and their educational systems had options other than to move the different children to special classes, including an option so obvious that it required great effort to ignore. But ignore general education did. The numbers of children pronounced exceptional mushroomed.

THE GROWING RIVER OF SPECIAL EDUCATION CHILDREN

The decade of the 1980s began as our cooperative special education school closed. The very special of the districts' special children were assimilated within their home schools. That the children did not receive the level of educational and psychological services previously provided at the special school created barely a stir from school district administrators. Most of the parents who first complained bitterly that their children were receiving little attention in their new classrooms ultimately quieted. Even those school officials whose ears (and hearts) were receptive to the parents' concerns could not stem the gathering momentum. Special education's attention had turned sharply toward its new population: a growing number of children not finding success within the public schools' curriculum, children now labeled exceptional, requiring resources beyond the regular classroom. There were no earthen banks to contain the flow of newly designated "exceptional," disabled children. The river swelled to overflowing.

> In less than a decade, the ailment spread from virtual obscurity to something well beyond epidemic proportions. It has no single name, no universally accepted symptoms, and no discernible anatomical or biochemical characteristics which can be diagnosed in a clinic or laboratory....Before 1965, almost no one had heard of it, but by the beginning of the seventies it was commanding the attention of an armada of pediatricians, neurologists and educational psychologists, and by mid-decade, pedagogical theory, medical speculation, psychological need, drug company promotion and political expediency had been fused with an evangelical fervor to produce what is undoubtedly the most powerful movement in—and beyond—contemporary education.[1]

FOCUS: THE RIVER IS OUT OF CONTROL

As it widened its path and churned its fury, the river seized all kinds of resources, dollars, certainly, but considerably more. Personnel, classrooms, and supplies had to be diverted to meet the demands created by the ever-growing numbers of labeled, mildly involved students. It became increasingly apparent that if the trend continued, if more and more children were said to need an educational program different from what regularly trained teachers provided, there would not be adequate resources for children requiring very special accommodations or children requiring little more than an exciting, innovative teacher.

Warnings were not heeded. Time, past and present, only produced new exceptionalities, some real and justified, some scarcely believable.

As the 20th century comes to its close, the river is out of control.

NOTE

1. Schrag, P. & Divoky, D. (1975). *The myth of the hyperactive child and other means of child control.* New York: Dell Publishing Company.

3

Judging Exceptionality

The recently arrived, newly designated "exceptional" children were an enigma to all of us who worked at the self-contained special education school. Their respective public school district administrators shared only that the new youngsters were reading below grade level, that their math skills were delayed, and that their writing was immature and limited. We were told by the public school administrators that the children certainly were bright, but that in light of their measured intelligence, their classroom work was less than their teachers (and perhaps their parents) expected. Although we were informed the new children were handicapped,[1] we were advised by school officials that the children's handicap, and its physiological cause, could not be seen directly. The schools' information did not help us understand why some administrators believed that our isolated special education facility, rather than their own public schools' classrooms, was better suited to provide the youngsters with what they needed to help them improve their academic skills.

Within days of their arrival, the new students met many of our school's very special children. A few of the new students were fascinated by our small population of blind, multiply handicapped preschoolers, a couple of whom, roughly 4 years of age, had recently started to walk (stumble forward would perhaps be more accurate). None of our toddlers were toilet trained, all had to be fed by staff, and most had verbal communications skills amounting to little more than quiet hoots and two-note songs. As the consulting school psychologist, I occasionally stowed away on the floor of the deaf-blind classroom, off to one of the brightly decorated corners, watching the new students as they hovered close to their recently adopted younger classmates. I was not surprised by what I observed: The children's different skill levels were painfully obvious. The term "handicapped," no matter how it could be interpreted, did *not* fit the new, very able children sent to us from the public schools.

DIFFERENT PERSPECTIVES

The bulging public school reports accompanying the new students contained endless pages describing their academic and behavioral problems. Invariably, a sophomoric summary would suggest what the new arrivals couldn't do and might *never* do. The tone cast by the bleak reports contrasted sharply with our orientation toward the multiply handicapped children at our facility. We had long since discovered that knowing what a child was presently not doing was of doubtful worth. A session or two with a deaf and blind, nonambulatory youngster, who didn't read or write or recognize a single number, was sufficient to teach us to search for what a youngster had mastered. The public school officials who had written their deficit-describing summaries had yet to learn that lesson. Each report came thicker and heavier than the previous one, documenting all that was perceived deficient with the new children. We wanted some statement of what a child could do, like a warm ray of sunlight streaming through dark, icy clouds. Rarely was the light discernible.

In fact, the public school officials seemed intent on building the strongest case possible for removing a youngster from his or her home (public) school. Frequently the officials suggested that a child's future would be compromised, literally endangered, unless a new, out-of-class placement was found. The pictures painted by school personnel to fortify their recommendations seemed purposely desperate and brushed with such pointless phrases as "the child has minimal brain damaged" or "he suffers from diffuse organicity." Our staff would read the narratives and vague references to brain injury, then glance toward our very special kids as they struggled to balance on two frail legs or walk a wide hallway without seizuring. The proposition that the newly arrived kids had suffered brain damage that was now responsible for their poor classroom achievements seemed stretched.

The public school's stance was confusing. Its officials seemed unalterably bent on convincing themselves that their dissimilar school children were somehow handicapped. We concluded the officials had found themselves under pressure to explain and accommodate an unexpected increase in the diversity of their student populations. The school officials, apparently, chose to explain the increased student diversity by judging that something was wrong with the children who were different from some heralded statistical norm. This seemed convenient, if nothing else. Nevertheless, resigned to the school districts' tagging highly capable children "disabled," we welcomed the youngsters and did what we thought their home schools might have done: We identified the students' academic strengths and weaknesses and then found capable teachers to teach them.

STARTLING COSTS

In the beginning, the numbers of children exhibiting problems with their public school assignments who were judged officially disabled or exceptional were relatively few. Because of state funding formulas, public schools could quite easily absorb the extra dollars needed to pay for whatever additional services were recommended for the children. No one suffered from those costs. Who could have known that the required expenditures would increase from a relatively paltry $250 million in 1977 to well over $2 billion less than 2 decades later.[2]

EXPERIENCES IMPACT PERCEPTIONS AND STRATEGIES

Our staff's views toward exceptionality differed from those held by school officials primarily because of differences in our experiences and training. Most of us had cut our teeth on very complex, multiply handicapped children, often working with them for hours, daily in isolated institutional, residential, or clinical settings. Only rarely had the public school administrators been more than introduced to such children. Certainly they were never expected or required to develop tight, replicable intervention programs for such demanding, multiply involved children. Their graduate studies simply did not include those experiences or requirements.

The Desert Children: Master Teachers

Had the public school personnel worked with children similar to those living at the Arizona desert institution that was my graduate school laboratory for nearly 3 years, their judgments and attitudes surrounding the concept of disability would have been very different. Perhaps problems related to a child's struggle with reading, writing, or mathematics might not have seemed so grave, warranting something as dramatic as tearing a child from his or her classroom, busing the youngster to a faraway out-of-school placement. But the public school officials who were sending us their able children hadn't been taught by those very special desert youngsters who had been my mentors. Little wonder that the public school officials' perspective on what constitutes a handicap or disability was so narrow.

The Lessons

Time: 1966 to 1969
Location: Phoenix, Arizona
Facility: State Residential Institution

Some of the kids living at the residential facility were confined to stabilizing wheelchairs. A few could move little more than their eyes as they watched the stirrings of others. Some were born deaf or had become so from the continued pounding of their ears by their own violent hands. Others were blind. Some were burdened by skulls too large or too small. Others were ravaged by ruinous genetic or metabolic anomalies yet to be discovered or named. Some, for personal safety, required constant restraint, by having their hands shackled or their heads covered by protective helmets. Others were given free reign to wander be-cause they would rarely move but a few feet from where they were once placed. Some gave no indication they knew where they were or who they were. Some were so physically self-abusive that invasive psychosurgery and electric shock joined the list of other treatment considerations. Some, without warning or eas-ily determined reason, would dart toward sharp corners of a table or metal bed and flail their heads against the objects' cutting edge. Having done so, with fore-heads reddened, swollen, and profusely bleeding, they would turn their attention to benign activities as if their personal confrontation with the sharp objects had never occurred. All of the children had been seen and evaluated by the institu-tion's physician and nurses. Medical science at the time offered little assistance.

K was my first teacher. I was a brand new doctoral student and she seemed to know it. She was nearly 7 years old when we met. She was a mosaic[3] Down syndrome child with small recessed eyes and the longest tongue I had ever seen. She was a veritable string bean: height—normal; weight—soaking wet, maybe 25 pounds. She squealed when happy. Squealing and crying were her only vocalizations. The nerve-jarring sound of her teeth grinding was constant, but her flattened teeth were the least of her problems. She had congenital, bilateral cataracts that had been removed surgically years earlier. A pulmonary aortic window was discovered and left unrepaired. She was nonambulatory, nonverbal, wore diapers, and was fed only pureed food. Along with perhaps a dozen or so other children, she was confined to a small antiseptic-smelling building where she sat or slept all day and night in a crib suited for a child half her size. While awake, sitting with legs crossed, she would place the thumb of her right hand deep into her mouth and forcibly push the tip of her right forefinger against the lower lid of her right eye. I would discover that K's eye-poking served an important purpose for her. It modified her visual field, providing a moment of internal optic stimulation. For much of K's isolated day, those self-initiated internal flashes of light were her only stimulation. Unfortunately, K's habituated eye-pressing had compromised what limited vision she possessed. K had been prescribed thick, heavy glasses to assist her in visually discriminating her environment. She refused to wear the uncomfortable devices, throwing them to the ground whenever they were placed in front of her eyes. Her par-ents had purchased straps for the frames, allowing the glasses to hang against her gaunt chest. Most often, the institutional aides who cared for her in her cottage kept the glasses and their straps safely hidden in a drawer. I was assigned to teach her to wear her glasses. I was told she would become permanently blind if she failed to wear them throughout her waking day. She was a great hugger and teacher.

N lived at the institution under the supervision of a houseparent with eight other girls, all roughly 10 to 12 years of age. She was a chunky, sturdy youngster who wore an eye-catching smile as she lumbered through her wak-ing day. She had great difficulty remembering much beyond a few colors and alphabet letters. An unexpected, and relatively serious, problem had emerged. Several of N's house-mates had begun physically assaulting her because she continually used their toothbrushes and hairbrushes. Under the supervision of a graduate student, the housemother showed N how to recognize her own toiletries. The task of remembering her own name was very difficult for the young girl.

B was 10 years old, deaf, blind, nonverbal, and diapered. He slept with arms and legs restrained in a framed crib. The knuckles on his right hand were smooth: The bony protuberances had been leveled flat by years of his small fist smashing against the side of his skull. A genius graduate student, now a university professor in the state of Florida, provided the child alternatives to his self-destruction.

Three children resided in the same cottage as K. Two were 4-year-olds, both Down syndrome children, the third was 5 years old, with an unknown etiology. All were bright-eyed and seemingly flush with capabilities. Only on rare occasions did they feel the warmth from the sun. Their cottage was supervised by two poorly paid and inadequately trained attendants. All the children were dynamos, and the poorly trained attendants were ill-prepared to meet even their simplest needs. The three children were particularly active. Although not walking, the children required only moments to scoot happily the length and width of the cottage, often entangling themselves in bedsheets and broomsticks. To make their own lives easier, the attendants tied ropes around the waists of the three youngsters, securing the ropes' opposite ends to a center supporting column inside the building. The tethering provided the children with some 4 feet within which to maneuver, affording the attendants more time to do nothing. When graduate students confronted them about their restraining of the children, the attendants weakly offered that the children couldn't walk anyway because they were retarded. When asked if they thought being tied to a pole might impede the children's ability to walk, the attendants answered no. Graduate students taught the children to walk within months. The attendants were upset by the children's progress.

C would lead a dozen or more professional people on a roller coaster ride that would first take them to the peak of joy and celebration, then drag them mercilessly through the deepest despair. Only a handful of people knew her when she was free of her shackles. I first saw her when she was barely 4 years old. She had already fractured her own skull with her small fists. The noticeable line of dead tissue that ran from the center-most follicle of blonde hair to the bridge of her small nose testified to the strength of those fists. I watched her progress from being strapped spread-eagle to her cottage bed, from wearing a faded straitjacket that kept her from damaging herself, from wearing a football helmet covered with chicken wire so her hands could not damage her face, to laughing and skipping to sleeping unrestrained at a new friend's house to exploring the joys of a supermarket, and to experiencing the pleasures of a fast-food joint, and tasting a marvelously greasy hamburger. I watched two psychologists give her life.

There were countless other children, most of them laughing with pure glee at the slightest change in their immediate environment. The presence of a familiar face or the sound of a welcomed voice produced waving arms and smiles that threatened to spread full circle. The outdoor playground was a kaleidoscope of carefree children, some running, some hobbling, some dragging themselves toward seesaws and modified merry-go-rounds. It didn't mattered that many of the children had never spoken and that, despite years of schooling, some recognized only a few letters of their names or that many required assistance with feeding and toileting or that some had not seen a mother or father in years or that some had never seen their mother or father. Their enormous spirit and determined drive to drain the small cup life had offered was astounding.

The Direction for Intervention

All the residential children had suffered loathsome congenital or adventitious physiological insults seriously impacting their abilities. These traumas never harassed only reading or handwriting. They would assault half a body or an entire brain. Little about them was ever hidden. These anomalies, however, no matter how extreme, did not adversely affect our attitude or focus as we assisted the youngsters. We were taught to give a mere passing thought to speculations or confirmations of brain damage or other purported physical limitations. To dwell on either was viewed as a poor use of time. Instead, we were disciplined by the children (and our professors) to clearly identify what the children could accomplish and what assets they possessed. We were to direct our energies toward what the children were doing that was facilitating or impeding their growth and development. We were continuously to ask ourselves what would help the children to become more independent and accomplished. We were to search for what we could do to better assist the children. We were to hold ourselves accountable for their progress.

We were advised to see each child as an individual, to respect individual differences, to be less concerned with how one child compared with another, and to be more concerned with how the child compared with his or her own earlier skill levels. We were taught to be patient and relish each accomplishment a child made, no matter what its size, or the time it took to achieve. The concepts of handicap and disability were unnecessary.

We never failed. Success was defined as being better today than yesterday, regardless of the task or assignment. Each of the children succeeded: Each child gained in skill acquisition, self-assurance, knowledge, and confidence. In these respects, we all succeeded.

The lessons the children taught us were invaluable and indelibly etched. They were tools as important as those carried by a physician in a handbag. They would always be at our fingertips.

1. Find out what each child can do

2. Build upon each child's strengths

3. Be problem-directed, solution-oriented

4. Monitor the effectiveness of strategies

5. Be responsible and accountable

6.   Focus on the children

7.   Protect the children's integrity

Exceptional Like All Children

Judging whether the children at the desert institution were exceptional was an irrelevant exercise for us. Like all children, they were exceptional. Our determinations required nothing beyond directly observing the children's struggles, regardless of their severity. Our eyes and ears would tell us if a particular child needed assistance. Helping that child learn to walk was approached with the same zeal as helping him learn to tie his shoelaces or recognize a name or read a word. We were taught to focus on the child, what he was doing, and what he needed to do next. "Exceptional" was a term for poets and philosophers. It carried no utility for the practitioner who was dedicated toward assisting children to grow physically, emotionally, educationally stronger. All children were exceptional, special, and unique. Surely public school officials understood that. Surely public school officials agreed that if a child was struggling with shoelaces or clarinet playing or learning to read words, the child was to be assisted, immediately, effectively. The desert children taught us that lesson. They would have taught public school officials the same.

THE PUBLIC SCHOOL ARENA

My transition from graduate school training and the desert institution's children to the marvelous special education school in Colorado was a natural progression. The script could not have been better written. The multiply involved children at the special school were equally remarkable, and the desert institution's lessons equally applicable. I was fortunate to have spent so many glorious years there. But that experience, too, would end. After 20 years with Denver's great university and countless hours spent at the special education school, the Arizona desert would once again offer me a new challenge and a new hat to wear. A chance meeting with a prominent Arizona university professor presented an opportunity for me to be part of a public school system responsible for some 55,000 youngsters. The position's responsibilities provided what seemed a perfect arena in which to put into practice the essential attitudes acquired earlier in the same Arizona desert:

1.   Each child was capable in his or her own right.

2.   Each child had assets from which to build.

3.   Each child, distinct from those children in a surrounding group, was able to learn, to succeed, to be better today than yesterday.

Essentials always remain constant.

A Working Laboratory with Great Promise

I had become part of a public school system charged with the responsibility of educating large numbers of young people, a system that had embraced a mission that could not be misinterpreted: "All children can learn; all teachers and administrators are responsible for teaching them." The system's standard seemed to forewarn that if a school employee found fault with any part of its message, employment should be secured elsewhere immediately. No exceptions, no excuses. Children first, the slogan promised.

Expectations of Assistance

Although I had consulted with many school districts over the years, I had stayed far removed from their politics. I always had been asked to help their children and teachers, but never to assist administrative personnel develop districtwide policies or evaluate educational procedures already in place. My interest was with kids and interventions, teachers and what they needed for their students, and parents and what they demanded for their children. In the past, my favorite phone call was from a district special education director announcing a new child and a need for a new program. I'd dash from my university office, anticipating the challenge the new youngster would bring. If, after evaluation, my colleagues and I believed the child would benefit from a special academic or social experience, from a modified piece of adaptive equipment, or from added time with a particularly able teacher or therapist, I'd meet with the district special education director and list what services were needed. The child would receive whatever was essential—that was axiomatic. Refusing a child assistance was not an option. I had come to expect that all children would receive what was necessary for their successful growth and development. The new adventure with the desert public school system began with the belief that nothing had changed.

Initiation

The first days in the school district were spent making new friends, reading through unfamiliar forms and schedules, renewing certifications and credentials, and consuming platters of the best Mexican food in the world. I had been assigned to one of the district's two administrative "service centers." The facilities were responsible for coordinating special education services to the district's students. My role was to visit classrooms to develop programs for students who were experiencing academic and social/behavioral problems. Unlike the other district's psychologists, I was not assigned to any particular school or intervention team. Instead, I was given free reign to visit any school or school-related program within the large district. I was expected to work closely with the numerous special education teams throughout the district's territory. For a practitioner who prized working directly with all sorts of children and their mentors, the job was incomparable, perfect. It was as though I had returned to the desert residential institution.

My first appointment came on my third day with the district. I was asked to observe a self-contained special education classroom, serving some ten boys between 7 and 9 years of age. I was told only that the principal had requested some assistance. I was fresh with excitement. The baptismal ceremony lasted nearly 2 hours. The effect lingered long after.

The Pupils

I sat quietly at a worktable located at the far side of the small room. I had seen similar students, I just hadn't seem so many grouped so closely in quarters more suited for two-thirds their number. I had witnessed similarly contagious and disruptive antics, I just hadn't seen them so frequent or furious for such extended periods. Most of the kids had a violent edge to their movements, an edge easily capable of inflicting pain with a slashing fist or forceful push. They fed off each other as though their actions had been choreographed. If one quieted, another member of the cast would make certain the respite was short-lived. Those youngsters not so overtly volatile sat huddled in their chairs or stood quietly in a corner, avoiding eye and body contact. The jumping, dashing and hurting, the name calling, the loud sardonic laughing, and the undisguised threatening ceased for moments only for want of a few breaths. Nothing that passed before me carried any resemblance to school as I had known it. I saw no group or directed individual instruction, no books opened to information that was to be learned, no sentences written, no problems solved or attempted. What pencils and crayons were within reach of the children were used more for projectiles than for what the manufacturers had intended.

The Teacher

Throughout the bedlam, the slender, pale teacher stood unmoving in the front of the room, remaining close to the chalkboard, her eyes following a particular child or two who dashed by. Occasionally, a verbal warning would cross her lips, but the words went unheard and unheeded. I thought that her stance might be part of a treatment scheme that I had yet to discover. As the minutes passed, I became more convinced that her posture was defensive: It was safer to be on the sidelines of the playing field. The teacher's aide stayed seated and uninvolved in the frenzy. She did not stir until requested by the teacher to corral the children and take them outside for their recess period. The youngsters departed noisily, leaving behind a swath of discordant sounds that hung in the air like a blast from a fire truck's siren. They were not quiet or self-managed as they descended upon the hallway. The other children in the school would know these special kids were on their way outside.

The teacher joined me at the table. She was a very pleasant, articulate woman, perhaps in her 40s, as quiet and moderate as the children were noisy and unruly. Embarrassed by what I had seen, she offered a half smile that quickly gave way to a furtive sigh hinting of exhaustion and discouragement. This was her second year with the children, she shared, her voice a near hush. She was trained as a high school English teacher and had recently relocated to the city. There were no suitable jobs available at any of the district's high schools. She had been advised by personnel that it would be wise to "get a foot in the door" of the district by accepting the position teaching these special kids. After 3 years she would have tenure and more leverage to use with the district to find a position more to her liking, one that would better fit her skills, she was told. I listened attentively. I felt for her. I caught her eyes and promised she would have my undivided assistance for as long as needed. She thanked me just as the youngsters charged into the room. Instinctively, I wanted to take control of the situation, to introduce some structure to the classroom, to tell the children something about respect, both for themselves and others. I knew such a bandaid would have created more problems. I calmed myself, admonished my heart to stop pounding, and walked briskly to my car. "Those kids are dead in the water," I growled to myself. "Why assign a teacher who, while certainly caring, has virtually no experience or skills to work with these difficult youngsters? She's a nice lady and all, but why should the kids get stuck with a teacher who unwittingly makes matters worse? Why would a school district's administration, with knowledge that the teacher's strengths were suited for an entirely different population, assign her to such a classroom? What was the district's payoff? What had happened to the district's commitment to all children?" I wanted some answers. I wasn't used to what I had seen. Back at my new office, I met with my colleagues. Their words were candid, although not appeasing.

No simple answers existed, none at least that completely satisfied anyone. The district was doing what it could, a psychologist told me without much conviction. There were lots of needy children throughout the system, resources were stretched pretty thin, and money was scarce. A few inservices, provided by the district, had been made available to the English teacher (and other district teachers responsible for similar children). Whether the inservices were practical and worthwhile was unknown. There were no larger rooms available for these children. Indeed, the children were fortunate to have the room they presently occupied. Several district principals had prevented the English teacher's children from being placed at their elementary schools. The children were too disruptive, the principals had whined to their supervisors. I was told central administration had not challenged the principals' views or self-serving autonomy. I reacted angrily: "The principals should have been fired!" I was told there would be no more support for this English teacher. Her program, according to the bean counters, was already very expensive. I was told the English teacher would have to make do with what she had. "Did her children have to do likewise?" I snapped. The district's slogan, with all its promises, had tarnished measurably.

Trenches

Weeks were spent with the English teacher and her pupils. She was a very competent and willing student, and her children's self-control and classwork improved measurably. Although the teacher and her students no doubt learned much from each other, they never should have been brought together as an educational unit. The children, already at serious risk for what the noted psychiatrist Thomas Szasz called "problems in everyday living," needed more than a gracious, empathic English teacher to guide them. That the district placed them under the same roof without sufficient training or assistance was not reconcilable. Their association would gnaw at me for many months to come, as would other troubling observations during that first school year, most particularly the fact that so many classrooms lacked the support they needed, leaving both excellent and poor teachers to fend for themselves.

The District's Children

The nature of my position guaranteed that I saw the district's most needy, and often disturbing, students. I witnessed few occasions where education as a system was proceeding as everyone hoped, where all kids were learning quality stuff and enjoying every moment of the experience. Even when summoned to a reputedly high-powered school where the kids were a cut above those living along the shores of "Lake Wobegon," it was not to enjoy a few moments with a finely honed model classroom program. Rather, it was to observe children who were raining havoc on everything within reach, youngsters who were moving themselves to the far edge of the normal curve.

Behavior Problems Not the Major Issue

Classroom disruption by a few rowdies who had not learned the true purpose of school was not the major problem, however. The number of well-behaved children who were asked to accomplished tasks without the benefit of necessary prerequisite skills or experiences was shocking. Many of these kids were measurably behind their class assignments before their assignments began. Equally troubling were the scores of delightful youngsters waiting to be challenged by material beyond what previously they had mastered. While the first group suffered with frustration, their more advanced counterparts lived with boredom. The prediction that some of the youngsters from both groups were the next band of rowdies was not rocket science.

Disheartening, too, were the students who seemed not to care about school in general and learning in particular. They showed little indication of an internal drive to better themselves academically. By all accounts, they had little external support to do so from family or friends. For those students, each passing week wedged more distance between their skills, what their teachers wanted those skills to be, and what their society would ultimately demand of them. Those children rarely understood fully their predicaments. It was not likely their parents understood either.

Many youngsters floundered in their classrooms. Without a particularly competent teacher, the quiet children—the easy ones—went unnoticed. It was astounding how many minority youngsters, some woefully behind in their studies, were not assisted or being assessed for special education for fear that singling them out would be interpreted by some as racially prejudicial. Allowing them to falter and fail, apparently, was an easier choice. All in all, only a relatively few students received a helping hand from a school professional other than their classroom teacher. It was painfully obvious that the school system did not provide assistance to its students on an as-needed basis.

Teachers In Need of Assistance

Many classroom teachers who worked endless hours preparing their students for tomorrow were as desperate for support as were their children. These teachers saw the galloping academic and social/emotional diversity everyday. They knew there were children in their classrooms who needed extensive help if improvement was to be accomplished. Some teachers handled the demanding differences by building within their rooms accommodating, multilevel, multigrade workstations that more accurately matched and pushed each child's acquired abilities. For those teachers it was a return in principle to the one-room, prairie schoolhouse where every student learned something every day. Sadly, other teachers ignored the glaring differences in their students' skills and interests. They seemed resigned to offer one worn instructional shoe for everyone to wear, hopeful to reach the shrinking numbers of average students. The desert school system seemed determined not to provide assistance to its teachers on an as-needed basis.

SPECIAL EDUCATION ASSISTANCE

I had not expected what I witnessed: teachers and students not receiving the assistance they needed. Something was in error. In the days of the Arizona residential center and the Colorado special education school, every youngster was aided when a skill- or school-related problem surfaced. There were sufficient professionals, well-trained and experienced, available to assist with a youngster's academic, motor, language, or social/emotional difficulties. The help was offered immediately and without fanfare. The special education school in Colorado, with the approval of the local sponsoring school districts, embraced a service-as-needed approach to helping the enrolled children. It was simple and effective. Need drove services. That may have been utopia. If it was, it was gone.

Need No Longer Sufficient

I learned that assistance for a struggling student was no longer axiomatic. Special education, out of necessity, had to guard its services more closely. The bulging numbers of newly designated exceptional children had so impacted resources that special education was forced to parcel out its assistance to only those children who now qualified as exceptional. The river had changed everything. Children had to qualify for assistance through a labyrinth of standardized tests and scores, placed within numerical formulas whose validities were as leaky as a sieve. Obvious need was no longer sufficient for help. Some needy schoolchildren failed to qualify for that help; the installed formulas guaranteed that outcome.

I'd sit in my desert office listening to my psychology buddies discuss the children they had seen recently who had failed eligibility requirements. Those children would not be served by special education, I learned. They would have to wait for a second round of eligibility testing, perhaps a year later, after they had slipped deeper into a hole many people were helping to dig. Need was acknowledged, but scores from the standardized tests the district required their psychologists to use were not sufficiently strained to warrant providing the children help with reading or math or writing. I watched my friends leave the office in the morning, test kits or district forms in hand, off to assess more children struggling with schoolwork, referred to special education by regular education teachers who seemed to possess no notion of what to do for the children. How many of those children, desperate for support, would also fail to qualify according to the psychologists' test numbers? I chided my buddies about the time they were wasting with their worthless standardized testing that was so unconnected to anything happening in the classroom. I'd dare them to dump their test kits and join me for the day working directly with the children and their teachers. We could provide the struggling children with direct assistance, immediately, effectively, I promised them. There would be no artificial qualifying for services, only observed need.

My friends, of course, could not join me. Despite the fact that the children and their teachers would benefit enormously from their presence, my buddies had no time for such luxury. Their job description called for them to spend most of their days determining which of the struggling children would be coded officially exceptional and eligible for services. Exceptionality had been removed from the pens of poets and philosophers and scientist-practitioners. It was now in the hands of politicians and bean counters.

SPECIAL EDUCATION ELIGIBILITY TESTING

Special education is supported by federal, state, and county dollars. Money available for its operations is based on the number of district children designated officially exceptional. From a budgetary perspective, the eligibility process is very important.

Eligibility: Dollars

The eligibility process also is very expensive, in terms of both supplies and professional time. Nearly 20 years ago, the cost of the process, including assessment and decision making, was estimated at $1,800 per each child assessed.[4] Today, the expenditure is suggested to be closer to $1,230 per child.[5] Both estimates, even if somewhat low or high, are enough to take one's breath away.

Most, if not all, of the 4,775,534[6] children presently being served by special education under Public Law 101-476 were required at some time to undergo some form of eligibility assessment. Whether we choose the low or high estimate, and whether we restrict our calculations to the most common (and controversial) exceptionalities that represent about 90% of the total numbers, we are talking from $5 billion to $8 billion in assessment costs!

Are Assessment Costs Justified?

Do the outcomes of this eligibility assessment process justify this enormous expenditure? That question will produce conflicting responses depending on one's perspective and job description. The researchers who provided the aforementioned figures, although separated by nearly two decades, provided similarly discouraging sentiments regarding the expenditures' value. The early view (1980): "[T]he practical knowledge gained from such [assessment] activities is marginal at best."[7] And the later opinion (1995): "[I]t has been suggested that these [assessment] results often provide little, if any, information regarding the instructional needs of students."[8] More recently it has been suggested that "[t]here...is absolutely no empirical evidence that the [most popular assessment instrument used by my school psychology colleagues to determine eligibility] leads to effective treatment, instructional programs, or strategies to improve academic skill or performance deficiencies."[9]

Noneligible Costs

The numbers of children presently served by special education, and who have undergone this expensive eligibility assessment, only hint at the total cost of this eligibility process. In addition to the nearly five million youngsters judged eligible and presently receiving services, an unknown but certainly sizable number of school children have been assessed formally and found not eligible for services. A school district's assessment costs are virtually the same whether one of its youngsters is or is not determined eligible for services. For each one million kids found ineligible for special education, the respective districts have spent probably close to $1.5 billion assessing the kids. You can bet the farm that most of those youngsters found ineligible during the first assessment attempt will be retested at a later date at nearly the same dollar outlay of the original assessment. There is no assurance they will be found eligible after the second assessment procedure. A third assessment attempt is possible. Again, the process is very time consuming and costly.

Eligibility: Numbers and Job Security

One beautiful desert morning, I was seated with several special education personnel in an elementary school's resource room discussing the educational future of a youngster. At the conclusion of the meeting, I was unexpectedly cornered by a participating therapist and asked if I knew any children at her school who might be eligible for special education status. I was surprised by her question. I hadn't met that many professional people who went out of their way to expand their caseloads. When asked why she wanted names, her response was telling: "If I don't find another child or two, I'll have to split my time between this school and others; there aren't enough special kids here," she divulged. Then she admitted honestly, "I don't want to leave this school." I realized full well what I was about to tell this woman was as useful as a rain barrel in Death Valley. Still I felt compelled to suggest, "Your school has some 350 kids. There are plenty of children who could benefit from your professional help." There was nothing cordial about her reaction. She actually snarled at me. "Tell that to the district!" she spat in my face. I had forgotten that need was no longer sufficient justification to serve children.

The desert school district was not alone with its faulty logic that only children formally labeled exceptional and placed on special education's roles need assistance. I had experienced similar district mentality years earlier when consulting for a school a thousand miles north of the desert. Fortunately, a very farsighted principal came to the rescue of nearly her entire student population. At the insistence of this principal, her school decided on its own to change the way it provided services to all its students. Not unlike other schools in the particular district, this school's standardized achievement scores were low and showing no signs of reversing their downward trajectory. Fourth and fifth graders exhibited reading levels closer to that of struggling first and second graders. Many students found writing a near impossible challenge, and others approaching middle school had virtually no math skills beyond double-digit addition. The children, not to mention their teachers, needed some additional help. According to the district's eligibility formula, most of the children weren't considered sufficiently exceptional for special education assistance, and thus were receiving no help from a very willing and competent special education teacher. It was a strange school system: The bottom of the kids' educational floor had dropped out, but they weren't eligible for assistance.

The elementary school's special education teacher, its principal, assistant principal, and a few of the school's staff, developed an assistance program that provided relatively immediate classroom support to any youngster enrolled at the school who needed academic help. (The school's parents were informed of the plan and they agreed it was worth a try.) About as creative as a fried egg, the program accomplished the main goal everyone desired: helping lots of children with their classwork and self-esteem. The project, however, produced an unexpected outcome from the school district's central administration that made various personnel at the school want to shriek, then take up a sword. Here's what happened.

The elementary school's approach eliminated the need for formal eligibility testing and special education labeling before a child was able to receive help from the special education teacher or her part-time aide. Any youngster enrolled at the school who needed help received it. Period. Since eligibility testing was no longer used by the school, there would be no new children from that school classified as exceptional and placed on special education's books. As it happens, school district's hire special education personnel based on numbers of identified special education children. They do not hire special education personnel based on numbers of children who might benefit from professional assistance. In this instance, "no new special education children" illogically translated into "no need for special education personnel." The moment the district's assistant superintendent for elementary education heard there would be no more designated special education children at the school, he instantly cut the aide's position and threatened to eliminate a portion of the special education teacher's position as well. Before the project commenced, the administrator axed (and was prepared to further ax) the people crucial to its success. When the white-hot elementary school's principal drove her daggered finger fully against the tip of the assistant superintendent's nose, threatening all manner of physical reprisal, he found it in his heart to rethink his logic. Smartly, he rescinded his order to eliminate the essential positions. While the district wasn't sharp enough to recognize the eventual outcome of its altered actions, it saved not only the educational health of a large number of students but also wheelbarrows full of money that later would have been spent on eligibility testing and special education placement. The operative word is "prevention."

Eligibility: Deviance

The previously mentioned therapist who requested my help in locating a child to bolster her caseload so she could maintain her position at the school successfully found a child enrolled at the school who (with a twist and a wink) qualified for her services. I knew the child well. He was a delightful kindergarten youngster whose classwork was excellent. He was, however, a little shy, and his communication skills were just beginning to blossom. The rules had been stretched to help the therapist (who no doubt assisted this child greatly—at no additional cost to the district). A system whose job availabilities are determined by numbers of eligible special children guarantees such soft deviance.

PROVIDING SERVICES: WAITING FOR CHILDREN TO WORSEN

I watched the desert's special education department do what it could to provide support services to the district's diverse children. Special education's slim budget combined with the excessive costs of eligibility testing demanded that its school psychologists monitor carefully the continuous flow of incoming referrals for special education evaluation. Psychologists were to make every effort to convince a referring regular education teacher to accommodate curriculum to match a child's unique academic needs, thereby allowing the student to stay in the regular classroom and off special education's rolls. If a psychologist's persuasion was successful, the regular teacher would rarely receive any assistance for the child who was struggling. Unless that teacher experienced a sudden jolt of responsibility for the child (along with some new skills), a lose-lose situation brewed. Without extra assistance or some fortuitous event, such as an out-of-school tutor provided by the child's parents, the youngster was certain to fall further behind in his or her studies. Inevitably, the frustrated regular classroom teacher would turn a deaf ear to arguments for further accommodations and would try once again to have the child found eligible for in-class assistance or out-of-classroom placement. If the child's classroom work had worsened sufficiently, special education eligibility would likely be awarded. Once more this seemed a curious system: A child's academic wound must begin bleeding profusely before attention is paid. This is an extensive waste of precious time. The term "prevention" is evidently asleep in the catacombs of the school system's vocabulary. A suitable fable was easy to locate.

> Once upon a time, there was a town whose playground was at the edge of a cliff. Every so often a child would fall off the cliff. Finally, the town council decided that something should be done about the serious injuries to children. After much discussion, however, the council was deadlocked. Some council members wanted to put a fence at the top of the cliff, but others wanted to put an ambulance at the bottom.
>
> In this parable, the idea of putting an ambulance at the bottom of the cliff clearly is foolish on many levels. Waiting for children to be injured and only then providing them with help is cruel and inhuman if the damage can be prevented. Further, it is needlessly expensive; an ambulance costs far more than a fence.
>
> Yet longstanding policies in...education...are very much like this ill-considered idea.[10]

ELIGIBILITY: SPECIAL EDUCATION'S SAFETY NETS, GENERAL EDUCATION'S EXCUSES

Of the many lessons I was taught by the desert experience, one was particularly troublesome: The uncontested concept that special education's most common exceptionalities represent something more than what a regular education teacher should be expected to accommodate in the regular classroom. This belief has set the stage for general education to believe it has a permanent safety net named special education. Such a perception creates the following bias: If a child isn't succeeding academically in the regular system, the only logical step considered appropriate by general education is to have the struggling youngster labeled exceptional. And it's happening in record numbers.

Those general educators who hold to the above perspective, choosing not to scrutinize their own curriculum systems, need to look at the shadow at their heels. They'll catch a glimpse of W. C. Fields' bulbous face reminding all of us that lunch is rarely free. Special education eligibility comes with costs that have little to do with dollars.

Infirm

"Special educators explicitly presuppose that school failure is pathological."[11] If a youngster is determined eligible for special education services, it means something is wrong with that child. A disorder or deficit, responsible for the child's classroom academic difficulties, is said to be present. More often than not, metabolic or neurological reasons are offered to account for the youngster's exceptionality.[12] More often than not, the purported physiological reasons are

undetectable. Eligibility requires only that the reasons be proposed, not substan-
tiated. Parents who sign documents attesting to their child's "learning disability"
are accepting the view that their child's neurology is defective.

Resigned

A child found eligible for special education will experience changes, some
welcomed, some unsettling. The child proclaimed "gifted" may wear the appella-
tion well. The child labeled " learning disabled" or "mildly retarded" may not.
The first child may wish to display the badge proudly, the second may wish to
hide it. Both youngsters may believe what is being said about them is true, the
first with joy, the second with resignation.

Exonerated

When a child's academic struggling is attributed to his or her exceptionality,
the regular educational system conveniently is off the hook. The child's purport-
edly marred physiology, like a whirlpool, snares everyone's full attention. Little
else is seen. A potential verifiable culprit, general education's curriculum, is ex-
onerated.[13]

> By positing biological bases for learning problems, the responsibility for
> failure is taken from the schools, communities, and other institutions, and
> is put squarely on the back, or rather within the head, of the child...moving
> the focus away from the general educational process.[14] If the child does not
> learn academic skills at the rate or level expected, or if he [or she] does not
> behave emotionally or socially as expected, too frequently it is assumed
> categorically that the fault lies within the child.[15]

So long as special education continues to hold to a neurological explanation
for students' learning differences, regular education need not monitor itself.
Regular education, not wishing to assume more responsibility for pupils' classroom academic difficulties, has remained painfully silent. Duplicity is suspected. It is not an exaggeration to suggest that the monstrous size of this issue
may ultimately bring down special education's house.

Eligibility: Cracks

> While at the copying machine outside my college office, I overheard a visit-
> ing parent furiously protesting her son's school's position to withhold
> placement in the school's accelerated program because he scored 95% rather
> than 97% on eligibility tests. Retesting would not be available for 6
> months.   In the meantime, he would be required to return to his regular
> class, a productive place for some students, but stiflingly slow-paced for
> him.

A first grader from an impoverished family was struggling with his class assignments. The school's special education teacher advised the child's first-grade teacher not to refer the child for eligibility testing, indicating that the youngster would not score poor enough on his achievement tests to be found eligible for help. She suggested the teacher wait until the end of the year to seek eligibility indicating that the child's scores would probably be low enough by then. The child's parents were not apprised of the regular education teacher's observations or the special education teacher's advice. The child would be required to languish for two-thirds of a school year in his regular classroom, a productive place for some students, but utterly devastating for him.

No matter the diligence and dedication of my desert school psychology buddies and our school district's many skilled special education teachers, the laws and regulations governing eligibility were (and are) so convoluted and open to error that enormous cracks existed (and continue to exist) within the eligibility system. Countless children descended (and continue to descend) through them each school day. The costs of these errors are incalculable. Given the present federal guidelines governing eligibility requirements, there is little professionals can do openly to right the wrongs.

To circumvent these large open cracks manufactured by special education's flawed eligibility system, slightly devious professional spins on behalf of struggling children are commonplace. Some 25 years ago, a school district sent a young pupil to our Colorado special education school asking us to evaluate his suitability for placement. Despite the fact the student was struggling miserably in all his academic subjects at his present public school and had grown increasing sullen at that school, it was apparent the referring district was not going to provide any assistance to this youngster if he remained in his regular classroom. To receive services at our facility, paid for by the school district, he would need to score below an 80 on a standardized instrument the district required for special education eligibility. Simply put, if the child scored higher than 80, he would receive no help. At the conclusion of the testing, the child's full score on the instrument landed directly on 80. The school district's cut-off score for assistance was 79. I knew the test well. It was punctuated by error. A single point disparity was as pragmatically meaningless as failing to call a storm a hurricane because its sustained winds were 74 mph rather than 75 mph. I fetched a brand new pencil from my briefcase. I changed the child's score to 79 and the district provided educational assistance to the child.

So long as numerical eligibility takes precedence over need, cracks in the system and circuitous ways of patching them will be as much a part of the system as a school's bell.

FOCUS: CHALLENGING THE ELIGIBILITY SYSTEM

Our country's past leanings toward providing assistance to unique schoolchildren has been less than storied. Our public schools historically have deemed it acceptable to deny entrance to children with even the mildest of disabilities.[16] By 1975, about three million children with disabilities were not receiving appropriate programming in public schools. Another one million were excluded totally from public education.[17] Today's leanings mirror those of the past: Large numbers of schoolchildren continue to go without essential assistance.

Congress Acted

The United States Congress attempted rectification of our public schools' deplorable history by passing Public Law (PL) 94-142 in 1975. This landmark legislation mandated a free public school education for every student regardless of the severity of the student's disability. The spirit and order of the law were clear: Students in need of help were to receive the assistance they required. That assistance was to be provided through the public schools. The law carried financial teeth. It was noticed.

Progress, Hindrance, and a Need for Change

While enormous progress has been achieved serving special children through PL 94-142, the very same law that shook the roots of public education has produced an unwieldy, ineffective means of determining who should and shouldn't be eligible for the mandated assistance. Special education's eligibility formula, driven by the federal law, is artificial, capricious, and built on spurious numbers. Scores and labels have taken precedence over children.[18]

My desert institution experience made it abundantly clear that the present special education eligibility system is not meeting the needs of today's students, teachers, or school psychologists. It has become a hindrance and it must be changed. With some license, I believe the following provides sufficient justification for that change:

1. The present eligibility system forces the identification of many children as disabled when by most any reasonable standard they are not. The term is misleading, excessive, contentious, and decidedly undeserved.

2. The system delays or prevents immediate, short-term educational assistance to pupils who with a little help would not fail or fall further behind. The system mocks prevention.

3. The system promotes the development of new, controversial exceptionalities to take the place of over-diagnosed exceptionalities. The

new exceptionalities are old ones, cleverly wrapped in differently worded statements.

4.   The system is so obscure that it provides little concrete direction to many parents who aren't certain how to obtain help for their kids. It compels parents to seek out lawyers who are all too happy to provide their own brand of clarification. It invites expensive litigation, draining near-empty school coffers.

5.   The system's artificial formulas pressure parents to spend large amounts of money to have physicians authoritatively claim the existence of an undetectable infirmity so school services will be provided.

6.   It interprets learning problems to be a function of intrinsic neurological anomalies. It conveys to parents that they have little responsibility for any portion of their child's school performance. It perpetuates the belief that the struggling child is the sole owner of his or her educational shortcomings.

7.   It has provided psychologists, teachers, and parents with definitions and guidelines so vague and amorphous as to border on worthless.

8.   It supports the notion that two educational systems are needed, one regular and one special, each frequently finding it difficult to communicate and work with the other. Both, out of necessity, have become stridently territorial.

9.   It forces school districts to scramble to meet federal demands that often appear unattached to anything that transpires in the classroom. Threats of loss of federal revenue fuel a district's frenetic activity.

10.   It is diverting scarce money needed for curriculum materials and professionally trained personnel in order to maintain an eligibility-service delivery system that provides little benefit to classroom teachers or students.

11.   It requires enormous dollars to be spent on verifying what everyone already knows: A child is having problems with school. It causes someone to name the problem, as if that name will magically translate into some procedure to assist the child.

12.   It requires highly trained, competent psychologists and special education teachers to spend much of their professional time administering standardized tests that have little to no classroom value or application. For financial reasons, test authors and publishers love the present eligibility system.

13.   It requires trained professional people to adopt a discrepancy model that is not a discrepancy model to verify the existence of a purported problem that is not verifiable.

14.   It requires school professionals, who should be working with kids, to spend megahours with forms and more forms and even more forms to keep the wolves from the front door. The forms rarely provide the classroom teacher with usable information. No one reads the forms.

15.   It reinforces the belief that regular teachers aren't sufficiently capable of working with exceptional children. It provides grounds for the regular teacher to make the exceptional child someone else's problem. It lets the regular school system off the hook.

16.   It sets a search, identify, and placement mentality rather than a system effort to develop classroom accommodations. It is not a problem-directed, solution-oriented model.

17.   It is preventing schoolchildren with wide-ranging abilities from receiving the help they need.

Judging a child's exceptionality, and providing services on the basis of that determination, cannot be accomplished through artificial numbers and unconnected formulas. Special education's eligibility system must be thoroughly modified. We know precisely what to do. We have the mechanics and the heart. Do we have the courage?

NOTES

1. Officially, the term "handicapped" would not be replaced with the term "disability" until 1990 with the passage of public law (PL) 101-476.

2. U.S. Department of Education. (1995). *Seventeenth annual report to congress on the implementation of the Education of the Handicapped Act.* Washington, DC: Author.

3. A form of Down syndrome where not all of a youngster's cells contain the additional 21st chromosome.

4. Mirkin, P. K.(1980). Conclusions. In J. Ysseldyke & M. Thurlow (Eds.), *The special education assessment and decision-making process: Seven case studies.* Minneapolis: University of Minnesota Institute for Research on Learning Disabilities.

5. Bradley-Johnson, S., & Johnson, C.M., & Jacob-Timm, S. (1995). Where will—and where should—changes in education leave school psychology? *Journal of School Psychology, 33,* pp.187-200.

6. *Seventeenth annual report to congress on the implementation of the Education of the Handicapped Act.*

7. Mirkin, P. K. (1980). Conclusions. In J. Ysseldyke & M. Thurlow (Eds.).

8. Wang, M. C. (1991). Effective school responses to student diversity: Challenges and prospects. *State Board Connection: Issues in Brief, 11,* 8-12.

9. Gresham, F. M., & Witt, J. C. (1997). Utility of intelligence tests for treatment planning, classification, and placement decisions: Recent empirical findings and future directions. *School Psychology Quarterly, 12,* 249-267.

10. Slavin R. E. (1996). Neverstreaming: Preventing learning disabilities. *Educational Leadership, 53*, p. 4-7.

11. Skrtic, T. M. (1995). The functionalist view of special education: Deconstructing the conventional knowledge tradition. In Thomas M. Skrtic (Ed.), *Disability and democracy: Reconstructing (special) education for postmodernity.* (pp. 65-103). New York: Teachers College, Columbia University.

12. Coles, G. S. (1978). The learning-disability test battery: empirical and social issues. *Harvard Educational Review, 48*, pp. 313-340.

13. Tomlinson, S. (1982). *A sociology of special education.* London: Routledge & Kegan Paul.

14. Coles, G. S. (1978).

15. Gardner, W. I. (1977). *Learning and behavior characteristics of exceptional children.* Boston: Allyn and Bacon.

16. Smith, D. D., & Luckasson, R. (1992). *Introduction to special education: Teaching in an age of challenge.* Boston: Allyn and Bacon.

17. Rothstein, L. F. (1995). *Special education law* (2nd ed.). New York: Longman Publishers.

18. Barry, A. L. (1995). Easing into inclusion classrooms. *Educational Leadership, 52*, pp.4-5.

4

Discrepancies: The Basis for Special Education Services

Before special education's eligibility formula can be changed, its weaknesses must be brought to the table for examination. An important first step is to have a clear understanding of the role discrepancies play within that formula. We begin by looking at two critical classroom barometers that fuel special education's eligibility issues:

1. How a student is expected to do in school

2. How a student is doing in school

CLASSROOM EXPECTATIONS, SCHOOL PERFORMANCE, AND DISCREPANCIES

Professional and parental expectations held for a student are the benchmark from which to predict what a student should do while in school. Classroom expectations are derived from numerous sources, including a student's age, scores on tests said to estimate aptitude and intelligence, teacher observations, established norms, comparisons with other youngsters, and on occasion, parental wishes or demands. In the simplest terms, parents (and teachers) expect a pupil to do well in school.

How that pupil actually is doing in school is a separate, but equally critical, issue. That barometer is derived most often from standardized achievement scores, classroom assignments and quizzes, teacher observations, and other school-performance measures. When compared, the two factors—expectations for a youngster's school-related achievements and that youngster's actual classroom performance—generally lead special education professionals in one of two directions:

1. If during school a student is meeting everyone's academic expectation, no apparent academic discrepancy exists, resulting in little cause for concern.

2. Conversely, if during school a student fails to meet everyone's academic expectations, if classwork is below or considerably above expectations, a discrepancy is often said to exist.

Discrepancies are extremely important. Whether they occur in school or everyday life, they alert us to the possibility of a problem that may warrant our immediate, careful attention.

Familiar Discrepancies

A discrepancy exists when an observation is different from what was expected. Most adults, for example, do well with an internal body temperature of 98.6 degrees F. If a probing thermometer measures a body temperature of 103 degrees F, a discrepancy of 4.4 degrees exists. Recalling that a discrepancy alerts us to the possibility of a problem, the unexpected reading may suggest the body is fighting an infection, hence the reason the measured individual is feeling on the yuk side. It is quite possible, of course, the individual feels fine, and the observed numerical discrepancy has occurred because the thermometer is broken or the technician reading the gauge needs an eye examination. These latter two possible causes for the temperature discrepancy are very important.

Cause and Treatment

Discovering what is responsible for a discrepancy is essential. Treatment or intervention is most often chosen only after a discrepancy has been observed and its basis has been identified. If the proposed cause for the elevated temperature is an infection, the sufferer may respond well to an antibiotic (and a week on a private Caribbean beach). On the other hand, the cause and solution may have nothing to do with the patient: The examining physician may need to fetch a new thermometer, or the technician may need to purchase new glasses before driving home. Treatments differ depending on what is responsible for the discrepancy.

Discrepancies: Some Serious, Some Annoying

Some discrepancies foretell potentially serious health issues. A significant increase in blood pressure, sudden blurred vision, or acute sharp pains anywhere in the body are marked departures from what is expected. An equally serious deviation from expectations would be if a child has yet to take his first step or say his first word before his second birthday. Certainly each of the above discrepancies tells us to seek immediate professional help.

Discrepancies characterized more as inconveniences than ominous occurrences still demand our attention. Hearing nothing from a car's motor after turning the ignition key is an all too familiar and most unwelcome discrepancy. Tasting a favorite morning cereal in milk the Australians say has "gone off" may present a less familiar discrepancy, but one no less unpleasant.

SPECIAL EDUCATION'S DISCREPANCY MODEL

Clearly, discrepancies are central to the field of education. At this moment, special education continues to wrestle with two seemingly inseparable, challenging problems: determining which students are truly disabled and determining which struggling pupils to serve. At the heart of the field's dilemma lies the discrepancy issue. A brief look at educational history and the power schools held over the children who were to be serve will help place this problem in some perspective.

Ignoring Exceptionality

At the end of World War II, our public school system roosted comfortably atop its own empire, holding tight-fisted the power to decide who could and could not enter its revered classrooms. Children who were judged atypical or less than average were denied entrance. The numbers of children barred from public school were staggering. In 1970, a task force studying students from the Boston school area "found over ten thousand students excluded from public school classrooms because they didn't match school standards for the normal student."[1] Later in that decade it was estimated that well over a million school-aged children were denied education in schools simply because "they were different in some way."[2] While children without handicaps were required to attend school under our compulsory school attendance laws, children with handicaps actually were prevented from attending school. Indeed, one state supreme court justified excluding a young boy with cerebral palsy because he "produce[d] a depressing and nauseating effect upon the teachers and school children...."[3] Our public schools' posture was remarkably transparent: "We don't take *those* kinds of children." The schools' messages were equally clear: Those kids and their parents would have to find their own educational facilities, often limited to state institutions or expensive private schools. Many children remained tethered to an isolated room or two in their own homes.

Parents Scorned

Intolerable conditions, however, have a limited shelf life. Americans are fearlessly audacious when they become tired of being wronged. Parents with unique children who are snubbed by the educational system are no different: Inevitably, they will take to the sword to pry open public school doors. Parent-initiated movements to that end began many years ago. At the federal level, the years 1957 to 1966 saw the creation of national special education programs for which the political presence and influence of parent groups was at least partially responsible.[4] Legal suits against school districts, begun by these disgruntled parents who wanted their offspring to have a fair shake at whatever their futures held, confronted the schools' deplorable attitudes. Politicians, for multiple purposes, added their voices to the parents' chorus. Many state legislatures initiated paper changes declaring ideological shifts in their states' view toward serving the handicapped. For years, states, through permissive laws, gave their school districts the option of serving or not serving handicapped children. During the 1960s and 1970s, the passage of mandatory legislation by an increasing number of states was removing that option.[5] Doing something for *those* kids ranked with the honored apple pie and motherhood. The parents and their very special children were heard.

State Rulings

A 1969 ruling handed down by North Carolina typified the legislative stances beginning to surface across the country. The state's attorney general proclaimed:

> It is unconstitutional and invalid...to operate the public school system in a discriminatory manner as against the mentally retarded children and to allocate funds to the disadvantage of the mentally retarded child. Often a mentally retarded child develops fair skills and abilities and becomes a useful citizen of the state but in order to do this, the mentally retarded child must have his or her chance.[6]

In 1972, legal actions in Pennsylvania and the District of Columbia initiated a national move to improve education for all exceptional pupils within the context of regular education. Due process and equal protection became weapons parents could use to support their children.

> The judgments were handed down in *Mills v. The District of Columbia Board of Education* . The district court ordered that the Washington school system readmit all excluded children "regardless of the degree of the child's mental, physical or emotional disability or impairment,"[7] and in the *Pennsylvania Association for Retarded Children v. the Commonwealth of Pennsylvania* where fourteen families sued the State of Pennsylvania on the basis that their children with mental retardation were denied equal access to a public education. This case was prompted by state policy denying a public education to youngsters with mental retardation. During the legal proceedings, parents described their futile attempts to fight a system that arbitrarily and callously excluded their children from school.[8]

The Pennsylvania court case signaled a new era for special education: It guaranteed access to public education to children with mental retardation previously excluded from school.[9,10,11] The nation's conscience began to change.

> North Carolina: The General Assembly of North Carolina hereby declares that the policy of the state is to ensure every child a fair and full opportunity to reach his full potential and that no child as defined in this act shall be excluded from services or education for any reason whatsoever [Sec.2] (Chapter 1293, 1973 Session).[12]

> Kansas: [T]he board of education of every school district shall provide special education services for all exceptional children in the district...not later than July 1, 1979 [H.B. 1672, Sec. 6a].[13]

> West Virginia: A...statute...passed in March 1974 in West Virginia, calls for the education of all exceptional children between the ages of 5 and 23 years beginning July 1, 1974 [H.B. 1271].[14]

Governors stepped forward adding their support to the special children and their parents. The National Governors Conference, June 6, 1974, saw the adoption of a policy position stating firmly that "It should be the responsibility of each State, as an integral part of a free public education, to provide for special education services sufficient to identify and meet the needs of all handicapped children."[15] In his 1974 impassioned "Condition of the State" address to the state legislature, then Iowa Governor Robert D. Ray declared:

> Isn't it enough that a youngster be handicapped—mentally, physically or both—let alone never have a chance for education, or training or to learn and to live? Let us not be a party to further penalizing these human beings. You will have before you a proposal to modernize our delivery system for special education. It will make available to these young people, whoever they might be and wherever they might live, an opportunity to learn and be recognized as someone who belongs. Debate it, however long it takes, but pass it. [16]

A Victory of Questionable Worth

With support from advocacy groups such as the Association for Retarded Citizens, parental groups had accomplished a critical first step. They forced legislative and educational systems to acknowledge that all children were deserving of educational opportunities, even those who were different from the hypothetical average child. Buoyed by new state laws and federal court decisions, states were required to acknowledge that physical and intellectual differences were no longer sufficient grounds for school exclusion. Youngsters described as retarded, once seen as too unusual to be helped, now were allowed through the front doors of the educational system. Some educators and legislators saw that gesture as magnanimous. Some thought it was sufficient.

By 1974, nearly all states had in force mandatory legislation requiring educational opportunities for a segment of the handicapped child population. Unfortunately, "these mandatory requirements [were] ignored, and in virtually every state many handicapped children in need of special education services [were] unable to obtain them."[17]

CRITICAL ERROR: ACCOUNTABILITY NOT MANDATED

While the federal courts and state legislatures saw to it that the educational system could no longer keep its doors closed to any youngster, the same judicial bodies failed to mandate responsibility and accountability for each child's educational progress. This latter failing was an error of huge proportions. Legally, schools were required to provide cognitively and physically different children with a protective roof for a few hours a day. The schools weren't directed to do much else, however. It was one thing to let markedly different children into a building, it was another to have knowledgeable, dedicated professionals trained and available to serve them.

Without effective educational strategies, a child's classroom progress and growth, regardless of the child's strengths and weaknesses, becomes merely a wish. Without accountability, a child's failure to improve academically and socially as expected is easily and conveniently blamed on the child's exceptionality. Establishing blame for educational discrepancies within the child gives the school system license to be without fault.

Off the Hook from the Beginning

The general educational system and its personnel had been indirectly excused from holding themselves liable and answerable for what happened within their classrooms. Administrative and staff employment as well as subsequent job assurances were not tied to either a pupil's performance or a school's willingness to accommodate programs to fit each child. Educational methodologies used within school classrooms were protected from an objective, outside audit by any individual or organization interested in improving educational services. The general education school system had been let off the hook from the very beginning. That insulated position would have grievous consequences in the very near future. When systems and methods are not held accountable, exact causes for system failure remain a mystery. Without accountability or professional scrutiny, attributing cause to the wrong source can easily happen. Poor student achievement, like our "patient's" elevated body temperature, might be mistakenly attributed to internal physical difficulties rather than inaccurate measuring instruments or inadequate observations. In the absence of any systemwide accountability plan, the system and its truths are dangerously susceptible to all kinds of events, those small and those beyond belief.

MOSCOW: OCTOBER 4, 1957

In the United States, the fall of 1957 was noteworthy for several reasons. If you were a New York City schoolchild during October, you likely were one of the quarter of a million schoolchildren who were forced to stay in bed because of a ravaging epidemic of Asian flu. If you were a Little Rock, Arkansas, student, you were embroiled in Governor Orval Faubus' school desegregation confrontation at Central High School that challenged the collective conscience of the country. If you were Brooklyn born and bred, your mouth was frozen numbly agape, now that the preposterous rumors were firming that the beloved Dodgers were leaving Flatbush for the glitter of the far west.[18] If you were elsewhere in the country, comfortably distant from the above disquieting events, occupied instead by matters of the heart or pocketbook, the afternoon of October 4 administered a taste of fear the depths of which you had never before experienced.

> Late in the afternoon of Friday, October 4, New York teletype machines banged into motion. From Moscow came word that an artificial Earth satellite had been launched by the Soviet Union. The Soviet news agency Tass called the device *Sputnik*, a Russian nickname for "Artificial Fellow Traveler Around the Earth." The world's first man-made satellite and its instrumentation package, weighing 184 pounds, were circling the earth once every ninety-six minutes.[19]

Flight into Fear

By today's standards, the Russian's high aerial feat would earn barely a yawn from those of us accustomed to watching intrepid astronauts play golf from the moon's natural bunkers. But days' present and past have very little in common. Now we are bored with traveling metal spheres that clutter space. In 1957, they scared the begushions out of us.

> The Russian achievement produced in America a peculiar and definite mixture of depression and panic that lasted for months....[20]

> Democratic Senator Henry Jackson of Washington described the feat as a "devastating blow" to the United States and called upon President Eisenhower to proclaim "a week of shame and danger."[21]

> Survival anxiety was all too real, and national self-doubt ran deep. Dr. Elmer Hutchisson, director of the American Institute of Physics, reacted to the events by suggesting that the nation's way of life might be "doomed to rapid extinction."[22]

Education: Fault and Solution

Our hysteria usurped our rationality; a whipping boy and a quick solution were demanded by an uneasy American public. *Sputnik* generated an intense educational crisis fueled by persistent criticism of our educational system. "Reform of education to win the cold war became a temporary obsession in the media, in Washington, and throughout the country."[23]

> Sloan Wilson, author of the influential novel *Man in the Gray Flannel Suit* and education editor of the *New York Herald Tribune*...asserted that [our] schools had "degenerated into a system for coddling and entertaining the mediocre." [Wilson] was equally definite about the fact that the "outcome of the arms race will depend eventually on our schools and those of the Russians."[24]

> [Arkansas Senator J. William] Fulbright laid much of the blame for the *Sputnik* hysteria on [Health, Education, and Welfare's] past tendency to "deprecate Russian ability and accomplishments."[25] The [United States] was now paying dearly, [Fulbright] said, for its failure to appreciate tremendous Russian accomplishments in education.[26]

> Americans reacted to *Sputnik* by charging schools with failing to produce scientists and technicians needed for the U.S. to remain ahead internationally in technological development. American schools were compared with Russian schools and found deficient. The chief problem, critics believed, was lax standards. *Life* magazine compared the schooling of two boys; one in Moscow and one in Chicago. It reported that in the Soviet Union, "The laggards are forced out [of school] by tough periodic examinations and shunted to less demanding trade schools and apprenticeships....In contrast, American students lounge in classrooms that are 'relaxed and enlivened by banter,' and in which the 'intellectual application expected of [students] is moderate.' "[27]

Falling Bombs and Rising Standards

That the Russians had a spaceship traversing our heartland we thought capable of raining nuclear annihilation was dead-serious business. That we could hear its electronic pinging made it expressly real and threatening. We were a paranoid populous then: Peter Sellers' *Dr. Strangelove* and his flamboyant entourage were alive and well. We had cement bomb shelters buried deep in our backyards. We were advised to stock these refuges with supplies sufficient to last—no one knew how long. I remember being taught how to protect myself from an exploding nuclear bomb by assuming a fetal position under a wooden table at school previously used to display paper art projects. Most of my friends and I doubted the table would afford much protection from a bomb we were told could drop atop our heads. Still, practice sessions were frighteningly common.

The belief that *Sputnik* signified failings in America's educational system became widespread in late 1957. Americans seemed ready to accept the conclusion that the nation's scientific leadership, perhaps even survival, depended on changing its educational institutions.[28] The phrase, "changing educational institutions" meant revising school curriculum and demanding more from students. After *Sputnik*, standards were increased, textbooks were rewritten, achievement tests were renormed, and schoolwork became more formidable. Specifically, "standards for reading achievement were raised and students were tested more rigorously."[29]   While resounding cheers for the newly elevated standards were voiced by many adults throughout the county (they had already finished their schooling!), other less joyful sounds were being emitted by a different segment of America's population: Quite suddenly, school and its assignments were tougher for a whole lot of children.

Not Everyone Ready for Changes

Curriculum modifications were imposed quickly, catching many teachers and students ill prepared for what was now expected of them. Students, particularly, were not aware that distant politicians and educators had set forth new requirements and embraced new expectations for classroom performance. (It wasn't as if postcards were mailed to us indicating that we had better tighten our learning belts because we had to prove we were smarter than those dastardly high-flyin' Russians.) Students having problems with reading (or academic achievement in general) before the new curricula came to school were certain to experience increased difficulties after the playing field changed. Nothing tricky (or sage) about that fact.

DISCREPANCIES IN THE MAKING: REAL OR ARTIFICIAL?

In days before the *Sputnik*-enhanced standards, those benign *Ozzie and Harriet* days that seemed best depicted in black and white, less than enthusiastic student performance in classrooms created virtually no stir or admonition from many teachers and educational administrators. It was commonly accepted that some bright, capable students chose to use fewer than their full complement of cerebral cylinders during their school day. The capable students' preoccupation with matters noneducational was understood and tolerated. Discrepancies between performance and assumed ability were acknowledged and accepted. "Not ready to learn" or "not fully matured" were common, casual explanations offered to parents for their youngsters' inattentiveness or absence of academic excellence. Clearly there was an implied promise that we would wake one day with "readiness" and "intellectual maturity" turned on as though someone or some event had thrown the right light switch.

The chaos created by *Sputnik*, however, took education's common day-to-day humdrum and violently jerked it upside down. Under pressure to surpass the Russians, curriculum screws and vises were turned and tightened, exacting different effects on those of us who for many years had done little more than look forward to the 3:00 bell. Some of us took to the new, more rigorous curriculum requirements as though the nuts and bolts ratcheting presented no obstacle. Some of us, dancing with hormone-driven private dreams, paid no mind to the changes. (Some of us didn't even know any changes had occurred!) Others, however, certainly bright and capable children, routinely successful on the playground, at the beach, indeed nearly every place outside their classroom assignments, began to feel a persistent queasiness now that the new *Sputnik*-driven standards had come to pass: These students knew they were lost academically. Quite suddenly, they were forced to face requirements that were foreign and confusing, requirements for which they lacked prerequisite skills and basic understanding. Unlike many adults, these children were not cheering.

A Newly Discovered Explanation for Students' Academic Discrepancies

The observed discrepancy between these struggling youngsters' classroom performance and the expectations their parents and teachers held for their achievements widened daily. Understandably, this increasing gap raised serious concerns. The ability-achievement discrepancies were undeniable and they begged for clarification. Once we had explained student achievement that bumped along below expectations by looking inside the students and naming immaturity and an absence of scholarly readiness as the likely culprits for the students' disappointing classroom performance. Now, post-*Sputnik*, we looked inside the struggling students and announced that we had discovered a different cause for their poor achievement, something significantly more sinister than youthful disinterest and school system apathy and culpability. Had we been able to see the future, we might have given thought to reexamining the validity of that discovery.

CRITICAL JUNCTURE

Perhaps every professional field experiences a supreme moment when a singular decision significantly effects its future direction. Special education was presented with such a moment during those post-*Sputnik* early days of general education's intensifying curriculum requirements when it became clear to everyone that sharp, able youngsters were experiencing difficulty with their class assignments. The field recognized that these new children were different from those previously found on special education's roles. These children were not retarded, certainly not as that term was used to represent youngsters found in institutions and residential centers. Neither were they encumbered by seizures or readily apparent physical limitations. Special education knew what the children weren't, but little else. Why, then, were they not experiencing success with their school work? The field was at its seminal juncture, its choice point. Any number of answers to that question were possible (including a mismatch between general education's curriculum and a student's readiness for that curriculum). The answer chosen by the field would carry it into the future.

Special education made its choice and marked its course. The field could just as easily have gone in an entirely different direction. It didn't. It chose its antagonists. Nothing the Russians ever put into space matched what we did to ourselves.

Many children were unable to keep up [with the new classroom requirements and the sharply elevated standards], but few blamed the raising of standards [for the children's difficulties]. Instead, students who scored low on reading achievement tests were personally blamed for their failure....If a child didn't satisfy the new demands...the cause for the youngster's difficulties were "believed to be organic."[30] Hypothesized causes included minimal brain damage,[31] a maturational lag in general neurological development,[32] a failure of the brain to establish cerebral dominance,[33] or a failure to achieve certain states of neurological development.[34]

THE RIVER OF DISABLED CHILDREN

The numbers of youngsters experiencing achievement difficulties with general education's classroom curriculum, rightly or wrongly designated disabled by special education's eligibility formula, have steadily increased over the recent years. Precisely describing the characteristics of these children is not possible because special education in general and the field of learning disabilities in particular "has been, and continues to be, beset by pervasive and, at times, contentious disagreements about definitions, diagnostic criteria, [and] assessment practices."[35] Stepping beyond characterizing these children any more specifically than saying they have mild or general learning difficulties with respect to the educational curriculum presented them would be to invite all manner of justifiable professional criticism. For our purposes, knowing that the children, despite being able, are struggling to meet some voiced or measured academic expectations is sufficient.

If we look at data available from 1948 through the 1993/94 school years, the increasing numbers of children identified as having general learning problems (GLP) are evident. In 1948, some 82,000 children from a school population of approximately 28 million were considered to have mild learning difficulties. Ten years later, the numbers of the mildly involved children increased to 206,000. By 1968, the numbers increased to 750,000. Of particular interest, among those 750,000 mildly involved children were 120,000 youngsters said to have specific learning disabilities(SLD).[36] Three years later, during the 1971/72 school year, the total numbers of mildly involved children increase to approximately 1 million, roughly 167,000 of whom were said to be learning disabled. By 1988, while total school enrollment decreased by 6 million students, the numbers of youngsters designated mildly involved swelled to some 2 .6 million, of which nearly 2 million were said to be learning disabled.[37] And during the 1993/94 school year, the total number of mildly involved school youngsters were counted at about 3 million, 2.5 million of whom were labeled learning disabled.[38]

Special Education's Total Growth

Growth in the numbers of mildly involved school children over the past years (see Table 4.1) is predictable given the growth in our country's general

Table 4.1
Special Education Growth

Year	Enroll-ments	General Learning Problems	Specific Learning Dis-abilities	Totals
1948	28,000,000	82,000		82,000
1958	40,000,000	206,000		206,000
1968	50,000,000	649,000	120,000	769,000
1971/72	51,000,000	872,000	167,000	1,039,000
1988[39]	45,000,000	664,000	1,926,000	2,590,000
1993/94	49,000,000	553,900	2,444,000	2,997,000

population. One would expect some reasonable correlation between the two figures. But the federal government has suggested that special education's growth is out pacing that of the general population.

During 1993-1994, a total of 5,373,077 infants, toddlers, children, and youth with disabilities from birth through age 21 were served. Notably, that number represents 217,127 more than 1992-93, the largest yearly increase since 1976. "The rate of growth in the number of children and youth receiving special education continues to exceed the rate of growth in the number of birth through age 21 population....It also continues to exceed the rate of growth in the number of children and youth enrolled in school."[40]

The government's view that special education is growing more rapidly than population numbers might justify may be correct. Frankly, as we proceed over the next few chapters, you will recognize that because of serious definition and assessment problems associated with the identification of exceptional children, no one has an accurate account of which children are mildly involved or otherwise, or which children belong or don't belong on special education's roles. The true numbers of mildly involved, struggling children are less a factor than the accepted reality that special education's roles are continuously increasing. Shocking no one, costs needed for special education services have increased commensurately.

Federal Dollars

In 1975, when the Education for all Handicapped Children Act (PL 94-142) was signed into law by President Gerald Ford, federal costs required to provide assistance to the children designated exceptional were accepted as necessary and (politically) correct. We were told, "Cost was not an issue. The social value of ideals outweighed funding considerations."[41]

It was easy being generous in the early days of the 1970s. Relatively speaking, generosity didn't cost taxpayers much money. In 1975, the federal government paid states a skimpy $71 per each identified exceptional child for a total outlay of $250 million. Today, generosity comes at a much higher price. For the 1994 school year, the federal contribution of $413 per identified special child cost tax payers $2.5 billion.[42,43] While that figure might elicit an eye-blink or two, it represents little more than a kernel from an ear of sweet corn. That federal share of $2.5 billion for the 1994 school year, intended to help all states defray their special education expenses, didn't even cover California's cost of special education for the 1991/92 school year. Serving nearly 500,000 exceptional children, California's budget for special education programs and support services during 1991/92 topped a whopping $2.6 billion.[44]

State and Local Dollars

If one state can consume all of the federal government's monetary assistance for special education, it is apparent that the bulk of financial responsibilities for servicing exceptional schoolchildren falls primarily on the shoulders of state and local authorities. Attesting to this supposition, during 1987 and 1988, states provided 56% of the funds expended for special education programming across the nation, as compared with 36% from local resources, and 8% from the federal government.[45] The federal contribution has remained constant.

Predictably, the increasing numbers of identified exceptional children and accompanying budgetary strains have forced states to evaluate their special education funding and identification processes. The more money set aside for special education, the less money available for general education. California and Oregon have responded to growing fiscal pressures by capping the growth of special education aid, limiting the number of students eligible for reimbursement.[46] (Caps, of course, guarantee that some school children struggling with classwork will be refused assistance.) Massachusetts, Montana, Pennsylvania, and Vermont have revised their state payment formulas to detach special education reimbursement from the numbers of students on special education roles. Under this "disconnecting" funding arrangement, state money distributed to school districts for their special education costs are based on the total number of students enrolled in the school district rather than the number of students identified for special education services. Such a system breaks the link between funding and local policies that determine how students with disabilities are identified and placed in special education programs.[47] A note of extreme importance not lost to anyone is that reimbursement to school districts based on the total numbers of students enrolled rather than on numbers of special education students identified *eliminates* the need for special education's discrepancy-eligibility model.

A Drying Well

Many variables have contributed to the growing numbers of children receiving special education services. A few include parental demands, litigation (justified and otherwise), changes in state laws, federal mandates, increasing numbers of children raised in poverty, the country's conscience, schools' changing standards and attitudes, and even the rise in air pollution, as some have contended. Reasons aside for the moment, the river of exceptional children has stretched so beyond what was initially foreseen that accurate eligibility identification has taken on enormous importance. If identification mistakes were made prior to the late 1970s, particularly finding some children eligible for services when their academic discrepancies were minimal, the mistakes went unnoticed or were forgiven by most special education administrators. The Golden Goose was alive and magnanimous. Not so today. There's not enough money or teachers or rooms to be lackadaisical about finding a child eligible for special education services. School psychologists and diagnosticians across the country have been told to limit (if not deny) arguable eligibilities. Special education's budgetary bones are clean and brittle. Despite the fact that budgetary balancing is not supposed to influence the eligibility process,[48] it does so, nevertheless. "When school districts have plenty of money to spend on educating students with disabilities, diagnostic personnel are encouraged to locate and identify as many students with handicaps as possible. When funds are limited, however, concerns grow about the large number of students being declared handicapped."[49]

Budgetary restraints controlling the numbers of children being provided with special education assistance assures us that academically needy children will be passed over. What happens to these children who are left unassisted? It is a provoking question. Will they be revisited by special education at a later time? At a greater or lesser cost?

FUTURE ELIGIBILITY REQUIREMENTS

Special education does not possess a foolproof litmus test clearly revealing which school children are sufficiently exceptional to warrant special education services. School district psychologists and special education teachers, despite best efforts, experience difficulty deciding who legitimately warrants services. As a result, inadvertent over- and under-identification of children are inevitable and frequent, and both create serious problems for the field, the children, and administrative budgets at all levels. "Under-counting deprives...children of special services to which they are entitled; over-counting results in the inappropriate placement of students who are not handicapped, loss of valuable staff time, and increased expense of operating programs. Over-counting thus drains resources from other programs and students."[50]

While special-education spending continues to grow, funding has not kept up, forcing school administrators to "encroach" upon general-education revenues to pay the costs of special education. Over a quarter of all special-education program expenditures in California, on average, are paid from a school district's general fund...In 1991-92, the special education program in Los Angeles incurred a deficit of $154 million—a deficit recovered through nonmandated encroachment into the school district's general fund.[51]

Today, eligibility determination is a major thorn in special education's side. Over-identification appears especially troublesome. "If [it] continues to be rampant, it could result in the demise of [exceptional] programs altogether."[52] Devastating as that would be, under-identification guarantees something immeasurably worse. Recall the recent question of what happens to children needing classroom support who are left unassisted. True, we do save a few dollars by not providing services to those academically needy children when they first begin to stumble. At the moment we refuse them services, they are not placed on special education's roles, and they are not part of special education's budget. That's the beginning of a predictable sequence of events. Before that sequence ends, we will spend a small fortune many times over for failing to offer those children the educational platform they first needed to succeed in their classrooms.

It appears as though we are caught between a rock and a hard place. We have growing numbers of children who need special assistance to succeed in school. We do not have enough money to provide them all with special education services. Of those we turn down because their discrepancies aren't yet severe, many will be seen again—at increased costs. The issue of special education eligibility is perplexing and aggravating.

A HINT AT THE FUTURE

Decisions regarding future eligibility rules and regulations ultimately will be resolved at the congressional level. Federal legislation, initiated by various organizations (e.g., National Association of School Psychologists and Council for Exceptional Children) will set future policies. The 1995 Seventeenth Annual Report to Congress on the Implementation of The Individuals with Disabilities Education Act [IDEA] offers an inkling of what the future might hold regarding special education eligibility. In a series of guidelines developed by the Center for Special Education Finance (CSEF), the following consideration was suggested to states "attempting to revise their special education funding formals (sic)...."

States could fund and encourage the use of appropriate interventions for all students. Some argue that service option restrictions result in some students who need intervention services being identified as eligible for special education because that is the only way to provide them with intervention services. State funding systems that actively support alternative interventions for all students will be less likely to lead to special education program placements that are unnecessarily restrictive.[53]

The above guideline suggests offering "appropriate interventions to all students," something akin to a service-as-needed approach for all enrolled students in our public school. While it might be hard to imagine the logistics necessary to accomplish such a (controversial) feat in a school system that has an unfathomable number of parts and pieces that do not always mesh smoothly, its adoption would allow the dismantling of special education's troublesome eligibility system.

The Center's suggestion remains only a proposal. For the near and distant future, special education will adhere to its requirement that a child must be identified and labeled exceptional before assistance is offered. The field will continue to be guided by federal and state regulations that have remained virtually unchanged for more than 2 decades.

FOCUS: DECISION ERRORS

Maintaining adherence to these federal regulations is not without a price, however. They are open to easy misinterpretation. No matter the diligence of practicing school psychologists, these regulations contribute directly to an unknown number of horrific eligibility-decision errors, what the field designates "false positives" and "false negatives." False positives result in students being officially determined exceptional when they're not, and false negatives result in students being officially determined not exceptional—and not in need of special assistance, when they are. These errors do impact children's lives.

Many respected authorities in special education have placed in question the essential components of special education's discrepancy model and the debatable formula the field uses to determine which schoolchildren are to be assisted. The model and its formula guarantee eligibility-decision errors. We turn our attention to their essential components.

NOTES

1. Henley, M., Ramsey, R. S., & Algozzine, R. (1993). *Characteristics of and strategies for teaching students with mild disabilities.* Boston: Allyn and Bacon, p. 5.

2. Henley, M., Ramsey, R. S., & Algozzine, R. (1993).

3. Smith, D. D., & Luckasson, R. (1992). *Introduction to special education: teaching in an age of challenge.* Boston: Allyn & Bacon, p. 20-21.

4. Heller, W. H., Holtzman, W.H., & Messick, S. (1982). Placement in special education: Historical developments and current procedures. In Kirby A. Heller, Wayne H. Holtzman, & Samuel Messick (Eds.), *Placing children in special education: A strategy for equity* (p.32) Washington, DC: National Academic Press.

5. Abeson, A. (1972). Movement and momentum: Government and the education of handicapped children, *Exceptional Children, 39,* 63.

6. Abeson, A. (1972).

7. Mills v. Board of Education (D.D.C. 1972), 348,f.Supp.866, 878.

8. Henley, M., Ramsey, R. S., & Algozzine, R. (1993), p. 8.

9. Blake, K. A. (1981). *Educating exceptional pupils.* Reading, Mass: Addison-Wesley.

10. Abeson, A. (1972).

11. Smith, D. D., & Luckasson, R. (1992).

12. Abeson, A. (1974). Movement and Momentum: Government and the Education of Handicapped Children-II, *Exceptional Children,* 41, 2, p. 109-115.

13. Abeson, A. (1974).

14. Abeson, A. (1974).

15. Abeson, A. (1974).

16. Abeson, A. (1974).

17. Abeson, A. (1974).

18. Clowse, B. B. (1981). *Brainpower for the cold war: The sputnik crisis and national defense education act of 1958.* Westport, Conn: Greenwood Press.

19. Clowse, B. B. (1981), p. 6.

20. Clowse, B. B. (1981), p. 6.

21. Blow to U.S. Seen. (1957, October 6). *New York Times,* p.43. (See also The Race to Come (1957, October 21). *Time,* p.21.)

22. Clowse, B. B. (1981), p. 21. (See also *A birthday flexing of red biceps.* (1957, November, 18). *Life,* p.35, and Building brainpower. (1957, November 4). *Newsweek,* p. 96.)

23. Clowse, B. B. (1981), p. 28.

24. Clowse, B. B. (1981), p. 106. (see also Wilson, S. (1958), March 24). It's time to close the carnival. *Life,* p. 37.)

25. U.S., Congress, Senate (1958). *A collection of excerpts and a bibliography relative to American education and certain other educational systems.* S.Doc. 109, 85th Cong., 2d sess., *Senate Miscellaneous Documents* 2: 30.

26. Clowse, B. B. (1981), p. 16.)

27. Sleeter, C. E. (1986). Learning disabilities: The social construction of a special education category. *Exceptional Children, 53,* 46-64.

28. Sleeter, C. E. (1986).

29. Sleeter, C. E. (1986), p. 46.

30. Sleeter, C. E. (1986).

31. Strauss, A. A., & Kephart, N. C. (1955). *Psychopathology and education of the brain-injured child.* New York: Grune and Stratton.

32. Bender, L. (1957). Specific reading disability as a maturational lag. *Bulletin of the Orton Society,* 7, 9-18.

33. Orton, S. T. (1937) *Reading, writing, and speech problems in children.* New York: W.W. Norton.

34. Delcato, C. H. (1959) *The treatment and prevention of reading problems.* Springfield, IL: Charles C Thomas.

35. Moats, L. C., & Lyon, G. R. (1993). Learning disabilities in the United States: Advocacy, science, and the future of the field. *Journal of Learning Disabilities,* 26, 282-294.

36. Swanson, B. M, & Willis, D. J. (1979). *Understanding exceptional children and youth.* Chicago: Rand McNally College Publishing Company.

37. U.S. Department of Education. (1988b). *Tenth annual report to Congress on the implementation of the Education of the Handicapped Act.* Washington, DC.: Author. [Table 3, p.9. Note: Children under GLD heading now placed under heading of "mental retardation."]

38. U.S. Department of Education (1995) *Seventeenth annual report to Congress on the implementation of the Education of the Handicapped Act.* Washington, DC.: Author. [Table 1.6, p. 11.]

39. U.S. Department of Education. (1988b). *Tenth annual report to Congress on the implementation of the Education of the Handicapped Act.* Washington, DC: Author. [Table 3, p.9. Note: Children under GLD heading now placed under heading of "mental retardation."]

40. U.S. Department of Education. (1988b) [p. 7].

41. Ysseldyke, J. E., Algozzine, B., & Thurlow, M. L. (1992). *Critical issues in special education.* Boston: Houghton Mifflin Company, p.350.

42. U.S. Department of Education (1995). *Seventeenth annual report to Congress on the implementation of the Education of the Handicapped Act.* Washington, DC: Author. [Table 1.6, p. 11. Cost only includes Part B State Grant Program.]

43. Amount derived by adding Part B State Grant, Part H program during FY 1993, and Chapter 1 funds.

44. Beales, J. R. (1993). Special education: Expenditures and obligations, *Reason Foundation,* Policy Study No. 161, p.13.

45. Moore, M. T., Strang, E. W., Schwartz, M., & Braddock, M. (1988). *Patterns in special education service delivery and cost.* Washington, DC: Decision Resources Corporation.

46. Beales, J. R. (1993).

47. U.S. Department of Education (1995) Seventeenth annual report to Congress on the implementation of the Education of the Handicapped Act. [Table 1.6, p.116.]

48. Martin , R. (1992, July/August). Problems with severe discrepancy formula, *LDA/Newsbriefs,* p.3.

49. Ysseldyke, J. E., Algozzine, B., & Thurlow, M. L. (1992), p. 343.

50. Chalfant, J. C. (1984). *Identifying learning disabled students: Guidelines for decision making.* Burlington, VT: Northeast Regional Resource Center.

51. Beales, J. R. (1993).

52. Reynolds, C. R. (1990). Conceptual and technical problems in learning disability diagnosis. In C. R. Reynolds & R. W. Kamphus (Eds.), *Handbook of psychological and educational assessment of children* (p. 571) New York: Guilford.

53. Parrish, T. B. (1994). *Removing incentives for restrictive placements* . (Policy Paper No. 4). Palo Alto, CA: Center for Special Education Finance, American Institutes for Research, p. 120.

5

Eligibility: The Playing Field

Eligibility problems plaguing special education are not related to the important concept of discrepancies. Discrepancies as signs of potential problems, whether educational, psychological, or physical, are essential. Special education's difficulties with its eligibility model stem rather from the types of discrepancy formulas it uses to determine which school children qualify for its services. While there are several formats adopted by states to evaluate eligibility, two are most popular. The components of the first formula consider the student's actual classroom academic work as compared with the expectations professionals hold for that student's classroom work. If the difference between the student's expected and actual academic achievement satisfies a prescribed level of deficiency (usually two years below grade level), a discrepancy is said to be present and the student likely is declared eligible for special education classification and resource assistance.[1] The second eligibility formula is somewhat different. In this second case, eligibility for special education requires a meaningful difference between what the youngster is capable of accomplishing academically and what he is actually accomplishing in the classroom.[2,3] This second eligibility formula, requiring a discrepancy between a student's academic achievement and the student's predicted academic ability or potential, is referred to as the "ability-achievement" discrepancy model. All states and school districts employ some variation of the aforementioned discrepancy formulas to determine which of its enrolled children qualify for special education support services. However, there appears to be an increasing trend toward using the second formula, the ability-achievement discrepancy format for eligibility determination.[4] As you might predict, the concept of discrepancy is not without its problems.

DEGREES OF DISCREPANCY

Discrepancies vary, ranging from incidental to serious. For example, data suggest that most toddlers take to their feet and walk (with differing levels of success) at an average age of 12 to 14 months. A child not exercising that skill at 16 months has exhibited a discrepancy, although it is not likely to be judged serious. A child now 24 months who has yet to take a first step has also exhibited a discrepancy. While both measures differ from professional expectations, the latter will be viewed as more serious than the former. Likewise, the discrepancy exhibited by a youngster who is a lesson or two behind a teacher's expectations will not raise the same concern as would a youngster who is lagging a full year or two behind. That discrepancies differ in degree adds to the difficulty of pinning them down. The fact that two professionals can look at the same discrepancy and judge its foreboding differently compounds its accurate interpretation.

Tightening Eligibility Qualifications

In my professional circles during the early 1970s, most cooperating special education directors advised those of us working at the Colorado special education facility to always serve a child who we believed needed assistance. The qualitative seriousness of a discrepancy was not viewed as an absolute prerequisite to additional services. Our charge was to identify children who needed help and to provide it. Dollars, again, were plentiful, allowing criteria used to approve added services for children to be lenient. The river, of course, soon would alter those circumstances.

In the mid-1970s, as Congress debated major legislation that would guarantee educational services to children regardless of handicap, it realized it had no handle on the numbers of children who might qualify for special education assistance. Authoritative testimony presented during legislative hearings estimated that as many as 40% of the present school-age population could be classified as learning disabled depending upon which definition was adopted. Since every eligible child would receive some amount of funding, the dollar costs were potentially staggering.[5] A decade later, authorities reevaluated that 40% estimate and suggested that "by using the various measurement models employed among the states, 'an astute diagnostician can qualify between 50% and 80% of a random sample of the population as having a learning disability that requires special education services....'"[6] "Staggering" was upped an additional notch.

Severe Discrepancies

The real prospects of an unharnessable negative cash flow, its volume certain to be prodigious, alarmed congressional accountants. In an effort to reduce the foreseen flow of dollars, the government concluded that the term "discrepancy" was far too broad to be the sole criterion for providing students with special education assistance. To rein in the term "discrepancy," presumably to assist school-based diagnostic teams in more accurately judging which students really needed assistance from special education, the government required the term to be qualified by the descriptor "severe." A school's diagnostic team now had to determine that a struggling child's discrepancy between his abilities and achievements was severe before that youngster was determined exceptional and eligible for special education services. The team also had to determine what constitutes severe?

The legislative decision to tighten the term "discrepancy" was a knee-jerk reaction at best. It's hard to grasp how Congress and its special education advisors could have imagined that the qualifier "severe" would solve their eligibility-determination problems. Severe is open to a tantalizing variety of definitions and interpretations. At what point does a discrepancy become that extreme? This is a pesky question without an absolute answer, a question that can be answered only with a predetermined cut-off score ordained with the power to distinguish severe from anything less. In an effort to assist its personnel, the state of Oregon, for example, during the 1950s, informed its educational diagnosticians how the term "severe" was to be defined: "[C]hildren in grades 2,3,4 whose reading age...is one year below mental age' are said to exhibit a severe discrepancy; 'children above grade 4 whose reading age is two or more years below mental age,' were likewise exhibiting a severe discrepancy between ability and achievement."[7]

Oregon set a standard that made it easier for its diagnosticians to determine which children should receive services. As will be seen, the cleanliness of the score that objectified severe would produce the same problems befalling all cut-off numbers. If a young child's reading age was one year below mental age, that difference was interpreted as severe; if less than one year below mental age, that child's reading discrepancy was not severe enough for special education assistance. State officials could have chosen 6 or 9 months below mental age or grade level or average reading level of the class—or any other measure that fit their perspective.

The outcome of Oregon's efforts at defining the term "severe discrepancy" was predictable. Under Oregon's standard, some of the state's school children were designated as having a severe reading discrepancy while others were not. Said differently, some children struggling with reading were not struggling enough to meet Oregon's criteria for assistance. Clean cut-offs rarely allow for exceptions. In Oregon's case, border-line kids would not be served until their reading skills worsened. Well, at least the concept of severe was standardized.

Undoubtedly, incorrect decisions as to which children deserved extra services were made by Oregon's officials. The slippery qualities of mental age and reading age guarantee an educational basket with holes large enough for an entire class of children to fall through. Perhaps Oregon thought it had no other option but to use an artificial cut-off score to help it determine which children warranted extra support. That's too bad. One option was as close as their collective noses. Rather than wait for some of its children to acquire more severe reading problems, Oregon could have decided that all children having difficulties with reading were entitled to well-planned, effective reading assistance. Oregon could have concluded that any child who was experiencing difficulty reading was exhibiting a discrepancy, making the concept "severe" unnecessary and avoidable. Presumably, general educators with skills in teaching reading were already in the building; they already were working with the children in the classrooms. It wasn't as though they needed to go outside their school buildings to hire expensive consultants. All they needed to do was switch on their copious talents. One wonders what these general teachers expected from special education.

Table 5.1
Assessment Procedures

Procedure	Valid Discrepancy Score	Comments
Number of years below grade level	No	Very crude and inaccurate measures of discrepancy
Ability-achievement discrepancy scores	No	Serious methodological problems
Intra-test comparisons	Evidence inconclusive	Research findings contradictory
Profile analysis	Evidence inconclusive	Serious methodological problems

Multiple Determinations of Severity

Today, even though some states do provide guidelines to assist their school districts' diagnostic teams, the task of confirming the existence of a severe discrepancy remains vexing and controversial for most professionals. Some states suggest that two or more years below grade level represents a severe discrepancy; some suggest three or more years is more accurate. Other states, despite warnings that their methods are thoroughly unsound,[8] still use profile and subtest analyses from intelligence test scores to help gain a handle on what constitutes severe. Still others use graduated cut-off scores attached to grade levels in an effort to quantify severe and provide special education services.[9] For example, a high school tenth grader must be 3 years or more behind in reading achievement to be eligible for special assistance, whereas a first grader can receive some assistance by manifesting only a 1 year discrepancy between reading efforts and grade level expectations.

School districts have tried more than a dozen different procedures to help them determine if an observed discrepancy warrants being classified severe. Unfortunately, technical reviewers (see Table 5.1) have concluded that the evaluative procedures used to bring order to the concept of severe are generally weak if not flatly invalid.[10]

Commonplace Confusion and Inconsistency

Nearly 50% of the states leave the knotty interpretation of severe discrepancy in the hands of their local school districts.[11] The states' reluctance to make a definitive decision is understandable since the size of a discrepancy needed to reach severe proportions is not spelled out in [the federal] definition.[12] As a result, discrepancy size used to qualify youngsters varies from state to state,[13] and the variety of models and procedures for determining a severe discrepancy is presently countless.[14]

Unintentionally, the educational system and the federal government have taken the relatively simple concept of discrepancy and muddled it to a point where it accomplishes little more than closing doors to children who need assistance, while simultaneously opening them to divisive and expensive litigation. As it stands now, being declared eligible for special education services has less to do with any difficulties a child might be having in school than with the state and school district in which the youngster lives.[15]

THE REAL PURPOSE FOR THE TERM "SEVERITY"

While it might appear that the government's inclusion of severe in the discrepancy formula was to assist diagnostic teams in their evaluative process, the truth is that the term's addition to the discrepancy model was intended to save money by reducing the numbers of children being qualified for special education services.[16] I don't think it's possible to overstate the disastrousness of such thinking. While all our children are exceptional, the most exceptional and fragile are those first starting school. It is that group that has been most injured by requiring the qualifier severe to be a part of the discrepancy model. Why? I've personally witnessed the following similar lunacy.

> A [regular] first-grade teacher expressed concern about a student's performance and inquired about the possibility of testing the student for special education [eligibility]. The special education teacher informed the teacher that testing would not be helpful at this time because it is rarely possible to demonstrate enough of a discrepancy on a first grader to qualify the student for services....[T]he special education teacher advised the first-grade teacher that the best[17] strategy would be to wait until the child reached second grade when the likelihood of documenting a...discrepancy would be greater.[18]

The special educator told the regular teacher not to refer the child for eligibility testing because the child's school work, deficient as it was, wasn't deficient enough for the achievement discrepancy to be classified *severe*. The first grader, therefore, would have to wait a year or more, falling further behind in his school work, before receiving any assistance from special education. Before the system would provide the youngster a hand, the child might nearly have to disappear in the hole the system helped dig. The cost of extrication would have been far less had direct services been provided as soon as the child began to stumble. Recall that preventative fences are a lot less expensive than ambulances. (As an aside, you might wonder why the first grader's regular education teacher didn't do something dramatic for the struggling youngster such as teach him. Amazing things might have happened: He might have improved some of his skills.)

The Least of Special Education's Problems

The term "severe" has clouded rather than clarified special education's basic dilemma of who should be served. Its inclusion into the discrepancy formula only guarantees numerous errors in identification. It has provided school psychologists and other diagnosticians with an unsteady hook upon which to place their hats.

That said, the easily dispensable term "severe" is the least of special education's problems as it tries valiantly to identify which population to serve. Special education's discrepancy model is only as good as its ability to measure its critical elements, specifically a child's intelligence or intellectual potential and academic achievement. If we can't measure one or both of those elements, we can't know if any discrepancy between the two exists. The qualifier "severe" then becomes quite irrelevant. Let's turn our attention to the first of the discrepancy model's pivotal measures.

INTELLECTUAL POTENTIAL AND ELIGIBILITY

Intellectual potential represents the most significant component of special education's discrepancy model. Whether referred to as potential, aptitude, ability, capacity, or intelligence, the concept represents a measure of what a child should, by sheer brain power, be able to accomplish in school. It provides the basis upon which expectations for a student's classroom performance are made. It, therefore, represents half of special education's ability-achievement discrepancy formula and is centrally involved in the question of a student's eligibility for special education services.

IQs

Many of us have been taught that intellectual potential is measured by intelligence tests and is communicated by means of the familiar intelligence quotient or IQ. Many of us have come to rely on a child's IQ as an indication of what to expect academically from that child. Although it does happen, it is a very rare occurrence when a school psychologist or special education teacher discusses a student's qualification for special education without referring to the child's IQ. As a result, intelligence tests and their produced IQ scores are firmly established in special education's discrepancy formula: "...34 states [use] an IQ discrepancy definition to identify children as being eligible for special education services because of a language or learning disability. Even when [a] discrepancy [is] not formally codified, all but four states [use] scores on an IQ test as part of the [eligibility] process."[19]

The Veracity of Intelligence and IQ

But suppose we have been misinformed about IQ. Suppose our assumptions regarding intelligence testing and IQ scores are wrong. Suppose intelligence tests measure something other than what we say is intelligence. The severity of a discrepancy aside, suppose special education has no ability-achievement discrepancy to begin with. Because the vast majority of special education eligibility decisions are made only after weighing a youngster's intelligence quotient against academic achievements, the concept of intellectual potential and our ability to measure it are critical issues. If we conclude that intelligence is not measurable, if we acknowledge that the term represents something other than an estimate of a child's capacity or intellectual potential, then its use in determining which children should qualify for special education services is in stark error. The professional literature sheds very interesting light on these issues.

INTELLIGENCE: DEFINITION

[Writes a professor], "When I first taught a course called 'Intelligence' in the early 1960's, my predecessor kindly gave me his notes which included a list of over 90 different definitions of intelligence that he had found in the literature. I suspect that, if the list has not doubled in the last quarter century, it's at least half again as long. E. G. Boring's almost tongue-in-cheek definition, 'Intelligence is what the tests of intelligence test'[20] lays bare the essentially circular reasoning that characterizes much of the speculation about intelligence."[21]

Today, a universally accepted definition for intelligence still lies beyond our reach. Not surprising, we have yet to fully agree how best to measure that which we have yet to define. In 1967, during the Presidential address to the American Psychological Association, the same observations were made.

The nature of intelligence has been a favorite subject for contemplation and disputation for centuries—perhaps from the dawn of man as Homo Sapiens. The topic is being studied and debated today by educators, sociologists, geneticists, neurophysiologists, and biochemists, and by psychologists specializing in various branches of the discipline. Despite this attention and effort, however—or perhaps *because* of it—there appears to be no more general agreement as to the nature of intelligence or the most valid means of measuring intelligence than was the case 50 years ago. Concepts of intelligence and the definitions constructed to enunciate these concepts abound by the dozens, if not indeed by the hundreds. With so many diverse definitions of intelligence, it is perhaps not surprising that we cannot agree on how to measure intelligence.[22]

Love and Intelligence: What Are We Measuring?

Years ago while at the University of Denver, I joined a few colleague-friends as we tried in vain to define and measure the elusive construct "love." I watched as a long gray chalkboard was blanketed with bits and pieces of observable actions and behaviors, chemical mixtures and electrical states—all purely fictional of course, along with a beguiling list of private emotions thought to course through the heart when love was ripe. The exercise was more fun than serious. To the bitter end, a few clung to the belief that love was quantifiable and dissectable. At argument was whether love was a thing. Most said if it were, it would cease to exist. Intelligence, it appears, bleeds from the same wounds.

> The grammatical form [of intelligence] itself can be misleading. 'Intelligence' is a noun, and nouns often refer to things or objects. Even when we know perfectly well that intelligence is not a 'thing', but a sophisticated abstraction from behaviour, we may sometimes half-consciously endow it with a shadowy existence distinct and separate from the intelligent organisms which alone give it meaning, or more insidiously, think it is a 'thing' that these organisms 'have', rather than a description of the way they behave. This kind of misconception is often described as 'reification' of the concept. It is better, therefore, to think of the adjective 'intelligent' as more basic (and less dangerous) than the noun.[23]

INTELLIGENCE: NOT AN ENTITY

The above admonition to view intelligence as an adjective rather than a noun (or thing) was preempted more than 100 years ago by the man whose name would become most associated with intelligence testing, Alfred Binet. Professor Binet warned against considering intelligence an entity with finite boundaries. He viewed intelligence "not as a thing, or an amount, or something 'inside' a person, but an active transaction between individual and external stimuli."[24] His cogent thoughts would be echoed further nearly a century later by A. G. Wesman, former president of the American Psychological Association, who thought intelligence to be "the sum total of all the learning experiences [an individual] has uniquely had up to any moment in time...an attribute, [and] not an entity....."[25] Berkeley psychologist and author, Arthur Jensen, differed little. "It is a mistake," Dr. Jensen suggested, "to waste time arguing about the definition of intelligence, except to make sure everyone understands that the term does not refer to a 'thing'."[26] D. G. Doehring, summarizing the view of many psychologists in the 1960s and 1970s, not only agreed that intelligence is not an independent entity but suggested further that "...there is no...unequivocal set of measures of the capacity of the intellect...."[27] (This latter position, representing much more than an afterthought, is of enormous importance to our present discussion.)

Finally, scholar/humorist John Horn provided an appropriate cap to Alfred Binet's concerns of what intelligence is and is not. Dr. Horn shared the view that "[a] great mound and variety of evidence indicates that what is called intelligence is a mixture of quite different things—different attributes having different genetic and environmental determinants and different developmental courses over the life span...."[28] A year later, when asked, "What do I conceive intelligence to be?" he answered, no doubt wearing a cleverly painted Jack Nicholson smile, "This is rather like asking me: What do I conceive invisible green spiders to be? ...[C]urrent knowledge suggests to me that intelligence is not a unitary entity of any kind. Attempts to describe it are bound to be futile."[29]

Intelligence: Multiple Types

From the end of World War I to the present, a significant proportion of the educational community has held to an opinion that there is probably no...single definition of intelligence. They have held that intelligence is composed of numerous independent abilities, many of which, if not all, are supposedly modifiable, given the correct pedagogical or psychological intervention.[30]

Intelligence, whether as adjective or noun, can apparently be whatever we choose. In 1921, the much admired learning theorist and educational psychologist Edward Thorndike, hinting at the chameleon character of intelligence, went so far as to suggest, "There may be as many specific intelligences as one cares to name."[31] Knowing that special education's concept of intelligence has always been extraordinarily myopic, measured by a rather simple paper and pencil test, I decided to test Dr. Thorndike's casual attitude toward the topic and see how many different types of intelligences I could find over a quiet lunch hour. Skimming the dozen or so books I pulled from the library's stacks, I quickly discovered Dr. Thorndike's opinion was accurate. Happily, I first met folks affectionately referred to as "lumpers" and "splitters." I half expected them to be relatives of the Seven Dwarfs. Instead, I learned they were theorists who thought intelligence was either a general capacity or a compilation of different types of abilities.[32] Between them, I discovered "intelligences" to fit most anyone's preference.

1.   General Intelligence[33]

2.   Academic Intelligence[34]

3.   Fluid and Crystallized Intelligence[35]

4.   Biological, Psychometric, and Social Intelligence[36]

5.   Conceptual and Practical[37] Intelligence[38]

6.   Neural, Experiential, and Reflective Intelligence[39]

7.   Emotional Intelligence[40]

8.   Social Intelligence[41]

9.   (Intelligence that is the) biological adaptation between the individual and the environment[42]

10.   (Intelligence that is the) systematic collection of abilities or functions for processing information of different kinds in various forms[43]

11.   (Intelligence that is the) ability to attend, process information, and utilize those processes to solve problems[44]

12.   Howard Gardner's magnificent seven : [45]

    a. Logical-mathematical

    b. Linguistic

    c. Musical

    d. Spatial

    e. Bodily-kinesthetic

    f. Interpersonal

    g. Intrapersonal

13.   Robert Sternberg's—just about every mental process you can possibly imagine—Intelligence:

> Intelligence comprises the mental abilities necessary for adaptation to, as well as shaping and selection of, any environmental context...This context has physical, biological, and cultural aspects, which may interact....[I]ntelligence is not just reactive to the environment but also active in forming it....Among the core mental processes: (a) recognizing the existence of [a] problem, (b) defining the nature of the problem, (c) constructing a strategy to solve the problem, (d) mentally representing information about the problem, (e) allocating mental resources in solving the problem, (f) monitoring one's solution to the problem, and (g) evaluating one's solution to the problem. [46]

The variety within the above list is not surprising. As with a droplet of mercury, intelligence scatters in all directions with just the slightest nudge. The term has been squeezed, stretched and so enthusiastically revered and pummeled that it no longer holds any practical value in education's day-to-day operations. No matter its artificially imposed shape, intelligence, like love, rests beyond our fingertips.

The really interesting concepts of this world have the nasty habit of avoiding our most determined attempts to pin them down, to make them say something definite and make them stick to it. Their meanings perversely remain multiple, ambiguous, imprecise, and above all unstable and open— open to argument and disagreement, to sometimes drastic reformulation and redefinition, and to the introduction of new and often unsettling concept instances and examples. It is perhaps not a bad thing that our prize concepts have this kind of complexity and instability (some might call it richness and creativity). In any event, they do seem to have these properties, and therefore we would be wise not to expend too much of our time and energy trying to fix them in formal definitions.[47]

FOCUS: REMOVING THE MEASURE OF INTELLIGENCE FROM SPECIAL EDUCATION'S ELIGIBILITY MODEL

In a recent *New York Times* book review of David Perkins' *Outsmarting IQ: The Emerging Science of Learnable Intelligence*, Derek Bickerton assessed a major problem faced by professionals assigned the task of measuring someone's intelligence: "They are trying to measure something without knowing what it is." Mr. Bickerton then suggested that, "the I.Q. debate would most benefit from a hundred-year-moratorium. A century from now we may finally be able to assess intelligence without fuzzy thinking."[48]

Intelligence in any form or by any definition, as a prerequisite to eligibility, has no place in special education. That position, controversial for certain, is arrived at logically. Scholars and authorities from different centuries and decidedly different dispositions remind us that we have yet to agree on a quantitative or qualitative definition of the term. Despite roundly humorous efforts at estimating an individual's intelligence (e.g., estimating intelligence from skull circumference),[49] measuring what has yet to be defined is hardly possible. We've named a bushel basket of types of intelligences, yet schools use only one flavor in their formula, and a flavor whose veracity has been called into serious question at that. Assuredly, intelligence is more than we know and less than we imagine. For the time being, and forever, schools don't need it, either as a way to describe a child or as a thing a child is said to have.

Catastrophe or Blessing: Hold On to Your Hat

If we remove a psychologist's estimate of a child's intellectual capacity or potential from special education's ability-achievement discrepancy model, we no longer have an ability-achievement discrepancy. We have remaining a measure of a child's accomplishments on whatever tests of achievement the youngster's teachers and school have chosen to use. That prospect causes no arrhythmic heartbeat for seasoned psychologists and teachers who are quite comfortable working directly with diverse children possessing varying academic strengths. Conversely, the suggestion that the measure of intellectual capacity be removed from special education's eligibility process roars apocalyptic for others, producing in one instance a prediction that truly warrants a second, careful reading to fully appreciate the prophecy's absurdity.

> If we were to rely on achievement tests only we would largely serve low achievers...we would create a situation characterized by overrepresentation of students from language-different backgrounds, minority groups, and males....Relying only on achievement data is basically nonexclusionary in that it provides no criterion regarding who warrants special education programming.[50]

Wow! It is hard to escape the impression that according to the above author, intelligence tests somehow provide a floor-to-ceiling fence that keeps those kind of kids away, somewhere. Elitism aside, if the illusory measure of intelligence and potential were removed from special education's eligibility model, leaving only a student's classroom achievements to work with, all but a few educators would know exactly what to do: determine the child's academic entering skills and strengths and build upon them. A child's language, ethnicity, or gender (or potential) would not interfere with that process. Ironically, special education, in partnership with general education, would become nonexclusionary, the very outcome the above author feared. The collective fields would assume the responsibility to provide all students with access to a special education. Intelligence tests only interfere with that responsibility.

If we were to remove intelligence from special education's discrepancy model, in fact, if we were never to administer another intelligence test in school, the educational world, and particularly our schoolchildren, would do just fine. The question of eligibility for school related supportive services would be answered easily.

NOTES

1. Algozzine, B., Ysseldyke, J. E., & Shinn, M. (1982). Identifying children with learning disabilities: When is a discrepancy severe? *Journal of School Psychology, 20,* 298-305l.

2. Myers, P. I. & Hammill, D. D. (1976). *Methods for learning disorders.* New York: John Wiley & Sons.

3. Hunt, N. & Marshall, K. (1994). Exceptional children and youth. Boston: Houghton Mifflin.

4. Frankenberger, W., & Fronzaglio, K. (1991). A review of states' criteria for identifying children with learning disabilities. *Journal of Learning Disabilities, 24,* 495-500.

5. Martin, R. (1992, July/August). Problems with severe discrepancy formulas, *LDA/Newsbriefs,* p.3

6. Reynolds, C. R. (1985). Critical measurement issues in learning disabilities. *Journal of Special Education,* 18,451-475.

7. Oregon State Department of Education. (1955). *Information concerning certification of handicapped children. HC Bulletin 2--revised.*

8. Macmann, G. M. & Barnett, D. W. (1997). Myth of the master detective: Reliability of interpretations for Kaufman's "Intelligent testing" approach to the WISC—III. *School Psychology Quarterly, 12,* 197-234.

9. Cone, T. E., & Wilson, L. R. (1981). Quantifying a severe discrepancy: A critical analysis. *Learning Disability Quarterly, 4,* 359-371.

10. Berk, R. A. (1982). Effectiveness of discrepancy score methods for screening children with learning disabilities, *Learning Disabilities, 1,* 11-24.

11. Henley, M., Ramsey, R. S., & Algozzine, R. (1993). *Characteristics of and strategies for teaching students with mild disabilities.* Boston: Allyn and Bacon.

12. Hunt, N. & Marshall, K. (1994) *Exceptional Children and Youth.* Boston: Houghton Mifflin.

13. Hunt, N. & Marshall, K. (1994).

14. Reynolds, C. R. (1990). Conceptual and technical problems in learning disability diagnosis. In C. R. Reynolds, & R. W. Kamphaus, (Eds.), *Handbook of psychological and educational assessment of children: Intelligence and achievement* (p. 574). New York: Guilford.

15. Reynolds, C. R. (1990). Conceptual and technical problems in learning disability diagnosis. In C. R. Reynolds, & R. W. Kamphaus, (Eds.).

16. Mather, N., & Healey, W. C. (1990). Deposing aptitude-achievement discrepancy as the imperial criterion for learning disabilities. *Learning Disabilities, 2,* 40-48.

17. Interesting choice of words for a special education teacher to use. I suspect a first year college student minoring in education could develop a better strategy than waiting a full year to intervene.

18. Mather, N. (1993). Critical issues in the diagnosis of learning disabilities addressed by the Woodcock-Johnson Psycho-Educational Battery-Revised. Journal of Psychoeducational Assessment, Monograph Series, Advances in psychoeducational assessment, WJ-R Monograph, p. 103.

19. Frankenberger, W., & Fronzaglio, K. (1991). A review of states' criteria for identifying children with learning disabilities. *Journal of Learning Disabilities, 24,* 495-500.

20. Boring, E. G. (1923, June 6). Intelligence as the tests test it. *The New Republic,* pp. 35-37.

21. Lezak, M. D. (1988). IQ: R.I.P. *Journal of Clinical and Experimental Neuropsychology, 10,* pp. 351-361.

22. Wesman, A. G. (1968). Intelligent testing. *American Psychologist, 23,* 267-274.

23. Howe, M. J. A. (1988). Intelligence as an explanation. *British Journal of Psychology, 79,* 349-360. (See also Butcher, H. J. (1968). *Human intelligence: Its nature and assessment.* New York: Harper TorchBooks.)

24. Sarason, S. B., & Doris, J. (1979). *Educational handicap, public policy, and social history.* New York: Free Press.

25. Wesman, A. G. (1968).

26. Jensen, A. R. (1982). The chronometry of intelligence. In R. J. Sternberg (Ed.), *Advances in the psychology of human intelligence,* Vol 1. Hillsdale, N.J.: Lawrence Erlbaum Associates.

27. Doehring, D. G. (1978). The tangled web of behavioral research on developmental dyslexia. In A.L. Benton & D. Pearl (Eds.), *Dyslexia: An appraisal of current knowledge* (pp.123-138) New York: Oxford University Press.

28. Horn, J. (1985). Remodeling old models of intelligence. In Benjamin B. Wolman (Ed.), *Handbook of intelligence: Theories, measurement, and application.* New York: John Wiley & Sons.

29. Horn, J. (1986). Some thoughts about intelligence. In R. J. Sternberg & D. K. Detterman (Eds.), *What is intelligence? Contemporary viewpoints on its nature and definition.* Norwood, New Jersey: ABLEX Publishing Co.

30. Kehle, T. J., Clark, E., & Jenson, W. R. (1993). The development of testing as applied to school psychology. *The Journal of School Psychology, 31,* pp.143-161.

31. Thorndike, E. L. (1921). *The measurement of intelligence.* Bureau of Publications, Teachers College, Columbia University, New York.

32. Morris, C. G. (1990). *Psychology: An introduction.* Englewood Cliffs, NJ: Prentice Hall.

33. Spearman, C. E. (1927). *The abilities of man: Their nature and measurement.* New York: Macmillan Company.

34. Anastasi, A. (1982). *Psychological testing* (5th ed.). New York: Macmillan.

35. Horn, J. L. & Cattell, R. B. (1966). Refinement and test of the theory of fluid and crystallized intelligence. *Journal of Educational Psychology, 57,* 253-270.

36. Eysenck, H. (1988). The concept of "intelligence": Useful or useless? *Intelligence, 12,* 1-16.

37. Sternberg, R. J., Wagner, R. K., & Okagaki, L. (1993). Practical intelligence: The nature and role of tacit knowledge in work and at school. In H. Reese & J. Puckett (Eds.), *Advances in lifespan development* (pp. 205-227). Hillsdale, NJ: Erlbaum.

38. AAMR Ad Hoc Committee on Terminology and Classification. (1992). Mental retardation: definition, classification, and systems of support. (9th ed.) Washington, D.C.: American Association on Mental Retardation.

39. Perkins, D. (1995). *Outsmarting IQ: The emerging science of learnable intelligence.* New York: The Free Press.

40. Goleman, D. (1995). *Emotional intelligence.* New York: Bantam Books.

41. Cantor, N., & Kihlstrom, J. F. (1987). Social intelligence: The cognitive basis of personality. In P. Shaver (Ed.)., *Review of personality and social psychology* (Vol. 6, pp.15-34). Beverly Hills, CA: Sage.

42. Ault, R. L. (1977). *Children's cognitive development: Piaget's theory and the process approach.* New York: Oxford University Press.

43. Guilford, J. P. (1988). The structure-of-intellect model. In Benjamin B. Wolman (Ed.), *Handbook of intelligence: Theories, measurements, and applications.* New York: John Wiley & Sons.

44. Naglieri, J. A. & Reardon, S. M. (1993). Traditional IQ is irrelevant to learning disabilities--intelligence is not. *Journal of Learning Disabilities, 26,* 127-133.

45. Gardner, H. & Hatch, T. (1989). Multiple intelligences go to school: Educational implications of the theory of multiple intelligences, *Educational Researcher, 18,* 6.

46. Sternberg, R. J. (1997). The concept of intelligence and its role in lifelong learning and success. *American Psychologist, 52,* 1030-1037.

47. Flavell, J. (1985). *Cognitive Development* (2nd Ed.). Englewood Cliffs, New Jersey: Prentice-Hall, p. 2.

48. Bickerton, D. (1995, May 21). Get smart. *New York Times Book Review,* p. 9.

49. Gould, S. J. (1981). *The mismeasurement of man.* New York: W.W. Norton.

50. Meyen, E. (1989). Let's not confuse test scores with the substance of the discrepancy model. *Journal of Learning Disabilities, 22,* 482-483.

6

Measuring Intelligence

The fact is, we haven't removed the testing of intellectual potential from special education's discrepancy model. Daily, thousands of times, in schools and private offices, skilled psychologists administer intelligence tests yielding IQ numbers most often used to say something about children's intellectual capacities. It has been estimated that "[e]ach year, between 1.5 and 1.8 million intelligence tests are administered by school psychologists."[1] Once obtained, the numbers are compared against students' sampled classroom academic achievements to estimate whether the students' intellectual capacities are used to their fullest. A student with a high intellectual capacity is expected to do well in school. A discrepancy (and often a disability) is said to exist if a student with apparent high intellectual potential fails to achieve academically.

Despite a torrent of professional challenge and opposition, special education holds to the belief that intelligence and intellectual potential are measurable, that tests of intelligence measure that potential, and that IQ numbers indicate how well a child should perform in school. Aside from the annoying fact that intelligence has yet to be defined, evidence will show special education wrong. Evidence, too, will verify that intelligence tests are barely more than weak achievement instruments that have little connection with what happens inside a classroom. During IQ testing, intellectual potential, as if it were something that could be gleaned from an hour-long paper and pencil test, hardly enters the picture. And everything that has just been said has been known for years.

MAXIMUM CAPACITY

To some professionals, intelligence quotients foretell not just a student's intellectual capacity but the student's maximum intellectual capacity, the lid, if you will, above which the student cannot—or should not be expected to—go. Many schoolteachers, once hearing of a child's IQ number, speak of the now numbered youngster as though his or her scholastic prowess, or lack thereof, has been revealed as neatly and cleanly as if exposed by a surgeon's scalpel. Because their own schooling often fails to share the intimacies of intelligence testing and resulting IQs, a sizable portion of these teachers (and often the parents they speak to), do not realize that obtained IQ numbers aren't to be interpreted as fixed, unchanging numbers permanently etched on a child's forehead. Some 50 years ago, we learned that retest data yielded changes in IQ scores by as much as 50 points.[2] Specifically,

> Over the period from 6 to 18 years, when retest correlations are generally high, 59% of the children changed by 15 or more IQ points, 37% by 20 or more points, and 9% changed by 30 or more. Nor were most of these changes random or erratic in nature. On the contrary, children exhibited consistent upward or downward trends over consecutive years.[3]

Not surprisingly, the above changes were related to evolving environmental characteristics, one of which was, and still remains, schooling. Predictably, "the relationship between IQ test scores and educational achievement is reciprocal. IQ test scores change in response to the educational opportunities available to individuals."[4]

Pint Jugs

Teachers, sadly, are not alone in misinterpreting the fixed nature of IQ scores. One of my desert school psychology buddies had the disquieting habit of discussing children he tested by referring to their IQ numbers: "She's just a 100," he would inform a teacher who had expressed disappointment in a child's average school work. The implication behind his casually offered certainty was: "Don't expect much more from her, she's topped out" as if her crankcase could hold no more oil.

Cyril Burt's infamous "pint jug" owns the best metaphorical representation of this exasperating hyperbole. In the 1960s, Dr. Burt contended, "Capacity must obviously limit content. It is impossible for a pint jug to hold more than a pint of milk; and it is equally impossible for a child's educational attainments to rise higher than his educable capacity permits....[I]t was obviously nonsensical to try to force more education into the child's head than could be fitted in."[5]

Cyril Burt relied on IQ numbers to determine a child's capacity and the child's assumed intellectual limits. For this British psychologist, intelligence was primarily genetically determined. IQ numbers were thought to reflect a child's innate intellectual strength. Intelligence, Dr. Burt contended, was relatively fixed; it was transmitted from parent to offspring: Like father like son, Dr. Burt would say. Limited jugs, it seemed, were inheritable and measurable through intelligence tests.

Questionable Data

Cyril Burt took great liberties both with his data collection and ultimate determinations. It has been suggested that he knowingly fabricated his data.[6] Unless you enjoy sleeping on a bed of nails, it's hard to be comfortable with his conclusions. Fathers and sons do resemble one another, except when they don't; moms and daughters, of course, the same. That we inherit characteristics from our parents and their parents is not arguable, the specifics becoming more understood. Knowing whether intelligence in some genetically transmittable form is one of those specifics is a question another generation will have to answer. Concluding that there exists an unbreakable ceiling limiting one's intellectual pursuits is, to put it kindly, premature. It's also arrogant. We still have much to learn about the full power of our brains and the fullness of our intellect that resides somewhere within. Consider the following awe-inspiring children. The term "limits" seems starkly obscene.

I recently read an article about a young child suffering from severe seizures who underwent a surgical procedure to remove entirely one of her cerebral hemispheres in the hopes of providing relief from her seizures. Here is a youngster with truly half a brain who, postsurgically, was described by her physician in this way:

> Eight months [after surgery] and completely free from seizures, she frolics with her mother at a local pool...and runs with other four-year-olds at day care. The plasticity of a child's brain has let neurons in her left hemisphere make multitudes of new connections and take over many of the functions once performed by the right hemisphere. Therapy several times a week has helped, though it cannot restore full movement to her left side.
>
> She's a bright, lovely young lady who doesn't use her arm very well, says Dr. [John M.] Freeman. That's the bottom line.[7]

It is fair to say that the brain continues to teach us its lessons (and share all its marvelous secrets). It is enjoyable to watch disbelief cover the faces of graduate students who are astounded, first, by the fact that there exists a surgical procedure to remove an entire hemisphere: "Hemispherectomy takes half of the cerebral cortex, about 40 percent of the brain's volume—four billion of the 10 billion neurons whose electrochemical connections produce sensation, intellect, emotion, personality...studies of hemispherectomy patients have found no loss of IQ after surgery,"[8] and second, that someone survives such intrusion: "Over the past 30 years, [Johns] Hopkins surgeons have performed 68 hemispherectomies for seizure disorders, the majority done since 1985 by [Dr. Benjamin S.] Carson....Four patients died during or after surgery. One, who had undergone previous surgery elsewhere, remains comatose months after hemispherectomy...That most of the patients survive and recover so completely remains a perpetual surprise even to those who watch it happen, again and again."[9] And third, surprised that the now single-hemispheric individual can do anything, much less do anything well:

[Dr. Carson's] Beth [who had her left hemisphere removed at the age of 7] has a weak short-term memory that requires constant drilling to master schoolwork. In her junior year at a competitive public high school, she is placed in standard history and science classes but gets special education support for math and English; she studies doggedly and often makes the honor roll. She speaks fluently and articulately but lisps her Rs and SHs and still receives some speech therapy. [She] is the girl she was before surgery—more mature, but with the same wise-guy manner, the same guile-less empathy with the underdog, the same ability to charm. Plus, she can kill her brother at Ping-Pong, and he has both hemispheres.[10]

The young lady described by Dr. Freeman had her right hemisphere removed. Another child described in the same article was making equally impressive gains despite having his left hemisphere removed. It is noted that in a 2 month period, this nonleft hemispheric youngster made 9 months' progress in language use. Fabulous! (And I would remind you that both children, because of their seizure activity and subsequent necessity of staying close to home, had to have missed out on enormous opportunities for everyday learning experiences and schooling which certainly would have impacted what they had acquired through their diffi-cult, presurgical, years.) This is the bottom line: Placing limits and lids on our brain (whether we have two hemispheres or one) doesn't seem a very intelligent thing to do.

Working above One's Maximum Capacity

School achievement ceilings are erected, however. Despite psychologists' condemnation of Cyril Burt's perspective that intelligence is fixed, limited in size and scope, unchangeable, represented by IQ, or imprinted indelibly some-where beneath the dura mater in the cerebral cortex,[11] some school personnel, particularly during special education staffings, act as though intelligence is mea-surable and immutable and that reported IQ scores accurately represent a child's capacity to achieve academically. They appear unperplexed when a child with a low IQ score performs poorly in class. Now that they "know" the child's intel-ligence, and have in hand the telling, low IQ score, it's as though the child's aca-demic struggling is expected and warrants little more than acknowledging. As interesting and bewildering, some teachers are surprised when a child with a low IQ score achieves beyond where he should. It appears a child may be suffering a serious problem if he is observed to progress academically beyond his alleged maximum intellectual capacity.

While at the University of Denver, I had completed an instructional presen-tation to a group of local public school teachers on issues of diversity and accommodation, and customarily asked the group for questions. A woman stood, her expression earnest. "I'm concerned about one of my students," said the young teacher. "I fear the student is working *above* his maximum capacity." I couldn't tell whether she discerned my flinch.
"I'm not certain I understand," I confessed.

Not wavering in voice or body, the educator explained, "The child is getting 'A's' in my class yet his intelligence is only average, 100 IQ," she added informatively. Then hammering the nail fully, she advised the spellbound audience, "He should only be making 'C's'."

After a dozen seconds of thick silence, I fumbled, "You must be an exceptionally good teacher."

THE ABILITY-ACHIEVEMENT DISCREPANCY MODEL'S DEMISE

What is measured when we administer a standardized intelligence test to a school youngster? What meaning or value is rightfully given to a score obtained from such a test? Both questions have been raised countless times. Response variations are plentiful, and it may be that until an agreed on data-level definition of intelligence is secured, no answer can be entirely wrong or right. With respect to today's special education discrepancy model, the following, however, is clear:

1. If intelligence tests do not measure innate capacity or intellectual potential, then special education has no ability-achievement discrepancy. The removal of intelligence tests from special education's discrepancy formula would leave the field with only a standardized achievement measure upon which to make its service decisions.

2. If intelligence tests are achievement tests that reflect some of what a child has learned, then special education again has no ability-achievement discrepancy. If intelligence tests continue to be administered to schoolchildren, special education in effect would have two achievement measures from which to make its service decisions. The field's ability-achievement formula used by most states to determine if a child qualifies for special education assistance would more accurately be an achievement-achievement formula that would provide no information about intellectual potential.

3. If special education has no ability-achievement discrepancy model from which to determine eligibility, then laws forcing psychologists to use an invalid model to determine which children are entitled to receive special education assistance must be changed.

WHAT DO TESTS OF INTELLIGENCE MEASURE?

Test names, of course, do not tell us what tests measure. Shortly after joining the University of Denver in 1970, I received a flyer advertising a testing instrument requiring a 5 minute administration entitled: "Quickie Test for Brain Damage." I doubted anyone paid much attention to such an instrument, much less its claim. David Wechsler, who suggested in the early 1970s that "recognizing and identifying degrees of brightness and stupidity is what intelligence testing is all about,"[12] chose to title one of his tests the "Wechsler Intelligence Test for Children (WISC)." As I see it, neither brightness nor stupidity are anywhere on a list of what David Wechsler's test assesses. Many professionals contend that intelligence, the type needed to read and write and succeed with a teacher's curriculum, is also absent from Wechsler's list.

> The use of the term "intelligence" to describe what is measured by intelligence tests biases our answer to the question of the usefulness of intelligence tests... [T]he mere fact that tests of intelligence are given that name does not indicate that the name is served or well chosen. There is no simple clear cut procedure that permits one to determine that tests of intelligence are in fact measures of intelligence.[13]

MEASURING ENVIRONMENTAL INFLUENCES

> Intelligence test scores, at best, reflect highly circumscribed behavior elicited by an often unfamiliar person under highly restricted conditions (answering strange questions asked by a strange person in a strange place).[14]

While psychologists may not be measuring anything akin to school-related intelligence when they ask children questions from a test of intelligence, they are assessing a considerable number of factors that influence a youngster's final score on such instruments. These factors include, but are not limited to, a child's motivation,[15] the influence his parents or guardians have on his attitude and experiences,[16] as well as his skills at understanding test instructions and directions.[17] Also assessed, and perhaps as important, is the child's ability to effectively cope with being removed from his classroom, taken to an unfamiliar room, seated across from a bigger, older, adult-stranger, who closes a door, who requires answers to mystifying questions and exercises, and whose help with the questions and exercises is, by necessity, limited to near none. Psychologists know that each of these factors impacts the meaning and value of a derived score; each can produce a false or misleading score.

Assuredly, when psychologists administer an intelligence test they are assessing the dominant factor these tests of intelligence measure: what a youngster has learned from his or her many and varied environments. The power environments have on intelligence test scores is crucial to the question of whether intelligence tests should be a part of special education's eligibility formula. Their intended function, as determined by special education, is to assess intellectual capacity and potential. If instead intelligence tests measure what a child has acquired from his environment, then they are wrongly included within special education's eligibility formula.

Soaring IQs

The environment's influence on IQ scores was brought to the public's attention in a fairly recent *Newsweek* story.[18] While the research behind the magazine's story contained an incredible amount of poor science, it revealed how IQ scores are enhanced by a youngster's experiences. What is remarkable is the number of times the article, and its dubious findings, continue to find their way into the professional literature.[19]

James R. Flynn, a political philosopher from New Zealand, reported on soaring IQ scores observed from various countries throughout the world—"27 points in Britain since 1942 and 24 points in the United States since 1918." Addressing a conference on intelligence, James Flynn discussed the data he had summarized, analyzed, and published in a professional journal in 1987.[20]   His research consisted of critiquing test data collected decades earlier and sent to him by colleagues from 14 different countries. He compared the early test data with later test data to see if any changes in test scores had occurred.

Overlooking a Few Loose Ends

One need not be an experimental psychologist to recognize that the research was as mortally wounded as a frog flattened by a hard charging 18-wheeler. The data James Flynn analyzed were drawn from a frightful number of different psycho-educational instruments, some twelve to eighteen as best I could determine. The different tests presented many different exercises assessing an unknown number of different skills under different circumstances that defied consistency or administrative control. The subjects' willingness to cooperate with test administrators was unspecified (and no doubt completely unknown to James Flynn). The skills (and objectivity) of those who administered the tests were also an unknown and troubling variable. And the location (and conditions) where the tests were administered was a guess. Nothing was standard or standardized. Everything was about as random as where the next dandelion might sprout on an emerging spring lawn.   Tests used in Belgium measured a subject's ability with "visualization of shapes"; the Netherlands, and several other countries, had their subjects run paper and pencil mazes. Norway used story-formatted math tests with problems ranging from simple arithmetic to elementary algebra, along with verbal tests consisting entirely of word similarities. Canada used a mental maturity test along with various achievement tests.   New Zealand used an achievement test that assessed its subjects' acquired skills with vocabulary, verbal similarities and opposites, comprehension, information, reasoning, and arithmetic problems. The United States mostly relied on David Wechsler's tests, which assessed a portion of the above along with countless other variables. The analyzed scores were so scrubbed and filtered through statistical formulas that they could hardly contain any likeness to the actual answers the thousands of subjects gave during the thousands of administrations. Despite experimental error as thick as Mississippi mud, conclusions were drawn, including the view that the IQ growth across decades was too large to have much to do with gains in true intelligence. (It is amazing what some folks are willing to ignore in order to have something to say.)

The Power of Cereal Boxes

The greatest of the discovered gains James Flynn discussed came from tests that required subjects to solve puzzles and run mazes. (J. C. Raven's Progressive Matrices[21] was a popular choice in James Flynn's fourteen countries.)   Why did puzzle and maze scores increased so dramatically over the decades? Cereal boxes! Psychologist Wendy Williams from Yale University, an expert on the development of children's intelligence, explained:

> [M]uch of the IQ gain [in Flynn's study] may simply reflect the greater familiarity that today's kids have with the sorts of questions posed on the tests. Taking her data from wherever she can find it, Williams has been collecting kids' cereal boxes and fast-food bags. Both are covered with mazes and puzzles remarkably similar to what IQ tests ask. "In the 1930s a kid may never have seen a maze before finding one on his IQ test," says Williams. "It seems clear that the tests are not measuring innate, immutable intelligence, but a type of practiced learning and familiarity with the test questions." [22]

Psychologists who study children's developing cognitive skills have long recognized the power of cereal boxes and similar technologies to provide youngsters with information, useful or otherwise, that occasionally finds its way on to an intelligence test. While there persists disagreement over the stability of intelligence test scores,[23,24,25] many researchers picture IQs as passengers in a roller-coaster cart, influenced directly and measurably by the richness or poverty of a child's surrounding environment.

> Studies of individuals...reveal large upward or downward shifts in IQ. Sharp rises or drops in IQ may occur as a result of major environmental changes in the child's life...Even children who remain in the same environment...may show large increases or decreases in IQ on retesting... In general, children in culturally disadvantaged environments tend to lose and those in superior environments to gain in IQ with age.[26]

A current television ad campaign pictures delightful youngsters, destined 2 decades later to become world-class athletes, thanking their mothers (wouldn't you know) for purchasing a particular brand of cereal. "Thanks, Mom," a seated little one says happily, his feet dangling far above the floor. Most children today who score well on IQ tests could turn to their moms and dads and voice the same sentiments. It seems that a major condition associated with rising IQ scores relates to the extent to which parents take the time to "deliberately train... [their] child in various mental and motor skills which [are] not yet essential."[27] The raised IQ score clearly reflects the parent's effort at actively providing experiences to his or her child.

DELETING INTELLIGENCE TESTS FROM SPECIAL EDUCATION

Wendy Williams' interpretation of James Flynn's data, specifically the power the environment holds over test scores, provides strong support for deleting intelligence tests from special education's eligibility process. The reaffirmation that intelligence tests tap a small number of environmental experiences rather than measuring a child's innate potential, confirms that the tests should play no role in determining which children should receive special services. If the right cereal box can enhance a youngster's IQ score, we know clearly that an IQ test is a measure of prior learning of skills and knowledge, and "not...a measure of some underlying native ability." [28]

[L]ong ago most psychometricians, developmental psychologists, and educational psychologists gave up the belief that IQ test scores measured potential in any valid sense. Instead standard texts in educational measurement and assessment routinely warn against interpreting IQ scores as measures of intellectual potential. At their best, IQ test scores are gross measures of current cognitive functioning.[29]

No Measure of Potential or Capacity

We do not know of any IQ test authors or publishers who claim that their tests measure potential. In fact, IQ authors, for example [David] Wechsler,[30] make it clear that IQ test results are environmentally influenced and, at best, reflect a momentary level of intellectual functioning.[31]

Intelligence tests do not measure intellectual capacity; they never have. They cannot forecast a student's innate potential; they never could . No matter the skill of the examiner, intelligence tests can only capture a single moment of a child's marvelously mysterious, gloriously complex life. To think that a test with a few questions and like number of exercises could do more than graze the surface of that life is appalling. Intelligence tests have been placed in a discrepancy model of which they do not belong.

The field need only heed the advice of Alan Kaufman, colleague of David Wechsler, author of an impressive list of books discussing intelligence testing, to end its intransigent practice of including intelligence tests within its eligibility formula. From *Intelligent Testing with the WISC-R*, Dr. Kaufman decisively attests: "[One] does not equate IQs with academic potential and, indeed, one may declare the WISC-R IQ to be irrelevant or inaccurate information for understanding some children's functioning...IQs become harmful when they are...interpreted as valid indicators of intellectual functioning and are misconstrued as evidence of the child's maximum or even typical performance."[32]

INTELLIGENCE TESTS ARE ACHIEVEMENT INSTRUMENTS

[A]ll the controversy loses meaning for each specific person referred for evaluation, when the clinician administers an IQ test to study and interpret just what the person has or has not learned.[33]

Intelligence tests are achievement tests at best, poor ones to be sure, that allow the psychologist to interpret what a child has or has not learned. Based on their sparing sample of materials,[34] intelligence tests provide a glimmer of what experiences have brushed a child's mind, an inkling of a child's past and present nourishing or impeding environments. They do not measure a child's capacity to learn; they do not afford an understanding of why a child might be struggling or succeeding with reading, writing, or mathematics.

Intelligence tests' conceived questions and scenarios can be as foreign to a child being tested as is the child's language and culture to the examiner. For some children of all shades and cultures, the tests possess little content validity, a fact that accounts for a large portion of children's low scores. A point overlooked by the graduate apprentice caught in the swirl of securing a discrepancy formula score to satisfy a federal or state requirement is that a child who has not been exposed to the information required by the intelligence test may score low and "be called 'less intelligent' when the child simply has less factual knowledge."[35]

Old News

This view that intelligence tests are achievement instruments is not electrifying news emanating from the 20th Century's last years. The tests' true persona and limitations have been known well before the passage of public law 94-142.

1971: [Researchers have] demonstrated that tests of intelligence are basically similar to tests of achievement. Both kinds of tests involve performances depending upon previously acquired information, abilities, and motives...Both kinds of tests call upon the results of learning or experience.[36]

Not long after the above clarification, the most prestigious body of the American Psychological Association (APA) clearly set the tone for understanding the nature and value of intelligence tests. Why education and the federal government chose not hear the APA's message is speculation.

1975: The notion that a so-called intelligence test can somehow measure innate capacity or potential was considered and explicitly rejected in 1975 by a committee of testing experts, appointed by the American Psychological Association's Board of Scientific Affairs. The Cleary committee declared:

A distinction is drawn traditionally between intelligence and achievement tests. A naive statement of the difference is that the intelligence test measures capacity to learn and the achievement test measures what has been learned. But items in all psychological and educational tests measure acquired behavior....An attempt to recognize the incongruity of a behavioral measure as a measure of capacity is illustrated by the statement that the intelligence tests contain items that everyone has an equal opportunity to learn. This statement can be dismissed as false....There is no merit in maintaining a fiction.[37]

PREDICTORS OF SCHOOL SUCCESS

Special education has long known that "intelligence testing is neither an essential nor useful service"[38,39]; that results and scores from intelligence tests possess virtually no practical application to teachers or children.[40] The tests' questions and exercises shed no light on a child's day-to-day abilities to adapt successfully to his pressing environment,[41,42,43] and the tests "cannot be translated directly into educational practice."[44] They don't say anything about intellectual ability, and they offer nothing that would allow a parent (or teacher) to learn of a child's classroom achievements. Other than providing special education with the pretext of measuring potential, reducing eligibility decisions to an often brainless number game, why does the field use them? A prevailing view is that "Intelligence tests are good predictors of school achievement."[45] This is one of those, "yes, but" exchanges that leaves a sour aftertaste, like a bottle of cheap wine. Do intelligence tests predict school performance? Yes, but. Thirty-five years ago, we were counseled that conventional intelligence tests can "provide fair predictions of school success, assuming we do nothing exceptional to help or hinder certain students and thus destroy the prediction."[46]

Pragmatically Worthless Relationship

True, there is a relation between IQ scores and performance in school. But both variables are so vague that numbers characterizing their relationship are little more than estimates that for convenience and communication are assumed real and codifiable. Interestingly, the statistically massaged numbers used to exalt the relationship actually show their worthlessness. "[T]here is a correlation of approximately .50 between IQ and performance in school.[47] The overall value of .50 is...low enough to indicate that about 75% of the variance in school achievement is accounted by factors other than IQ."[48]

IQ Should Never Stand Alone

Side-stepping the statistics for a moment, the above quote's wording is curious and warrants some response. Note the author uses the abbreviation "IQ" twice. In both instances, it stands alone, unaccompanied by a companion word, as though, by itself, it represents some independent thing, some thing like "native intelligence," some thing an individual carries if not in-hand at least in-skull. The author, of course, is wrong. "IQ," unless popularized in one of rock singer Sting's songs,[49] must be accompanied by either the term "score" or "test." In other words, the correlation the author referenced is between IQ scores from an IQ test and school performance. It is nothing more magical than that. When a parent asks for his or her child's IQ, the reputable psychologist will clar-ify: "You mean the score the child received from an 'IQ' test." The psychologist should also share that the IQ test is only a weak achievement test, that the score itself isn't particularly revealing, and that it would be more productive to look closely at the youngster's acquired skills with reading, writing, and mathematics.

Back to the relationship issue. The quote's statistic ("...correlation of ap-proximately .50 between IQ and performance in school") tells us that a young-ster's performance in school is influence by many factors, most of which are un-der our control: teacher skills, class size, curriculum, materials, parental support and encouragement, the youngster's state of interest and motivation, a good night's sleep, decent food and health, to name just a few. Said differently (and speculatively), 25% of children's performance in school is a function of the chil-dren's intelligence—however defined, and 75% of their school performance is a function of our intelligence. (Don't get lost in the numbers; their message is more important than their calculation. If you square the correlation .50, change the resulting number into a percentage (.50 x .50 = .25 = 25%) then subtract that number from 100% you get 75%, which suggests pointedly that what teachers and school psychologists do is a lot more important than any presumption of what intellectual capacity resides in a child's brain.)

Despite our lack of consensus as to what is measured by intelligence tests, schools (as though they had no other choice), continue to spend mega-dollars and hours feeding special education's discrepancy model with what it needs to sur-vive: an IQ score that is interpreted to represent a child's capacity or aptitude to learn in school. If special education would remove its decades-old blinders, it would see that scores from IQ tests offer school officials little of value.

IQ Proponents Agree on Achievement Status

Intelligence tests are, once again, achievement tests, not measures of apti-tude or intellectual capacity. Their proponents, making every effort to keep them afloat when by all rights they should have been scuttled years ago, agree. Amazing! "The content of all tasks, whether verbal or nonverbal, is learned within a culture. The learning may take place formally in the school, casually in the home, or incidentally through everyday life. As a measure of past learn-ing, the IQ test is best thought of as a kind of achievement test, not as a simple measure of aptitude."[50]

Proponents have even found a beneficial use for IQ tests as achievement tests in an effort to justify their continued presence. "The WISC-R subtests measure what the individual has learned...from this vantage point, the intelli-gence test is really a kind of achievement test; not the same type of achievement test as reading or science, but a measure of past accomplishments. Since learning occurs within a culture, intelligence tests obviously must be considered to be culture loaded. Treating the WISC-R as an achievement test may actually have vital social implications. [It has been noted][51] that poor performance on a test viewed as an index of achievement pressures society to apply additional educational resources to improve the children's achievement; in contrast, poor performance on a test interpreted as a measure of aptitude may be seen as a justification of the withdrawal of educational resources."[52]

Very Poor Achievement Tests

Standing naked in the wind, intelligence tests are unmasked as very poor achievement tests. As such, they have no place in special education's ability-achievement discrepancy model. Special education hired the tests because it was told the instruments measured intellectual potential. The salesman lied.

Their removal from the eligibility process will create room for a more efficient and effective discrepancy model that operates independent of any conjecture of a child's innate intelligence. At this juncture, special education and all of its professional personnel need to focus efforts on prevention in the regular education program rather than on qualifying children, based on IQ-achievement discrepancies, for special education programs.[53] The first step toward this needed attitude is to dislodge IQ scores and intelligence as a prerequisite to services. "[Alfred Binet]...firmly rebuked those who believed that 'the intelligence of an individual [was] a fixed quantity, a quantity that one cannot augment....'[54] '...[A] child's mind,' Binet said, 'is like a field for which an expert farmer has devised a change in the method of cultivating, with the result that in the place of desert land, we now have a harvest.'"[55]

FOCUS: A SHADOWY PICTURE OF CLASSROOM ACHIEVEMENT

We turn now to the achievement side of special education's eligibility formula. A student's achievement scores are intended to shed light on the student's academic progress in class. Ideally, that progress should drive all scholastic programming, including direct instruction, support, and academic challenge. If, however, we do not have a clear picture of a student's achievement, we may be forced to plan and deliver a student's classroom curriculum on the basis of the student's age, grade level, or scores from standard achievement instruments that fail to assess what the child has learned. Age, grade level, as well as standardized achievement scores, however, offer only a shadowy glimpse of what precise levels of reading or mathematics, science or social studies a student is prepared to challenge effectively. Age and grade level tell us how long a student has been enrolled in school. Neither figure can declare with certainty what the child has learned or is prepared to learn.

NOTES

1. Gresham, F. M., & Witt, J. C. (1997). Utility of intelligence tests for treatment planning, classification, and placement decisions: recent empirical findings and future directions. *School Psychology Quarterly*, 12, 249-267.

2. Honzik, M. P., Macfarlane, J. W., & Allen, L. (1948). The stability of mental test performance between two and sixteen years. *Journal of Experimental Education*, 17, 309-324.

3. Anastasi, A., & Urbina, S. (1997). *Psychological testing* (7th ed.). Upper Saddle River, NJ: Prentice-Hall, p. 326.

4. Brody, N. (1997). Intelligence, schooling, and society. *American Psychologist, 52*, 1046-1050. (See also Ceci, S. J., & Williams, W. M. (1997). Schooling, intelligence, and income. *American Psychologist, 52*, 1051-1058.)

5. Eysenck, H. J. & Kamin, L. (1981). *The Intelligence Controversy*. New York: John Wiley & Sons, p.94.

6. Mackintosh, N. J. (Ed.). (1995) *Cyril Burt: Fraud or famed?* London: Oxford University Press.

7. Swerdlow, J. L. (June, 1995). Quiet miracles of the brain, *National Geographic*, 187, 2-41.

8. Shane, S. (1997, April 13). An extraordinary, ordinary girl. *The Baltimore Sun,* p. 4j.

9. Shane, S. (1997, April 13), p.4j.

10. Shane, S. (1997, April 13), p. 4j.

11. Kaufman, A. S. (1990). *Assessing adolescent and adult intelligence*. Boston: Allyn and Bacon, p,60.

12. Wechsler, D. (1971). Intelligence: Definition, theory, and the IQ. In Robert Cancro (Ed.). *Intelligence: genetic and environmental influences.* (p. 10). New York: Grune & Stratton, p. 51.

13. Brody, E. B., & Brody, N. (1976). *Intelligence: Nature, determinants, and consequences.* New York: Academic Press, p.87.

14. Gresham, F. M., & Witt, J. C. (1997), p. 256.

15. Cronbach, L. J. (1960). *Essentials of psychological testing*. New York: Harper & Brothers.

16. Thorndike, R. M., Cunningham, G. K., Thorndike, R. L., & Hagen, E. P. (1991). *Measurement and evaluation in psychology and education.* New York: Macmillan Publishing Company.

17. Cleary, T. A., Humphreys, L. G., Kendrick, S. A., & Wesman, A. (1975). Educational uses of tests with disadvantaged students. *American Psychologist, 30*, 15-41.

18. Begley, S. (1996, May 6). The IQ puzzle. *Newsweek*, p. 70.

19. Detterman, D. K., & Thompson, L. E. (1997). What is so special about special education? *American Psychologist, 52*, 1082-1090.

20. Flynn, J. R. (1987). Massive gains in 14 nations: What IQ tests really measure. *Psychological Bulletin, 101*, 171-191.

21. Raven, J. C. (1938). Progressive Matrices. In O. K. Buros (Ed.). *Tests in print.* (p. 115) Highland Park, N.J.: The Gryphon Press.

22. Begley, Sharon. (1996), p. 71.

23. Wechsler, D. (1971). Intelligence: definition, theory, and the IQ. In Robert Cancro (Ed.). (Wechsler suggests the "...average test-retest change amounts to some 5 points (p.54).")

24. Honzik, M. P., Macfarlane, J. W., & Allen, L. (1948). The stability of mental test performance between two and sixteen years. *Journal of Experimental Education*, 17, 309-324.

25. Jensen, A. R. (1969). How much can we boost IQ and scholastic achievement? *Harvard Educational Review*, 39, 1-123.

26. Anastasi, A. (1988). *Psychological testing* (6th ed.) New York: Macmillan, p. 340.

27. McCall, R. B., Applebaum, M. I. & Hogarty, P.S. (1973). Developmental changes in mental performance. *Monographs of the Society for Research in Child Development*, 38(3, Serial No.150).

28. Albee, G. W. (1980). Open letter in response to D.O. Hebb. *American Psychologist*, 35, 386-387.

29. Stanovich, K. E. (1991). Conceptual and empirical problems with discrepancy definitions of reading disability. *Learning Disability Quarterly, 14*, 269-280.

30. Wechsler, D. (1974). *Manual for the Wechsler Intelligence Scale for Children-Revised*. New York: Psychological Corp.

31. Baldwin, R. S., & Vaughn, S. (1988). Why Siegel's arguments are irrelevant to the definition of learning disabilities. *Journal of Learning Disabilities*, 22, 513.

32. Kaufman, A. S. (1979). *Intelligent testing with the WISC-R*. New York: John Wiley & Sons, p. 2-13.

33. Kaufman, A. S. (1990), p. 26.

34. Salvia, J. & Ysseldyke, J. E. (1978). Assessment In special and remedial education. Boston: Houghton Mifflin Company.

35. Siegel, L. S. (1989). IQ is irrelevant to the definition of learning disabilities. *Journal of Learning Disabilities, 22,* 469-478.

36. Hunt, J. McV., & Kirk, G. E. (1971). Social aspects of intelligence: Evidence and issues. In Robert Cancro (Ed.). *Intelligence: genetic and environmental influences.* New York: Grune & Stratton. (See also Humphreys, L.G. (1962). The nature and organization of human abilities. In M. Katz (Ed.), *The 19th Yearbook of the National Council on Measurement in Education.* Ames, Iowa.)

37. Eysenck, H. J., & Kamin, L. (1981). *The intelligence controversy*. New York: John Wiley & Sons, p. 94.

38. Macmann, G. M., & Barnett, D. W. (1997). Myth of the master detective: reliability of interpretations for Kaufman's "Intelligent Testing" approach to the WISC-III. *School Psychology Quarterly*, 12, 197-234.

39. Reschly, D. J., & Ysseldyke, J. E. (1995). School psychology paradigm shift. In A. Thomas & J. Grimes (Eds.), *Best practices in school psychology--III* (pp.17-31) Washington, DC: National Association of School Psychologists.

40. Gresham, F. M., & Witt, J. C. (1997).

41. Kaufman, A. S. (1990). (Kaufman indicates..."[T]he biggest weaknesses were the Wechsler scales' inability to measure real-life problem solving situations or to relate meaningfully to vocational interests and decision making.")

42. Snyderman, M., & Rothman, S. (1987). Survey of expert opinion on intelligence and aptitude testing. *American Psychologist, 42*, 137-144. (authors explain...[Respondents] --661 experts in intelligence testing--...cited the inadequate measurement of 'adaptation' to one's environment' as one of the main weaknesses of intelligence tests.)

43. Frederiksen, N. (1986). Toward a broader conception of human intelligence. *American Psychologist, 41*, 445-452. (Researcher appealed...for a broader conception of human intelligence, stress[ing] the need to supplement traditional IQ tests with "realistic simulations of real-life problem situations.")

44. Sternberg, R. J. & Wagner, R. K. (1982). Understanding intelligence: What's in it for educators? (ERIC Report 227-110(ED)) Washington, DC: National Commission on Excellence in Education (ED).

45. Kaufman, A. S. (1979), p. 14.

46. Smith, R. M. (1969). *Teacher diagnosis of educational difficulties.* Columbus, Ohio: Charles E. Merrill, p. 45.

47. Matarazzo, J. D. (1972). Wechsler's measurement and appraisal of adult intelligence (5th ed.). New York: Oxford University Press, p. 285.

48. Kaufman, A. S. (1990), p. 18.

49. Sting, *Seven Days*, Ten Summoner's Tales, A & M Records.

50. Kaufman, A. S. (1990).

51. Flauger, R. L. (1978). The many definitions of test bias, American Psychologist, 33, 671-679.

52. Kaufman, A. S. (1979), p. 11.

53. Berninger, V. W., Hart, T., Abbott,R., & Karoosky, P. (1992). Defining reading and writing disabilities with and without IQ: A flexible, developmental perspective. *Learning Disability Quarterly, 15* , 103-118.

54. Eysenck, H. J., & Kamin, L. (1981), p. 91.

55. Binet, A. (1909). Les idees modernes sur les enfants. Paris: Ernest Flamarion. Cited from G.D. Stoddard. (1939). The IQ: Its ups and downs. *Educational Review, 20*, 44-57.

7

Measuring Classroom Achievement

In recapping, special education uses students' scores from standardized achievement tests as part of its discrepancy model. The field compares the measured academic achievement scores with the students' IQ scores. Special education assumes as a matter of practice that students with elevated IQ scores should perform quite successfully with the basics and beyond of reading, writing, arithmetic. A discrepancy is said to exist if the relationship between the students' classroom achievement and estimates of their intelligence is contrary to expectations. If the discrepancy between those two measures is severe, special education eligibility and the label "learning disabled" are often awarded. I have suggested the model presents several contentious issues.

FAMILIAR PROBLEMS

You are familiar with two insurmountable problems rendering special education's eligibility model inefficient:

1. The field has no definition or measure of native intelligence, nullifying a prediction of normal intelligence and intellectual potential. Without the estimate of potential, there can be no measured discrepancy between ability/potential and achievement.

2. The federal government's qualifier "severe" is too relative and shapeless to aid in determining which children should and should not receive services. As it stands, the ill-conceived term serves only to delay (or perhaps prevent) needy students from receiving special education assistance.

NEW PROBLEMS

Special education's academic achievement measure, the third component of its eligibility formula, presents us with an additional problem. The most popular achievement instrument adopted by special education to complete its eligibility decision making taps very little information from a student's classroom curriculum. This standardized achievement test tells us nothing about a student's day-to-day classroom achievements. In actual practice, special education teachers use this instrument for its normative box scores that are contrasted with a student's presumed measure of capacity or aptitude to ascertain the presence or absence of an artificial, numerical discrepancy. Good teachers gain virtually no practical instructional value from its total or subtest scores.

Pointedly, if eligibility were not an issue, special education's skilled psychologists and teachers would never use any part of the standardized instrument special education most often has chosen as part of its ability-achievement discrepancy model. Because special education has maintained its obsession with issues of eligibility, the field's standardized achievement test serves two purposes: providing a number to be compared with an IQ score and keeping self-serving lawyers at bay.

SPECIAL EDUCATION'S STANDARDIZED ACHIEVEMENT TESTS

Eligibility for special education services is a legal issue. From a governmental perspective, it has little to do with educational need, compassion, or science. Today, compliance with the federal mandate that requires special education to demonstrate the existence of a significant ability-achievement discrepancy before a student can be eligible for school services has become a burden that saps the field's energy and resources.

To satisfy that federal mandate, special education administers achievement instruments to help it answer questions of eligibility.[1]   Whether the selected instruments used by special education's professionals measure actual classroom achievement or tell a teacher precisely where within his or her curriculum a student is either succeeding or faltering is quite irrelevant to the purpose of the assessment: supporting or negating the presence of a severe discrepancy between ability and achievement.

Purpose for Assessment

It is important to recognize that the purpose for assessment always defines the instruments to be used. If, for example, the purpose for a youngster's academic assessment was to answer questions about how that student's general informational standing compared with members of a group (a measure that beyond boasting-rights holds virtually no practical importance for classroom teachers), then a norm-referenced instrument, such as The California Achievement Test, would be chosen.[2] If, on the other hand, the purpose for school assessment was to answer questions about what that student had learned from his or her classroom curriculum (or perhaps needed to learn from that curriculum to become more successful with schoolwork), then criterion-referenced tests directly related to a student's classroom curriculum, such as informal inventories, checklists, classroom quizzes, and teacher-made or commercially produced academic probes, would be the assessment instruments of choice.[3,4] As it turns out, justifying eligibility for support services represents special education's major purpose for requiring its professionals to spend hours administering its standardized achievement measures. Discovering a student's specific academic strengths or weaknesses, or what a particular student has or has not achieved in the classroom, astonishingly, is unrelated to that administration.

Weak Measure of Achievement

That special education's most popular achievement test is a poor measure of a student's classroom accomplishments seems not to bother the field or the federal government whose laws drive special education's policy. So long as eligibility for services remains the predominant concern of the field, an inadequate measure of classroom achievement will suffice. The field has been aware of the limited value of its standardized achievement test from its initial adoption but has chosen to overlook its weaknesses. Its strength, which has been to provide a magical number for special education's eligibility formula, has taken precedence.

Same Questions from Maine to Montana

Special education's most preferred achievement test presents the same items to all children regardless of where they live, what school they attend, or what curriculum they have experienced at their home school. The test's multiple forms barely broaden its coverage. The diagnostician administering the achievement test will not know which of the test's items suitably reflect the child's experienced classroom curriculum. Whether the test items and student's curriculum match is pure guess. If special education's achievement instrument sampled each student's classroom curriculum thoroughly, if the results of the assessment described how each child fared with respect to that individual classroom curriculum, and if there was assurance that each child was in fact exposed to the curriculum being assessed by the achievement instrument, then special education would have an excellent achievement measure. The field's most preferred test does none of that. Its worth, therefore, is highly problematic. To be considered sound, an achievement test must measure the curriculum to which a student is exposed.[5] If an administered achievement test presents items unrelated to what a pupil has experienced, or asks questions about material a pupil has yet to experience, the achievement instrument is said to have poor content validity. Unless a test's content reflects the content of the curriculum the pupil has experienced, the obtained results are meaningless.[6]

Limited Numbers of Questions

Out of necessity, a time-consuming standardized achievement test adminis-tered to many thousands of youngsters across the country can only afford to sample a small portion of what any child might have experienced in his or her classroom. Certainly tests that inadequately sample a child's curriculum can hardly provide an accurate picture of a child's academic accomplishments or edu-cational needs. Not much achievement is tapped by the few of questions pre-sented to a grade-school child being assessed with the very popular Woodcock-Johnson-R achievement test.

Form A of the Woodcock-Johnson-R[7]

1. Less than 60 items are used to assess letter-word identification span-ning grade equivalents from kindergarten through college levels. A to-tal of 4 items are used to assess 3rd grade letter-word identification skills, 3 items are used to assess 4th grade letter-word identification skills, 3 items are used for 5th grade.

2. Less than 60 items assess mathematical calculation, kindergarten through college; 4 items are used to assess kindergarten level skills, 3 are used to assess 2nd grade level skills, 3 are used to assess 6th grade.

3. Less than 45 items are devoted to reading comprehension, kindergarten through college. Only 4 items carry a grade equivalent of 3rd grade; 2 items are grade equivalent at 5th grade; 2 at 6th grade; 1 at 7th grade.

4. Fewer than 40 synonyms, fewer than 40 antonyms are used to assess sixteen plus years of school experiences pertaining to vocabulary ac-quisition.

Form A of the Woodcock-Johnson-R will miss much of what an assessed student knows. Indeed, the test's calculations hardly depict the achievement ef-forts of any tested child. Because only a few items are presented to each student, a question or two capriciously hit or missed can measurably over- or underesti-mate a student's skill, playing havoc with special education's eligibility and clas-sification decisions. Of course, not all standardized achievement tests are the same. Some over- and underestimate more than others. Not surprisingly, when questions of special education eligibility arise, the achievement test administered, rather than the child, may be the most critical variable.[8,9]

Deficiencies: Old News

Nothing new has been stated. Professionals administering the above stan-dardized achievement component know that the test captures no more of a child's true school achievements than a human eye captures the depth of the universe. For decades, special educators have been aware that their achievement tests sampled only fragments of relevant classroom information and were not capable of providing regular classroom teachers with practical information that would help either themselves or their students experience greater success.[10,11,12] More than 10 years ago, the most prestigious of special education journals, *Exceptional Children*, published by The Council for Exceptional Children, clearly described serious weaknesses inherent in the standardized achievement tests being administered by special education.

> Whether standardized instruments used with a student contain curriculum materials covered by his teachers is indeterminable. Given the seriousness of pending decisions, assuming representation is a dangerous and unnecessary gamble.[13]

> [A major problem with standardized achievement tests]...is that they are developed by test production firms which must service an entire nation, a nation with very diverse curricular preferences. If the test agencies spelled out, in unambiguous detail, exactly what it is their tests measure, many educators would find that the test's emphases did not match the local curriculum. They wouldn't buy the test. But test publishers subsist on the sales of their tests. They get out of this bind by describing their tests in very general terms, thereby picking up the classic Rorschach dividend of allowing people to see what they want to in an ink blot. This practice results in many educators using tests which are, in reality, not consonant with local curricular emphases. Mismatched measurement and instruction yields misleading data and spurious conclusions.[14]

Spurious conclusions, of course, guarantee occurrences of false positive and false negative errors, particularly with children whose classroom curriculum experiences differ markedly from materials found on standardized achievement tests. Despite efforts toward fair assessment, standardized achievement tests are culturally and socially biased resulting in the misclassification of minority children.[15] Interestingly, with respect to standardized achievement tests, the term "minority," as just used, is misleading. A child's ethnicity is not the issue. Any youngster from any location in the United States can undergo a biased administration of a standardized achievement test if he or she is required to answer questions about academic and social material the child has yet to experience. The assumption that school attendance, age, or grade level guarantee exposure to the materials the test authors have chosen is ludicrous. Making the assumption that a minority child's acculturation is similar to that of the norm group upon which the test was developed is worse.

> Acculturation is the most important characteristic in evaluating a child's performance on a test. To the extent that a child's acculturation differs from the acculturation of those on whom a test is standardized,...decisions based upon [those] test results...may actually be both invalid and biased.[16]

GENERAL EDUCATION: EXCUSED ONCE MORE

It is altogether puzzling why a regular teacher would refer one of his or her students to special education for a standardized achievement assessment. What's to be learned? The teacher already knows the youngster is struggling with (or excelling in) some or all of his class assignments. Assuming the general education teacher has maintained any contact with the curriculum being used in the classroom, the teacher certainly can identify the exact assignments and activities that are creating difficulty for a youngster. Why request a standardized achievement test that will ask the child a bare minimum number of questions, the answers to which the regular teacher should already know? What could the regular teacher possibly hope to gain? These are fair questions. Let's see why our teacher's request for standardized assessment is so perplexing.

Comparing Students

First, standardized achievement tests are used to compare student's academic performance with the mythical "average" student. The teacher will find little value in that information. "In standardized testing, test tasks are presented under standard conditions so the student's performance can be contrasted to the performance of the norm group. The resulting data are comparative; the student's level of functioning is described in relation to typical or average performance."[17]

Knowing that a youngster compares favorably or unfavorably with other children from his or her classroom, much less with average children from another state, says absolutely nothing about the referred youngster's specific academic problems, strengths, or where within the teacher's curriculum the youngster best fits. Besides, the regular teacher, assuming he or she is still breathing, is keenly aware the youngster's classroom performance varies from that of other students. It's time to move beyond that issue.

Instructional Assistance

Second, special education's standardized tests provide little or no instructional assistance to the classroom teacher.[18] Standardized achievement tests assess general performance over broad subject areas. The tests were not designed to improve teacher strategies; the results simply are not specific enough to provide direction for instructional planning,[19] and efforts toward that end have been described as "hopeless."[20]

The student in question is struggling with very specific problems, probably making consistent, daily mistakes with the same classroom materials. The teacher needs practical ideas that will result in adaptive curriculum and modified instructional strategies. That issue needs to garner our undivided attention. "[T]eachers need to be able to link assessment results to curriculum and instruction...The disadvantages of basing instruction on the result of achievement tests are well known, the principle drawbacks being that measurement is infrequent and there is no assurance that the items on the test reflect the skills contained in the curriculum used in the classroom."[21]

If Not for Instructional Assistance, Then Why?

Third, and perhaps most puzzling, is why the regular classroom teacher would request a highly trained, certified special education teacher, to spend hours with an academically struggling child, asking questions, summarizing data, and writing lengthy reports that will provide the requesting regular classroom teacher with no instructional assistance? Assuming that regular classroom teacher has been attending to the youngster's academic efforts and has kept minimal records, even just legible scribbles on a notepad, the teacher knows which math problems the pupil consistently misses, which words are unknown or unpronounceable, which letters are misidentified or written backwards, and which concepts seem thoroughly mystifying. The pupil has been with the teacher for months, certainly weeks, which translates into hundreds of hours of direct observation in and out of the classroom. The teacher has presented the child with dozens and dozens of assignments and has had the opportunity to ask the child voluminous related questions to help clarify the child's answers, errors, and confusions. What could our regular teacher obtain from a diagnostician who will be with the child under sterile conditions for 60 minutes or so, who will ask the child to complete a few math problems, identify a few words, and pronounce a few letters? Why would the general teacher seek test data from a standardized achievement instrument? Why indeed? "[Standardized tests] are convenient and expedient means of classifying and excluding children from regular education and have thus fostered the creation of a dual education system."[22]

Safety Net

The ever-present quest for special education eligibility serves as the impetus for this poor use of professional time. In most states, without the standardized achievement test data, a struggling child cannot be found eligible for special education services. Without eligibility, the regular teacher is not likely to receive any support, and to his or her dismay, the difficult youngster is not likely either to be pulled from the regular classroom or assisted within it.

Despite expressed views that [standardized tests] are unreliable and unvalidated for the purpose of determining which children have characteristics consistent with mildly handicapping conditions,[23] the search for eligibility forces the belief that achievement tests, when used with intelligence tests, will help identify children who are exceptional. That flag, once pinned on a child's baseball cap, can become a convenient excuse for general education to continue avoiding its responsibility.

FOCUS: REMOVING STANDARDIZED ACHIEVEMENT MEASURES FROM ELIGIBILITY DECISIONS

In the absence of a standardized achievement option, regular teachers would be required to assess their own students using the curriculum found in their individual classes. General education would be reminded that assessing students' strengths and weaknesses and adapting curriculum to fit each student's uniqueness is its responsibility, whether or not a student is declared officially exceptional. Special education has provided excuses for general education to avoid looking at its own house ever since the passage of Public Law 94-142. There will be no system changes unless those excuses are banished.

The achievement component of special education's discrepancy model provides little direct help to children or their teachers who are, respectively, struggling with learning and teaching reading, writing, and mathematics. The achievement component does little to help educational teams determine which children truly are in need of special services. Eliminating standardized achievement tests as part of an eligibility formula would logically follow from the removal of special education's intelligence tests. Separately, the two measures provide special education with virtually nothing of practical value; together they paint a false picture of science when what exists is psychometric alchemy. "Though the formula method may have some appeal because it requires relatively less clinical competence and judgment, the fact remains that reducing an important diagnostic decision to a mathematical equation gives a false sense of objectivity to a contrived procedure that is still essentially subjective."[24]

NOTES

1. McLoughlin, J. A., & Lewis, R. B. (1990). *Assessing special students.* Columbus: Merrill Publishing Company.

2. McLoughlin, J. A., & Lewis, R. B. (1990).

3. McLoughlin, J. A., & Lewis, R. B. (1990).

4. Thorndike, R. M., Cunningham, G. K., Thorndike, R. L., & Hagen, E. P. (1991). *Measurement and evaluation in psychology and education.* New York: Macmillan Publishing Company.

5. Taylor, R. L. (1989). *Assessment of exceptional students.* Englewood Cliffs, N.J.: Prentice Hall.

6. Salvia, J., & Ysseldyke, J. E. (1985). *Assessment in special and remedial education.* Boston: Houghton Mifflin Company.

7. Woodcock, R. W., & Johnson, M. B. (1989). *WJ-R Tests of Achievement, Form A.* The Riverside Publishing Company.

8. Good, R. H., & Salvia, J. (1988). Curriculum bias in published, norm-referenced reading tests: Demonstrable effects. *School Psychology Review, 17*, 51-60.

9. Jenkins, J. R., & Pany, D. (1978). Standardized achievement tests: How useful for special education? *Exceptional Children, 44*, 448-453.

10. Deno, S. L. (1985). Curriculum-based measurement: The emerging alternative. *Exceptional Children, 52*, 219-232.

11. How well do textbooks match? (1980). *Communication Quarterly*, 3,2.

12. Jenkins, J. R., & Pany, D. (1978).

13. Special issue: Curriculum-based assessment. (1985). *Exceptional Children,* 52, 193-304.

14. Popham, W. J. (1974). An approaching peril: Cloud-referenced tests. *Phi Delta Kappan*, 55, 614-615.

15. Winikur, D., & Wohle, R. (1984). Toward program based special education and school psychological service-delivery system. Cited in, J.E. Galagan. (1985). Psychoeducational testing: Turn out the lights, the party's over, *Exceptional Children*, 52, 288-299. (See also Preliminary Report of the NASP/NCAS Task Force. (1984). Report on School Psychology and Advocacy Third Working Draft .)

16. Duffey, J. B., Salvia, J., Tucker, J., & Ysseldyke, J. (1981). Nonbiased assessment: A need for operationalism. *Exceptional Children, 47,* 427-434.

17. McLoughlin, J. A., & Lewis, R. B. (1990), p. 72.

18. Heller, K. (1982). *National Research Council Special Task Force Report.* Washington, DC: National Academy Press.

19. McLoughlin, J. A., & Lewis, R. B. (1990). Assessing special students. Columbus: Merrill Publishing Company, p. 173.

20. Tucker, J. (1985) Curriculum-Based Assessment: An Introduction. *Exceptional Children,* Vol. 52, No. 3, 199-204.

21. Blankenship, C. S. (1985). Using curriculum-based assessment data to make instructional decisions. *Exceptional Children, 52,* 233-238.

22. Hersh, R., & Walker, H. (1983). Great expectations: Making schools effective for all students. *Policies Studies Review*, 21, 152-154.

23. National Coalition of Advocates for Students. (1985). Barriers to Excellence: Our Children at Risk.

24. Simpson, R. G., & Buckhalt, J. A. (1990). A non-formula discrepancy model to identify learning disabilities. *School Psychology International, 11*, 273-279.

8

A Move Toward Exclusion

When the new children from the public schools came to our special education facility in Colorado during the 1970s, the issue of their intelligence was unimportant. If we had been told a child's real intelligence, that information would not have guided our efforts. We were too smart for such silliness. The magical quantity would not have helped us deliver effective educational services to any of our children.

We were equally unimpressed by standardized achievement scores that compared and ranked children or hinted of ambiguous grade level accomplishments. Learning that a youngster was in the 27th percentile in reading told us she needed help with reading, something her regular classroom teacher knew. Learning that the child was reading at a second grade-level told us what it should have told the professionals at her school: where, roughly, to begin assessing her mastered skills.

Eligibility for extra services was not an issue for us. None of our students was excluded. The fact that regular education had been given license to send able children to our facility for assistance the public schools could have provided was mystifying. Those of us at the Colorado special education facility were problem directed, solution oriented, and nonexclusionary. We couldn't understand why the public schools weren't the same.

A CRITICAL CHOICE: CATEGORICAL EXCLUSION

We were not unique. Other professionals in the field of special education had preempted our position by decades. Consider the early 1900s when special education began to stretch its arms. Elizabeth Farrell, who later with others would form the Council for Exceptional Children, clearly wanted every student, including those deemed exceptional, to receive whatever was necessary for them to benefit optimally from school.[1]   She was problem-solution oriented. Students, she proposed, were not to be ill-served or excluded from educational opportunities. "Selected eligibility" was not a phrase in her vocabulary. In the late 1960s, Professor Ray H. Barsch, a recognized authority in special education, suggested with incisive simplicity that it would be best to define a child with a learning disability as "any learner who fails to benefit from an existing curriculum into which he has been placed."[2]   Had education followed his advice, it would have been unnecessary for special education to have invented its own brand of an IQ-achievement-driven eligibility formula. General education, with special education's assistance, would have provided services within the school and on the spot to all children who experienced trouble with classroom curriculum. Insightfully, this scholar foresaw the future and warned "that a narrow definition [of exceptionality] would lead to massive exclusion" of students from supportive school services. He understood the consequences of a system that failed to provide supportive services to students in need.

Ray Barsch's words, calling for assistance to all children experiencing difficulty with their schoolwork, went unheeded. A powerful group of special educators (and parents and legislators) chose to make special education an exclusive field. Special education would not be open to all children who needed help. It would not be a consultative field, available on an as-needed basis to general education for the benefit of all schoolchildren. The voices of these proponents for exclusivity were more strident than others who disagreed with their position. As often happens, louder voices prevailed. Special education would serve a select group of children who manifested a discrepancy between their presumed abilities and obtained scores on standardized achievement tests. These children would be called disabled. "With great reluctance by many," special education "adopted a categorical discrepancy definition. This definition has been soundly criticized on almost every conceivable ground *except* undue exclusion of children."[3]

A Misguided Choice

The field's adoption of the categorical discrepancy model was an error of enormous proportions. The adopted model forced the focus of special education toward eligibility, categorical identification, and school placement issues. Had special education's ability-achievement discrepancy model not been fabricated, had the idea of handicap-identification not won out, several beneficial and essential outcomes would have occurred.

1.   Responsibility for educating all children would have remained on the shoulders of general education.

2.   Special education would not have provided general education with excuses to avoid that responsibility.

3. Special education could have spent past decades building and refining a substantial arsenal of workable, effective educational strategies for all children and their interested teachers.

Special education had in hand a viable option to its eligibility/placement mentality. It chose to say no to that option. It moved instead toward a narrow population of able students the field chose to call disabled, resulting in needy children with a wide range of strengths and weaknesses being ignored by both regular and special education. Special education's decision to select its eligibility/placement model would not be without thorns.

Identification Errors

It is puzzling why special educator's would have considered their discrepancy model adequate to the task of determining who was and who wasn't deserving of additional school-based assistance. Accurate definition and identification of special education's obscure, often indecipherable exceptionalities that are educationally irrelevant and overlapping[4] has been a fundamental problem for the field ever since it chose to move beyond such venomous classifications as "dull," "defective," and "idiotic."[5] That the categorical placement system is based more on administrative convenience and influence of special interest groups than on sound educational practice has been clearly documented.[6]

An examination of [our] 'classificatory' labels strongly suggests that there really is no classification system within special education. What might appear to be a system is, in reality, an unsystematic crazy quilt of labels. The categories and labels do not constitute a scientific classification system. First, there is no common logic, criteria, or order within the scheme. Second, the various classificatory labels come from different disciplines, reflect different perspectives, and serve no single purpose. The crucial and fundamental inadequacy of current special education classification is simply that the scheme does not serve educational purposes.[7]

The discrepancy scores from special education's intelligence and achievement tests could do little to objectify or clarify difficulties classifying the educational and cultural diversities students brought to school. Why special education's decision makers did not see that their tests were certain to produce unacceptable errors in diagnosis, classification, and program placement is difficult to explain. While at the University of Denver, I witnessed an honored colleague at the University of Colorado investigate the state's ever-increasing numbers of children designated exceptional, particularly those classified as learning disabled. One had the sense the state was suspicious of the rising numbers of children so classified. Its suspicions were confirmed. "[A] representative sample of 1,000 cases were analyzed both quantitatively and qualitatively...Only 28% of the...cases met strict criteria for LD; another 15% showed weak signs of the handicap. The remaining 57% were better described by other indicators."[8]

Wasted Assessment Costs

From its inception, special education's categorical discrepancy model produced immediate overidentification of exceptionality all across the country. It invited general educators to automatically assume that children who failed to meet classroom expectations were encumbered by a disability that required something beyond good teaching. Quite suddenly, the numbers of children being referred for special education assessment skyrocketed. During the early 1970s, assessment costs garnered minimal attention. That changed as the river rose. The astonishing amount of money burned by special education's assessment process, money that never reached the children in the classroom, jolted the bean counters with the impact of a wooden two-by-four to the nose. "The ever-growing numbers of children classified as learning disabled (LD) has staggering cost implications. As noted[9]...much of the...cost is excessive[10] and wasted. Almost half of the special education budget for LD pupils is eaten up by assessment and staffing.[11] Also noted, [is] the cost, not measured in dollars, of the never ending referrals to special education."[12]

General Education's Failings

A measurable portion of general education's numerous failings with students who learn differently can be traced directly to special education's categorical discrepancy model and its generous, ever-present parachute. The discrepancy model informed regular education that some children who learned differently had a hidden neurological disability that required teaching techniques regular teachers could not provide. Regular education was encouraged by special education to refer troubling students to special classes taught by special education teachers. Regular education was told its teachers did not have to review their teaching procedures or learn new skills or check their attitudes toward challenging children. A segment of regular and special education met together beyond closed doors and decided that it was acceptable for regular education to turn its back on children who were struggling in the classroom. The complicity was clear: "...[R]egular and special education teachers have colluded to relieve regular teachers of responsibilities for teaching children functioning at the bottom of their class."[13] Regular education, sufficiently cued, gladly did what it was told. Special education's caseload swelled to bursting.

> The discrepancy model fuels overreferrals to special education. Because there is no consensus about the characteristics of a student with a learning disability, special educators continue to accept hard-to-teach students into their classroom. As long as the discrepancy formula continues to be widely accepted as an evaluation guideline, the quality of special education services will be diluted, and general educators will have no need to reexamine ineffective teaching practices.[14]

A Clear Suspicion of Disability

Given permission to look the other way, some regular education teachers learned to take advantage of special education's limitless safety net. While many teachers and school principals worked diligently to adapt materials for children who were experiencing academic difficulty, others from both professions didn't. These latter, indifferent educators began to refer students for special education evaluation upon seeing the first ripple of educational or social difference. Quite obviously, this wasn't supposed to happen. A youngster was not to be referred for special education evaluation unless there was a clear suspicion of a disability. Public Law 94-142 contained a clause stipulating unmistakably that only students suspected of being handicapped may be evaluated. The purpose for this "suspicion of disability"[15] clause was to reduce incidence of casual referral to special education by regular education teachers. Regular teachers were expected to exhaust all procedural adaptations when faced with a difficult student before referring that youngster for special education evaluation.

Some teachers decided not to work that hard. They discovered early that it was easier to hand the problem over to special education personnel who had previously intimated that it was acceptable to pass the buck to their corner. There's no misinterpretation; professional territories were being staked.

> "Studies have recently demonstrated that the governing 'suspicion of disability' standard has been either ignored or subordinated to the subjective and chaotic referral methods of individual teachers.   Teachers have manifested a pervasive propensity to refer students who 'bother them.' The result is a haphazard, idiosyncratic referral method whereby different teachers refer different types of students because different student traits bother them."[16] "Overwhelmingly, teachers then expect these myriad types of referred students to be tested and testing to produce special education placement."[17]

Special education was quite suddenly available to take care of struggling children by removing nearly all of them from the regular classroom. Once eligibility was approved, regular teachers washed their hands of the problem. There was no need to see if the struggling children, rather than being the problem, were products of a problem that was conveniently overlooked.

Professionals who watched from the sidelines and offered no objections to special education's ubiquitous safety net failed to (or chose not to) see a potentially calamitous problem. If general education continued its unwillingness to evaluate and adapt its curriculum, then referrals to special education would be never ending. Regardless of how many difficult children were removed from a regular classroom, another struggling or disturbing child would soon surface and try a teacher's patience, assuring yet another referral. Distributions of students, no matter how skewed in the desired direction, always have a lower end. When instructional programs are not geared to individual student's strengths, differences in performance will be observed. A system prone toward explaining differences through disabilities will ensure that more children will be said to be disabled.

As increasing numbers of children are classified as handicapped and removed from regular classrooms for special instruction, there has been a dramatic reduction in the range of abilities among children who remain within the general education system. Concurrently, as national standards for excellence are being raised, the number of children at risk for school failure is growing dramatically. Without provisions to prepare students for [these] higher expectations through effective instructional programs, many ["at-risk"] children may also be identified as handicapped and placed in special education. This climate, in which children are tested and labeled as failures or as handicapped in increasing numbers, creates an urgent need for reexamination and change in the system which provides access to services.[18]

A CALL FOR CHANGE

Special education's eligibility process is unnecessarily time consuming, expensive, and thoroughly inefficient in the task of determining which children need extra services. If a teacher seeks special education assistance with a child, the eligibility process can take months from the time that teacher first sounds an alarm to when a favorable eligibility decision might be made. The eventual evaluation will cost roughly $1,500 in supplies, professional time, report writing and phone calls--assuming no lawyer is seated at the table. (The stakes are much higher in that latter circumstance.) At the conclusion of the evaluation and the accompanying dollar expenditures, a decision might come down that the evaluated student doesn't qualify for any additional assistance through special education. Under the worst scenario, that student, still possessing the same academic difficulties and deficiencies, will be returned to the teacher who made the initial referral. It has not escaped the attention of many professionals that the process exemplifies a poor use of precious time and dollars. Some scholars and practitioners have suggested our resources rather than being spent on "determining who is 'special' and who is not could be better used to provide services to all who need it, regardless of any presumed handicap."[19]

PREVENTION: SERVICES AS NEEDED

Special education's eligibility model contains no redeeming features. It causes an over-identification and an under-serving of children. As distasteful as is the former, the latter is worse. The model excludes measurable numbers of young children from receiving the help they need, even though they are the youngsters most likely to experience benefit from such assistance. It is hard to be impressed by the wisdom of professionals whose actions say that struggling youngsters warrant no assistance because they have yet to be completely swallowed by failure. Excluding these children from special education's assistance only sets them further back, it doesn't send them away. When they return, as the present eligibility model guarantees, their fermenting needs will be more costly than had they been helped as soon as the need arose. Perhaps, finally, the time has come

...to move away from the significance of the concept of disability as it is presently implemented through public policy. In many respects, definitions of this sort require a child to fail before services can be provided. There is ample evidence that children who are at risk for language and/or learning problems can be identified early in their development. In addition, there is evidence that the effects of remedial efforts are much more effective when the child is younger....It may be desirable to begin to de-emphasize the concept of disability as it is presently tied to eligibility for services and begin to devote more resources to methods for early identification and intervention.[20]

Perhaps, finally, we can look at serving all children, immediately, effectively, declaring, as some have,[21] that any student who is achieving poorly warrants special consideration and interventions that make a difference.

The Skeptics

The time has come to institute a general/special education policy that provides services to all children, on an as needed basis, and is designed to protect the integrity and value of each child, to leave no child behind, and to challenge and produce daily success for all children and their teachers. No artificial formulas. No fabricated, slippery eligibility requirements. No months of frustrated waiting for assistance, either for children or their teachers. Instead, public schools that are fashioned to become problem directed, solution oriented, and nonexclusionary.

Skeptics say it can't be done. They won't say it shouldn't be done, only that it can't be done. Read carefully. They express their pessimism in such a way as if hoping they are wrong.

Constructively, [advocates] wish...us to focus on academic deficits and to provide appropriate remediation to all children and adolescents who need it. This is a utopian vision to which we all aspire. But practicalities constrain the attainment of such a vision. The most obvious and dominant constraint is the taxpayer's gripe against the increases in school taxes that would be necessary to enable the arrival on earth of such a utopia.[22]

(Please note this point of clarification: No tax increase is necessary. A service-as-needed model can begin with most schools' present staff. While additional staff would be helpful, and in the future will be needed, we can begin a model change without any additional cost to taxpayers.)

FOCUS: A NEW RIVER OF CHILDREN

1. We have no ability-achievement discrepancy model. We have no measure of intelligence and we use weak measures of student achievement to assess what they know. Despite warnings against doing so, we give life[23] and

value to numbers so statistically trampled that they tell us nothing about an individual child who is struggling.

2. Special education must stop providing excuses for general education. So long as the flawed discrepancy model is used to justify extra educational services, the message to general education is that it owns none of the child's scholastic problems. So long as special education persists in explaining academic failure as being due to intrinsic neurological anomalies, general education can comfortably avoid facing its own "appalling decline in quality."[24]

> [T]oo many children have been labeled inappropriately by...a system that attempts to meet the needs of too many children who are unsuccessful in regular classrooms....The problem is not just a special education problem. The general education community needs to provide broader alternatives for marginal students other than special education.[25]

3. "Approximately 80-90% of the students in special education are served in categories for the mildly handicapped--the most unreliable and scientifically controversial categories."[26] Special education's flawed discrepancy model fuels these controversial categories. A huge portion of these designated disabled children would be help effectively and immediately, and removed from special education's roster, by requiring regular education to adapt and accommodate its curriculum to fit each child, regardless of the child's age, grade level, or prior curriculum accomplishments.

4. Special education must evaluate how best to use its professionals. My school psychology buddies in the desert spent close to 80% of their time administering, scoring, and summarizing tests to satisfy the insatiable appetite of special education's eligibility model. They were forced, by entrenched governmental rules and regulations, to pay homage to the beast even while treating it with full disdain.

We need to step forward and initiate a systemic change. Efforts to modify the system will not be easy. Scholar John Horn has advised us.

> I have noted that when beliefs become imbedded in a culture, they can become very resistant to change. Such inertia represents one of the reasons why we persist in using hodgepodge concepts of general intelligence. This cultural inertia is imbedded in federal and state laws that require children to be classified in accordance with hodgepodge measures—or example, for the purpose of determining eligibility for special education programs. Such laws virtually force...psychologists to give obeisance to a false belief.[27]

In fairness, not all of my desert school psychology colleagues objected to their daily IQ testing routine. Some enjoyed the predictability of their schedules. But more of my psychologists friends wanted out from the yoke of intelligence testing. More wanted to be in the classrooms, working directly with teachers and children, solving problems. Special education's discrepancy model, with its reprehensible requirement of services only after eligibility, virtually kept them in their small rooms, seated across from a child, separated by a test-covered desk. There were no confrontations there. There was no chance to impact a faulty educational system or analyze a child's gradually increasing disruptive classroom behavior or confront a lazy professional who only wants to know if it's lunch time. "A waste," I rebuked my friends as they left the office with their IQ test kits to find a severe discrepancy. These inordinately competent people were required to genuflect to a phantom model. You may as well administer intravenous Valium to a corpse.

5.   Special education's tightening of its criteria for eligibility (by adding the term "severe") to reduce expenditures and the numbers of children served will not prevent the river's flow. It will only divert its path.   Let me share a recent experience.

My college dean and I were meeting with the principal and vice principal of a local elementary school to discuss a modified lab school for our special education graduate students and the school's pupils. At the close of the meeting, I asked the vice principal for the size of his school and the numbers of identified special education pupils. I learned the school served some 760 children, 75 of whom were designated "special education." "How many learning disabled kids?" I inquired, expecting near forty.

"Twelve," he remarked, after the information illuminated his computer's screen.

"Twelve?" I reacted with wide-eyed surprise.

"That's it," he verified. "We have twelve LD kids."

"What about the other sixty-three children?"

"One has spina bifida, three are multi-handicapped, and fifty-eight are speech and language impaired." I was shocked.

I met my speech pathologist wife for dinner and announced in animated disbelief that this quiet rural school carried 58 speech and language kids on its special education roles. She was unruffled. "Come on," I poked at her. "No way are there fifty-eight kids with speech problems at that school. Ten maybe...and even that number is too high. What's going on?"

"The kids are probably having problems in class, not keeping up with their work," she suggested without much emotion. "Probably a small number have legitimate speech and language problems. The rest are having difficulty with their assignments; they're being found eligible for special education services."

"Through speech and language classification!" I exclaimed.

The next day, I visited with the vice principal of the rural school. "Special education is concerned about eligibility," he reminded me. "We are concerned about getting kids help. We will use whatever means necessary to accomplish that goal. It's easier establishing eligibility through speech than LD," he explained matter-of-factly.

6. Speech and language classification is not the only (alternative) conduit presently being used in the never-ending search for additional education assistance for children having problems in school. There's another one just itching to provide a colossal infusion of children onto special education's rolls. The Seventeenth Annual Report to Congress tells us that second only to the frightening increase in traumatic brain injuries, "other health impairments" showed the largest growth of any other special education category from 1992-93 through 1993-94, a mind-boggling 26.1%: "The increase in the number of students with other health impairments appears to be the result of growth in the service population. Specifically, the number of students with attention deficit disorders (ADD) appears to be increasing."[28]

The 17th Annual Report's judgment that "ADD appears to be increasing," is amusingly understated. ADD/ADHD is epidemic. The river has carved a new path. Unless we make some major changes in how general and special education do business, the whole boat is going to capsize.

Special education's current discrepancy model misses too many children. We need a system that immediately sends help to youngsters when instruction produces frustration and avoidance. Focusing our attention toward a child's suspected disability is pragmatically meaningless. Withholding our assistance while we debate a disability's existence borders on being criminal. That children differ from one another, that many fail to accomplish in school what we wish for them is so basic as to be minutiae.

NOTES

1. Hallahan, D. P., & Kauffman, J. M. (1994). *Exceptional children: Introduction to special education* (6th ed.). Boston: Allyn and Bacon.

2. Barsch, R. H. (1968). Perspectives on learning disabilities: The vectors of a new convergence. *Journal of Learning Disabilities, 1,* 7-23.

3. Bateman, B. (1992). Learning disabilities: The changing landscape. *Journal of Learning Disabilities, 25,* 29-36.

4. Smith, R. M., & Neisworth, J. T. (1975). *The exceptional child: A functional approach.* New York: McGraw-Hill.

5. Hardman, M. L., Drew, C. J., & Egan, M. W. (1996). *Human exceptionality: Society, school, and family.* Needham,Mass: Allyn and Bacon.

6. Reschly, D. J. & Ysseldyke, J. E. (1995). School psychology paradigm shift. In A. Thomas & J. Grimes (Eds.), *Best practices in school psychology--III* (pp.17-31) Washington, DC: National Association of School Psychologists.

7. Smith, R. M., & Neisworth, J. T. (1975).

8. Shepard, L. A. & Smith, M. L. (1983). An evaluation of the identification of learning disabled students in Colorado. *Learning Disability Quarterly, 6,* 115-127.

9. Hagerty, G. J., & Abramson, M. (1987). Impediments to implementing national policy change for mildly handicapped students. Exceptional Children, *53,* 315-323.

10. Shepard, L. A. & Smith, M. L. (1983).

11. Shepard, L. A. & Smith, M. L. (with Davis, A., Glass, G. V., Riley, A., & Vojir, C.) (1981). *Evaluation of the identification of perceptual-communicative disorders in Colorado.* Boulder: CO: Laboratory of Educational Research.

12. Shepard, L. A. (1987) The new push for excellence: Widening the schism between regular and special education. *Exceptional Children, 53*, 327-329.

13. Shepard, L. A. (1987), p. 328.

14. Henley, M., & Ramsey, R. S., & Algozzine, R. (1993). *Characteristics of and strategies for teaching students with mild disabilities.* Boston: Allyn and Bacon, p. 152.

15. Galagan, J. E. (1985). Psychoeducational testing: Turn out the lights, the party's over. *Exceptional Children, 52*, 288-299.

16. Ysseldyke, J., Thurlow, M., Graden, J., Wesson, C., Deno, S., & Algozzine, B. (1983). Generalizations from five years of research on assessment and decision making. *Exceptional Educational Quarterly, 4* , 75-93.

17. Ysseldyke, J. E. (1983). Current Practices in Making Psychoeducational Decisions About Learning Disabled Students. Cited in Galagan, J. E. (1985). Psychoeducational testing: Turn out the lights, the party's over. *Exceptional Children, 52*, 288-299.

18. Position Paper: Advocacy for Appropriate Educational Services for All Children. (1985). *National Coalition of Advocates for Students and the National Association of School Psychologists.* Boston: Author.

19. Graden, J. L., Zins, J. E., & Curtis, M. J. (1989). The need for alternatives in educational services. In Janet L. Graden, Joseph E. Zins, & Michael J. Curtis (Eds.), *Alternative Educational Delivery Systems: Enhancing instructional options for all students.* Washington, DC.: NASP.

20. Francis, D. J., Fletcher, J. M., Shaywitz, B. A., Shaywitz, S. E., & Rourke, B. P. (1996). Defining learning and language disabilities: Conceptual and psychometric issues with the use of IQ tests. *Language, Speech, and Hearing Services in Schools, 27*, 32-143.

21. Siegel, L. (1989). Why we do not need intelligence test scores in the definition and analysis of learning disabilities. *Journal of Learning Disabilities, 22*, 514-518.

22. Wong, B. Y. L. (1989). Concluding comments on the special series on the place of IQ in defining learning disabilities. *Journal of Learning Disabilities, 22*, 519.

23. Kaufman, A. S. (1979). *Intelligent testing with the WISC-R.* New York: John Wiley & Sons, p.2.

24. Bateman, B. (1992).

25. Report of the Special Education Advisory Committee Task Force on Perceptual-Communicative Disorders in Colorado. (1981). *Colorado Department of Education,* Denver, Colorado.

26. Reynolds, M. C., Wang, M. C., & Walberg, H. J. (1987). The necessary restructuring of special and regular education. *Exceptional Children, 53*, 327-329.

27. Horn, J. L. (1985). Remodeling old models of intelligence. In Benjamin B. Wolman (Ed.), *Handbook of intelligence: Theories, measurement, and application.* New York: John Wiley & Sons, p. 269.

28. To Assure The Free Appropriate Public Education of all Children with Disabilities. Seventeenth Annual Report to Congress On the Implementation of The Individuals with Disabilities Education Act. U.S. Department of Education. 1995, p. 11.

9

Learning Disabilities

A 'Rumpelstiltskin fixation'...[a term coined by Dr. Alan Ross]...characterizes the preoccupation of some...with whether a given child who manifests a learning disability is or is not brain-damaged. That question and related questions of etiology and classification often dominate...evaluations and staff conferences as if everything depended on that one answer. In a well-known fairy tale the chance for the princess to live her life happily ever after depends on her discovering the name of an ill-tempered dwarf. As a result she goes to great lengths to learn his name, and upon doing so, earns her salvation. Many clinicians and educators seem to engage in similar fairy-tale behavior. They act as if, could they but give the condition a name, the child would be saved.[1]

The late, much admired Samuel A. Kirk gave us the categorical term "learning disabilities" in 1963.[2,3] The formal birth occurred at an April 6 Chicago meeting, sponsored by the Fund for Perceptually Handicapped Children. Parents had gathered to discuss concerns about their children's school difficulties and to express their dissatisfaction with having their children referred to as "retarded" or "brain damaged," the two predominant labels used to account for the children's unexpectedly poor classroom performance. Dr. Kirk joined the parents in their objections, pointing out that neither term carried much practical value for educators. He further explained that neither was likely to entice the federal government toward providing funds to support necessary classroom accommodations for these special children. He shared with the parents that in his recently published textbook, *Educating Exceptional Children*,[4] he had begun to use a new term to describe otherwise bright youngsters who were performing below expectations. He suggested the term could serve as a suitable alternative to the many confusing labels (e.g., dyslexic, brain injured, perceptually handicapped, neurologically impaired, aphasic[5]) used to explain a myriad of school-related, academic difficulties being exhibited by a diverse group of children.[6] The term struck a receptive chord with the parents. During that seminal business meeting in Chicago, "learning disabilities," as a separate category of exceptionality, was born.[7] Dr. Kirk's intent for the term was clear: "The concept of learning disabilities...encompass[es] the heterogeneous group of children not fitting neatly into the traditional categories of handicapped children....[These are] children who often appear quite normal in most respects but have marked disabilities in one area or another."[8]

SUPPLANTING "EDUCATIONALLY RETARDED"

Most compelling, was that Samuel Kirk's proposed label conveyed to the Chicago parents that their youngsters, although struggling with some schoolwork, were still "quite normal." Being given permission to once again believe their children were normal was no small benefit. A few years earlier, these same parents were told their children were "educationally retarded,"[9] a term capable of eliciting suffocating fear. That "learning disability" was a softer, more kindly term, that it gave hope that a child's personal sky might still be his only limit, made it enormously appealing. That it was also an enigmatic construct with little chance of clear definition and even less chance of telling a teacher precisely what to instruct was irrelevant. It supplanted the thoroughly demeaning term "retarded." For that, Samuel Kirk should be roundly applauded.

THE CHOICE POINT AGAIN

That applause, however, must be brief. Samuel Kirk, who a quarter of a century later, would describe learning disabilities as only "a catchall phrase that's been used to describe all different kinds of learning problems,"[10] failed to seize a precious opportunity to provide those Chicago parents with crucial alternatives when searching for solutions to their children's learning difficulties. Samuel Kirk, as a representative of special education, stood at a pure, choice point, a rare and pivotal position where a respected leader can score a clear, determined path for others to follow, research, and perfect. Special education that very day held in hand the opportunity to offer the Chicago parents a plan of action that would have directly and immediately benefited their youngsters' classroom achievements. That day, the field could have signaled general education to be alerted to and prepared for a wave of student diversity that would require its comprehensive, unfaltering commitment and cooperation. Special education as a profession could have accomplished so much.

1. Special education could have rejected the position that an educational disability was a necessary prerequisite to additional school-based services.

2. Special education could have rejected the position that a student's difficulties with reading, writing, and mathematics were due primarily to a physiological error hidden within a student's central nervous system.

3. Special education could have directed its efforts toward assisting general education to adapt teaching styles and materials to accommodate the normal diversity of all its students.

4. Special education could have directed its efforts toward assisting general education to develop an accountable system where all children would experience academic success regardless of their entry level skills, educational history, or unique perceptual and cognitive strengths.

5. Special education could have refuted the belief that educational difficulties and differences were synonymous with educational disabilities.

6. Special education could have turned its back on a pathological disability model. Rather than becoming a deficit-oriented field, where a student's faults and perceived limits were the first items communicated, special education could have turned its energies toward identifying students' strengths and building programs based on those strengths.

Pathology Embraced

As we know, special education chose otherwise. With one breath it proudly disavowed "brain damage," with the next it celebrated "brain dysfunction." It chose to use impressive clinical terms that convinced many parents "that their children [had] some irredeemable congenital or pathological disorder."[11] The conscious choice of the term "intrinsic" adopted by special education's definition of learning disabilities conveyed clearly the position that the child owned the problem: "*Learning disabilities* is a generic term that refers to a heterogeneous group of disorders manifested by significant difficulties in the acquisition and use of listening, speaking, reading, writing, reasoning, or mathematical abilities. These disorders are intrinsic to the individual and presumed to be due to central nervous system dysfunction."[12]

Pathology Hidden

There has been a marked resurgence of interest in dyslexia since Geschwind's (1962)[13] reintroduction of an anatomical basis for reading disorders...Geschwind, et.al., (1968)[14] demonstrated conclusively that the left planum temporale, a triangular area behind the auditory gyrus of Heschl (a part of the auditory association cortex), is usually larger than the right. Other asymmetries also were documented.[15] (See added note.)

Despite lengthy, instructionally worthless authoritative claims, similar to the one above, that a physical basis for certain academic difficulties had been conclusively demonstrated, special education knew it would not be able to verify the neurological deficiencies it said were responsible for classroom learning problems. That inability to verify, however, appeared of small consequence. The field announced that the neurological errors were hidden, and the matter effectively was closed. The word "presumed," included within the body of the learning disability definition, seemed to the profession a sufficient hedge. (Science, of course, rarely allows for such arrogance. The chopping block is covered with the blood of decapitated presumptions.)

> No matter whether brain structure and activity were inferred, pictured, or mapped; whether the brain was directly examined; or whether drugs were used to influence brain activity, no body of evidence has confirmed—and much of it has repudiated—the many neurological-deficit interpretations.[16]

> The evidence from studies using formal neurological examinations...is especially damaging to the neurological impairment explanation. Surely, if the neurological thesis were to find support anywhere, it would find it in the techniques and science available to neurologists. Unfortunately for those who held this thesis, studies of borderline symptoms, soft signs, have uniformly failed to contribute to the diagnosis of academic underachievement.[17]

Despite the above compelling perspective, special education maintained its posture of attributing academic discrepancies to a child's supposed defective neurology.

Creating a Need to Identify

The field, of course, needed to develop a way to identify which schoolchildren were said to have this improbable neurological impairment and be labeled learning disabled. Since these presumed disabled youngsters carried no discernible physical sign of their handicap, some mathematical formula that would help practitioners identify the children needed to be manufactured. The field chose to use an ability-achievement discrepancy formula similar to the one that had been established in the 1960s that was used to categorize children as "educationally retarded"—"The term 'educationally retarded' means that the child's achievement in one or more school subjects is below what would normally be expected of a child of his intellectual capacity."[18]

Overlooking Verification

Special education accepted its ability-achievement discrepancy model without thoroughly scrutinizing either of its crucial components. Had the field requested that impartial psychometric detectives investigate the validity of their tests of intelligence, they would have found reason to pause in their enthusiasm. Intelligence, they would have discovered, refused to be corralled or calibrated. Had the same investigators evaluated the relevance of special education's tests of achievement to a student's actual classroom curriculum work, they would have concluded that their discrepancy model had the reliability and resilience of a floating soap bubble.

No dispassionate sleuths visited special education's model, however. The discrepancy model received blanket acceptance as a valid means of identifying a disability that was not definable and verifying the presence of a neurological deficiency that was not measurable. Special education had built a name for the schoolchild's problem, had presumed a cause for that problem, and had lost contact with the child in the process. Few parents seated at the Chicago meeting would be aware of that latter consequence.

HOW LITTLE ANY OF THIS MATTERS

Fascinating and infuriating, all this exertion spent with definition, identification, and naming brain anomalies as cause for children's school-related difficulties means little and matters even less. Being given the label "dyslexic" or "learning disabled" does not illuminate the student's weakness, strength, or tutorial needs. Until we perfect microsurgery with dendrites, partial or total brain transplants, or are able to repair that previously mentioned mystifying triangular area behind the auditory gyrus of Heschl, being told that brain damage is responsible for the disability is technically wrong and educationally worthless: The purported brain-damaged child either will have to be taken behind the barn door and humanely done away with or taken into the classroom and provided instruction by some enthusiastic competent teacher. It's not a hard choice.

The Solution: So Simple, So Clear

Ironically, it was Samuel Kirk who endeavored to bring sense to the process of serving each child, regardless of speculations surrounding neurological dysfunction. It is too bad Dr. Kirk waited so many years after the Chicago meeting to set the right course for the field he loved and honored. We can easily speculate where special education would have gone had Dr. Kirk's following words been spoken sooner—

> From an educational point of view, the cause (etiology) of a condition rarely is relevant for remediation. To know that the etiology of a learning disability is brain injury or cerebral dysfunction does not change the educational program. Teachers use a developmental curriculum, starting where a child is and helping the child move the developmental ladder step by step.[19]

Samuel Kirk's observations and advice were painfully uncomplicated. "Starting where a child is and helping the child move the developmental ladder step by step" requires no assignment of category or disability. It requires no talk of eligibility or artificial discrepancies. It requires no expensive time-consuming formal standardized assessment. It requires no comparison of children to determine who is educationally normal and who is not, who is educationally better and who is worse. It requires no classification of exceptionality, no pressure to justify "severe" or substantially less. It requires a teacher who knows where a child is in relation to the teacher's curriculum, a teacher who understands a developmental curriculum, a teacher who can and does choose to effectively match the two measures, a teacher who is willing to look at the results of his or her strategies to see if they need modification.

If it is so painfully uncomplicated, why then does special education continue with its defective ability-achievement discrepancy model? The answer: artificial eligibility! So long as eligibility for services is mandated, the name "learning disability," or a suitable facsimile, will be needed before a child can be caught by a safety net that has begun to show signs of wear.

The Rallying Point

Samuel Kirk's term "learning disability" emerged that 1963 day in Chicago pristine fresh, without tatter or stain. Like Neil Armstrong's rocket, it ascended flawlessly. It was, for a growing number of parents struggling with a confusing hurt felt for their children, a virtual godsend. It became a flag around which the parents could rally. It served as vehicle for their honorable cause of vindication: It would prove that their children, casually and summarily dismissed as lazy and retarded, were neither. It gave the parents what they had been lacking: the ways and means to fight an insipid educational system not yet bound by law to accommodate the children's diversities, a system content to place everyone on the same bus driven by the same driver.

> [W]hen dealing with large numbers of children, it is simpler to classify them by age and set up schedules. It is far less trouble, at least for the authorities, when everyone does the same thing at the same time in the same sequence. Schools that are organized in this fashion function exactly like assembly lines in factories; as one critic has noted, the main purpose of going to school seems to be to get to the next grade.[20]

Sometime after 1975, the child-advocacy rally turned politically ugly, and this cohort group of disenchanted parents went for the school system's jugular. They became singularly demanding in their cry for action on behalf of their children. Public schools were placed on notice: They would accommodate—the law now required them to do so! Samuel Kirk's term, intact for the moment, was both pennant and wedge used to force open general education's tutorial doors.

The Flood

The term "learning disabilities," however, was stretched too far by its advocates. First, minimal variations in students' learning and classroom performance were dubbed a disability, and children who deviated ever so slightly from the mainstream were taken to places outside the regular classroom where their hidden neurological disabilities were better "fixed" (presumably). By the mid-1980s, it was estimated some 1,000 people per day were being told they were learning disabled.[21] (Those numbers, of course, represented only those individuals who had passed the litmus test of having a "severe" discrepancy. Perhaps another 2,000 individuals each day were deemed a wee short of being disabled, but likely to reach that discrepancy during the next assessment go-around after they had fallen further behind in their studies.) By the 1993-94 calendar year, individuals designated as learning disabled composed a group larger than all other exceptionalities combined. The term was being used to explain all sorts of deviant cognitive, academic, and social activities not originally intended, including not being able to find one's car in a shopping mall's parking lot.[22]

The river of school kids, tagged now as disabled, had broken free of its intended banks, their numbers rapidly drowning the educational system. Examples are everywhere. They are very revealing.

A small, rural school, 15 minutes from my office, has seventy-six third graders, divided among three classes. Twenty-four of the third-grade children have been referred and found eligible for special education services, either for learning disabilities or speech and language difficulties, the latter used in place of learning disabilities to obtain special education assistance with reading and writing assignments. During the second week of the school year, one of the third grade teachers announced she intended to refer ten additional students from her class for special education evaluation. (The total cost for evaluation and assessment for the new ten referrals will approach $15,000 to $18,000.) The teacher reported the children were not prepared for their third grade spelling assignments; the teacher stated the children should be taught in a smaller group where they could receive individual assistance. Chances are that only five or six of the teacher's ten will meet special education criteria, bringing the total of special education third graders to twenty-nine out of the original seventy-six. If only five children are found eligible for special education, the third grade will have 38% of its students enrolled in special education.   During the early 1970s, while Congress held hearings on the Education for the Handicapped Act (PL 94-142), apprehension was expressed that perhaps some 40% of the school age population might be labeled learning disabled.[23] That view, at least at one school in this small town, seems no longer a concern but a reality.

A Broker Term

The term "learning disabilities" originally served many useful purposes, not the least of which was asserting that schoolchildren who required greater accommodation and individualization during instruction time were not to be dismissed as lazy or just stupid. The notion that a learning disability was something to have, something that could interfere with school progress provided able students with relief from a system not often sympathetic to the classroom learning problems they were experiencing.[24,25]

At best now, learning disabilities is an unnecessary broker term. It's an empty "middle-man," an extra layer of impeding bureaucracy. When used, it requires extensive explanation and clarification before a student's strengths or academic weakness are communicated. Standing alone, the term cannot convey any clear decisive message for it has become an "umbrella"[26] covering an endless array of differences in school children's academic and social activities. The slightest kneading is all that's necessary to change the term's shape and appearance and allow it to take on an explanatory role for a child "who stuttered, who teased the family cat, who could not deal with geometry in the 10th grade but who otherwise was getting along well in school, who had night terrors; who was diagnosed by the family psychiatrist as depressed."[27]

The term has become cause célèbre for a legendary list of unsuitable, bothersome behaviors, capable of frazzling the calmest parent. Professor William Cruickshank tells of his experiences when conversing with parents concerned with their children's behaviors:

> Parents in their concept of learning disability have talked with me about nail biting, poor eating habits, failure of the child to keep his room neat, unwillingness to take a bath, failure to brush teeth. Teachers have questioned me about disrespectful children, children who will not listen to the adult, children who are sexually precocious, children who are aggressive— all in the belief that these are learning disability children. One parent asked me if the fact that his college-student son wore long hair and he "suspected" lived with a girl outside his dormitory was the result of a learning disability![28]

And without much effort, the term "learning disabilities" can mean most anything anyone chooses:

> An analysis of LD would suggest that it means many different things as opposed to one thing. Consequently, it is difficult to capture any essence for LD, and a real definition for LD seems not possible....It is unlikely that any combination or permutation of words defining LD will ever be universally accepted as "the" definition.[29]

Or it can mean nothing:

> I believe that if we continue trying to define learning disabilities by using ill-defined concepts, we will forever be frustrated, for it is an illusive concept. We are being bamboozled. It is as though someone started a great hoax by inventing the term then tempting others to define it. And lo and behold...task forces and others have taken the bait.[30]

LEARNING DISABILITY

> [T]he entire concept [of learning disabilities] is dated and flawed. With enough...testing...close to half the population can be classified LD; with money attached to the classification there is a lot of impetus to put any kid that needs more help into LD programs, particularly in resource-strapped

schools. The model comes out of 1950's and 60's thinking about intellectual function and is so outdated as to be embarrassing.[31]

However we describe the term learning disability, whatever properties we
invest within it or definition we bestow upon it, the fact remains we have no
measure of it, no way of knowing whether it is real or merely a convenience.
Our collective ignorance aside, the label learning disabilities was an inevitable
outcome of general education's stubborn refusal to recognize and accommodate
for the increasingly diverse learners who were attending post-*Sputnik* elementary
and secondary schools. Too many of these youngsters were experiencing problems with classwork to have remained unnoticed. Too many professionals, suspicious of their increasing numbers, wondered why the children were struggling.
Too many parents refused to accept the ignorant professional line that their children were "educationally retarded." Unrelenting forces demanded an explanation
for the children's classroom difficulties.

No Single Cause

Several options were available to special education, including the most obvious: that no single, identifiable variable was responsible for the children's perplexing academic performance. Schools certainly had a hand in the children's
problems, as did the children's parents and the children themselves. Special education could have declared there was no needle in the haystack, that a single,
simplistic answer was unacceptable, and that it was incumbent upon general education to stop looking for excuses and to concentrate its energies on curriculum
accommodation. It didn't happen. Samuel Kirk stepped forward and gave the
parents—and general education—learning disabilities. Something neurological
was interfering with the children. No other options were heard.

Arguably, Samuel Kirk never intended learning disability to be an identifiable "it" that was seen and measured like an arm that was fractured or a rash that
was spreading. His intent, in part at least, was to propose a term that would
take the place of "brain damaged" or "mentally retarded," two terms previously
used to described children who were experiencing problems with reading, writing,
and mathematics. But learning disabilities today satisfies so many varied personal and professional agendas that it has become impossibly murky. It has
evolved to represent a vague construct complicated by substantial heterogene-
ity.[32] It represents so many idiosyncrasies that it provides no categorical value.
Each learning disabled individual is his or her own star, making the term quite
useless when applied to an entire group. Because "each child, adolescent, or
adult with a learning disability is unique, [because] each shows a different combination and severity of problem...,"[33] Samuel Kirk's term "learning disability"
no longer says anything meaningful about any of them. It is time we get past
the attempt at a consensus definition and onto the children who need assistance.

When it comes to finding the definitions of learning disabilities, we should
forget about it, at least for now. Far too much time, money, and space in
textbooks and journals have been taken up by this futile mission. Those

concerned with this goal have sought the answer by administering one test after another, giving multiple tests, and like alchemists of old, carefully selecting and combining subtests and items from many tests. The thinking is, apparently, that if the proper battery of tests, subtests, or items can be blended and then administered and if the proper multivariate analysis is employed, then we will be able to tell who is really learning disabled and who isn't (the pretenders!). And further, if our tests and measurements are highly sophisticated, we will know about the many subtypes of learning disabilities. Wrong![34]

ELIGIBILITY

It matters little to the classroom teacher that learning disabilities is a term with multiple definitions and parameters or that the eligibility process used to identify a child as learning disabled is scarcely more than an expensive game of numbers and creative wits. The regular classroom teacher, up to his or her neck in frustration with a student or two, cares little for truth or accuracy in labeling; that teacher, at the very least, wants help and respite. While in the desert, I saw the pressure brought to bear on school psychologists to find difficult children eligible for special education services. I heard the teacher's attitude as it was voiced loudly: "Something needs to be done, and now!" That desired something, most often, was separating a disturbing child from a distraught teacher—at least for a few hours a day.

While the eligibility process and its outcome are inconsequential to the classroom teacher, both capture the full attention of special education directors who are held accountable for the cost of assessment, the numbers of referrals, and the children designated as exceptional.

Admonition: Message from a Director of Special Education

Although learning disabilities is a somewhat nebulous category, there are [Federal and State] guidelines that have been established. I know that there is often pressure or a desire to place students who need help. Unfortunately special education is often the only available program for students needing some kind of help. However, we must keep in mind that only students who are handicapped and in need of special education can be placed. Any student who does not meet the criteria is illegally placed and when we are monitored, we will have to pay back any funds collected for an ineligible student. We can't afford to do this. Our numbers in the learning disability category, in particular, have increased in the last year and a half. Overall our numbers have increased by over 300 and we have added no more teachers. We cannot afford inappropriate placements, nor should we be labeling students as handicapped who are not.[35]

Dabbling With Guidelines

As the special education director noted, eligibility guidelines do exist. On paper, they are nearly as black and white as the letters used to convey them. Off paper, in real-life settings, their color is vague, and their elasticity is similar to that of a yard of saltwater taffy. We know eligibility guidelines vary from state to state and district to district. We know favorable eligibility decisions often depend on a street address. But a child's school district attendance area is not the only source of malleability in the eligibility process. A second source, perhaps surprisingly, stems from the examining psychologist's leanings toward the child being evaluated and the fairness of the evaluation process itself. Clinical judgment most assuredly enters the eligibility decision process. A psychologist may decide the test being used isn't suited to the child being assessed; the psychologist, for the benefit of the child, may tinker with a test's administrative rules.[36] I haven't met too many of my colleagues who haven't fiddled a drop when such fiddling brought the child a little closer to needed extra help. Such dabbling, beneficial or otherwise, does introduce additional variability into the eligibility process.

Certainly, a portion of school psychologists "go by the book" handed them by their school district. They know their numbers, norms, and standard deviations. They know their cut-offs and ceilings. They make little exception for a child's answer to a question or exercise. If an assessed child's test scores match the discrepancy requirements adopted by the examiner's school district, eligibility is usually approved. If the discrepancy is only close, approval is usually denied. These psychologists may not agree with the entire playing field, but they abide by their district's established rules.

Other psychologists, however, see weakness in the eligibility process and the instruments used in that process. They choose to manipulate the assessment playing field, believing their actions are sound and honorable. They recognize that acceptable answers to some questions on intelligence tests are dead wrong, out dated, and culturally ignorant. They find ways to have needy children ruled eligible for additional services. I tracked the following discussion among several school district psychologists who were members of an Internet listserve and who were struggling with issues of eligibility.

Psychologist 1: Now, this is what puzzles me: Since there were no significant discrepancies, the [psychologist] determined that the...scores must not be good scores...so [he] chose to use the FLUID REASONING score of 124 on the [Woodcock Johnson] Cognitive test to use as an estimate of the examinee's OPTIMAL abilities. Using this score (124) the examiner was able to get a significant difference and say that a learning disability was present...My question is this: Is this a legitimate procedure? I thought Fluid Reasoning was a subtest. Is it appropriate to use a subtest score to use as the IQ score in computing a significant discrepancy? Wouldn't that be like using a high [intelligence test] subscale score to say it was a more accurate reflection of an examinee's IQ when all of the other subscale scores indicate otherwise?[37]

Psychologist 2: If this is indeed the way this psychologist proceeded with the evaluation and interpretation, it is obviously a sham. The psychologist was going to find a learning disability no matter what instruments he/she administered or what the scores would be![38]

Psychologist 3: Yes. It's BS. No learning disability exists, in my opin-ion...The psychologist is looking for data to support his or her opinion, and disregarding what the actual data are showing—that no learning disabil-ity exists! High [sic] unscientific, and perhaps bordering on unethical, I think.[39]

Psychologist 4: Let us consider a commonl [sic] example, which psychol-ogists do all the time. I don't know of any psychologist who would score the Verbal scale when evaluating a deaf child!   Yet the Wechsler [intelligence] instruments are often used. Would we use the Performance scale on a blind or paralyzed student? Of course not! In these cases we in-deed "a priori" throw out sub-tests because of the handicap. It's no big deal, and I doubt anyone would demand you use the full scale scores on these chil-dren. We may give out some verbal tests to a hard of hearing student, but have no intention of "scoring" it. We may just want to get an idea of what they can do. Similarly with a motor impaired youngster, we may give out Block Design but not use time limits, and certainly not score it. This is done all the time![40]

Psychologist 4: With regard to the recent discussion on full scale IQ's, abil-ity/achievement Discrepancy, LD, etc. I admit I've erred in using the term "throw outs" when discussing subtest scores...I started using the term "throwing out" instead of "partial out," which is not my intent or practice at all. We cannot "throw out" tests in the sense that we don't report them, i.e., pretend we never gave them. We must report them—but, as per my argument; "partial" them out from the full scale IQ—if it makes sense.[41]

Psychologist 2: If we begin down the path of "partialling out" particular subtests scores...what will keep unscrupulous (or merely stupid) practition-ers from redefining ability as the aggregate of only the top subscale scores...in the service of their clients?[42]

Psychologist 4: I remain committed to the idea that when there is strong evidence that a cognitive weakness...significantly affects...an IQ score, it does indeed make sense to parcel it out...before calculating an ability-achievement discrepancy....I am not in favor of deleting...scores just to be deleting scores, or selecting only those that are high to put the child in the best possible light...I do, however, believe there are times when it is neces-sary not to use a Full Scale score IQ and be "locked into" a global intelli-gence score.[43]

Psychologist 5: Perhaps the biggest issue regarding this topic is that of validity. What is it that we are measuring when we administer an individual intelligence test?   If we are attempting to measure overall ability (which appears to be implied in the call to identify a discrepancy between ability and achievement), then does not an individual's weaknesses as well as his/her strengths enter into the picture? If the "goal" is to "find" a severe discrepancy so that the student may receive services, perhaps the...model...is at fault.[44]

Psychologist 3: Unfortunately, [these] procedures are not new to researchers who have investigated the use of LDs in practice. The procedure of shopping around until a discrepancy exists between some cognitive measure and...achievement measures has been documented...over the last 15 years. It has the same aura as setting monkeys loose with typewriters, finding a coherent word or phrase and announcing discovery of new intelligence.[45]

That psychologists bend rules on behalf of selected students is a fact. Whether their approach falls within acceptable practice is not the present issue. Their actions, however, do add more variability to an already capricious system. The resulting eligibility coin can land heads or tails producing a false positive, a false negative, or a correct decision. Unfortunately, no examiner can know for certain which of the three possible outcomes have occurred.

While professional judgments and multiple sets of district guidelines do account for some of the capriciousness associated with special education's eligibility process, the major source of system variability and identification error remains the fabricated ability-achievement discrepancy model.

An Impossible Assignment

The above special education director admonished her district's school psychologists to avoid labeling students as learning disabled if they were not. She reminded them that falsely identifying a student as learning disabled is costly to the district and detrimental to the child. The director assumed her psychologists had available assessment instruments that would allow them to distinguish real learning disabled students from those really not learning disabled. The director's assumption, of course, was wrong.

No matter the credibility or conservative stance of an examining psychologist, the currently used intelligence and achievement instruments guarantee unknown numbers of eligibility errors. Difficulties responsible for those errors are unrelated to the tenuous nature of the learning disability category. The discrepancy model on which learning disabilities are awarded is flawed sufficiently to guarantee the very miscalculations the special education director needed to avoid.

FOCUS: DIVERSITY

Educators and psychologists spend far too much time trying to decide whom to serve or whether a specific student is eligible. They also spend too much time judging why specific students are having difficulty. In contrast, they spend far too *little* time deciding what to do with youngsters who experience difficulty—how to help them....We think efforts to separate disability from diversity are doomed to be difficult. [46]

Special education's discrepancy-eligibility model is no longer suited for the present educational arena. It is ill-equipped to handle the new group of diverse learners standing at America's educational doorstep. If we look at these new students through the opaque eyes of our intelligence and achievement tests, if general education is not required to change its curriculum delivery, these students' diversities will be easily mistaken as disabilities.

> A number of teachers will note readily that many, possible most, of the "learning disabled" students enrolled in their programs do not satisfy either the 1977 USOE or the NJCLD definition. This is because, in many school districts, all students who are thought to be able to profit from tutoring or remedial education are arbitrarily called learning disabled. As a consequence of such definitional liberality, the learning disability programs have become glutted with underachieving students, culturally different students, and poorly taught students.[47]

Special education does not have enough seats in its boat to carry them all.

NOTES

1. Smith, R. M. & Neisworth, J. T. (1975). *The exceptional child: A functional approach.* New York: McGraw-Hill.
2. Kirk, S. A. & Chalfant, J. C. (1984). *Academic and developmental learning disabilities.* Denver: Love.
3. Lerner, J. (1993). *Learning disabilities: Theories, diagnosis, and teaching strategies.* Boston: Houghton Mifflin Company.
4. Kirk, S. A. (1962) *Educating exceptional children.* Boston: Houghton Mifflin Company.
5. Ysseldyke, J. E. & Algozzine, B. (1990). *Introduction to special education.* Boston: Houghton Mifflin Company.
6. Hallahan, D. P., & Kauffman, J. M. (1988). *Exceptional children: Introduction to special education.* Englewood Cliffs, NJ: Prentice-Hall.
7. Kirk, S. A. & Chalfant, J. C. (1984).
8. Kirk, S. A. (1962), p. 41-42.
9. Magary, J. F. & Eichorn, J. R. (1960). *The exceptional child: A book of readings.* New York: Holt, Rinehart and Winston, p.410.
10. Kirk S. A & Gallagher, J. J. (1989). *Educating exceptional children.* Boston: Houghton Mifflin Company, p. 184.
11. McGuinness, D. (1985). *When children don't learn.* New York: Basic Books, p.3.
12. Hammill, D. D., Leigh, J. E., McNutt, G., & Larsen, S. C. (1981). A new definition of learning disabilities. *Learning Disability Quarterly, 4,* 336-42.
13. Geschwind, N. (1962). The anatomy of acquired disorders of reading. In J. Money (Ed.), *Reading disability, progress and research needs in dyslexia,* (pp.115-129). Baltimore: Johns Hopkins University Press.
14. Geschwind, N. & Levitsky, W. (1968). Human brain: Left-right asymmetries in temporal speech region. *Science,* 161, 186-187.
15. Richardson, S. O. (1992). Historical perspectives on dyslexia. *Journal of Learning Disabilities,* 25, 40-47. (Added note: The field continues to search for neurological causes for classroom difficulties despite the fact that no finding will impact teachers' abilities to do a better job. Findings will only give general education further reason not to look at its methods and responsibilities. Most

recently, *The Baltimore Sun* reported that Sally Shaywitz's work has verified that dyslexia is a neurological problem, not a result of "subpar intelligence or lack of effort." No doubt some general education teachers will use that information to explain why the children aren't learning. See *The Baltimore Sun*, March, 17, 1998, p. 12a-13a.)

16. Coles, G. (1987). *The learning mystic.* New York: Pantheon.

17. Coles, G. (1978). The learning disability test battery: Empirical and social issues. *Harvard Educational Review, 48*, 313-340.

18. Magary, J. F. & Eichorn, J. R. (1960), p. 410.

19. Kirk S. A. & Gallagher, J. J. (1989), p. 139.

20. McGuinness, D. (1985), p. 239.

21. Reeve, R. E., & Kauffman, J. M. (in press). Learning disabilities. In V. B. Van Hasselt, P. S. Strain, & M. Hersen (Eds.), *Handbook of developmental and physical disabilities.* New York: Plenum. [Reported in Patton, J. R., Payne, J. S., Kauffman, J. M, Brown, G. B., & Payne, R. A. (1987). Exceptional children in focus. Columbus: Merrill Publishing Company, p. 13.]

22. While working on this paragraph, an undergraduate college student entered my office to ask a question about a course I was offering on "The Psychology of the Exceptional Child." She wondered if the course would allow her to verify that she had a learning disability. When I asked her why she felt she might have a learning disability, she shared that she is forever forgetting where she parks her car when shopping at the local mall. She seemed quite surprised when I shared that I, too, often "lose" my vehicle under the same circumstances.

23. Martin, R. (1992, July/August). Problems with severe discrepancy formulas. *LDA/Newsbriefs, p. 3.*

24. McGuinness, D. (1985), p. 4.

25. Reiff, H. B., Gerber, P. J., & Ginsberg, R. (1997). *Exceeding expectations: Successful adults with learning disabilities.* Austin, TX: Pro-Ed.

26. Gelfand, D. M., Jenson, W. R., & Drew, C. J. (1988). *Understanding childhood behavior disorders* (2nd ed.). New York: Holt, Rinehart, and Winston.

27. Cruickshank, W. M. (1972). Some issues facing the field of learning disabilities. *Journal of Learning Disabilities, 5*, 380-388.

28. Cruickshank, W. M. (1972), p. 382.

29. Kavale, K. A., Forness, S. R., & Lorsbach, T. C. (1991). Definition for definitions of learning disabilities. *Learning Disability Quarterly, 14*, 257-266.

30. Lovitt, T. C. (1978). *Reactions to planned research.* Paper presented at the Roundtable Conference on Learning Disabilities. Minneapolis: Institute for Research on Learning Disabilities, p.3.

31. Willson, V. L. (May, 1996), 16:53:55 -0500 (Psychoeducational listserv.)

32. Mather, N., & Roberts, R. (1994). Learning disabilities: A field in danger of extinction. *Learning Disabilities Research & Practice, 9* , 49-58.

33. Learning Disability Association publication, 4156 Library Road, Pittsburgh, PA 15234.

34. Lovitt, T. C. (1989). *Introduction to learning disabilities.* Boston: Allyn & Bacon, p. 473.

35. Memo from Executive Director of Special Education and Pupil Services to School Psychologists (1992).

36. McLoughlin, J. A., & Lewis, R. B. (1990). Assessing special students. Columbus: Merrill Publishing, p. 91.

37. Dated 96-07-09 PSYCHOEDUCATIONAL_ASSESS

38. Tue, 9 Jul 1996 -0400 PSYCHOEDUCATIONAL_ASSESS

39. Tue, 9 Jul 1996 -0600 PSYCHOEDUCATIONAL_ASSESS

40. Taken from Tue, 14 Nov 1995 ASSESS-P

41. Fri, 17 Nov 1995-0500 ASSESS-P

42. Mon, 9 Nov 1995 ASSESS-P

43. Fri 17 Nov 1995 ASSESS-P

44. Wed, 15 Nov 1995 -0700 ASSESS-P

45. Tue, 9 Jul 1996 PSYCHOEDUCATIONAL_ASSESS

46. Ysseldyke, J. E., & Algozzine, B. (1995). *Special education: A practical approach for teachers*. Boston: Houghton Mifflin Company, p. 56-7.

47. Myers, P. I., & Hammill, D. D. (1990). *Learning disabilities: Basic concepts, assessment practices, and instructional strategies* (3rd ed.). Austin, TX: PRO-ED, p. 13.

10

Diversity: Students and Their Entering Skills

> Since the beginning of educational measurement no fact has been more frequently revealed, and its implications more commonly ignored, than the great variability in achievement of pupils in the same grade. [1]

The same student diversity that produced the learning disability label in the 1960s exists today, only to a greater degree. Presently, children know more and can do more than ever before, but as in the past, neither their everyday knowledge nor mastery ensures their success in school. Once again, the educational system is faced with bright, capable children who will not achieve grade level reading, writing, and arithmetic skills without professional support. The number of youngsters coming to schools requiring special assistance in order to be academically successful is astounding. Accommodating them represents the challenge for the next generation of educators.[2] It is not outlandish to argue that these exceptional children no longer represent the minority.

> We serve a large and growing proportion of students in general education settings who are younger, who have learning problems, and who come from homes with low levels of income, single parents, and/or little educational background...As such, students with these characteristics can no longer be perceived as outside the mainstream. These students constitute the school population we serve daily, and it is incumbent upon us to design and implement a suitable learning environment for them.[3]

DISABILITY MUST GIVE WAY TO DIVERSITY

Economic and social problems occurring far off school grounds promise the educational system a diverse range of student-entering skills and school-related attitudes that will challenge the patience and mettle of the most seasoned teachers and principals. Even schools formerly accustomed to serving affluent, educationally motivated children are seeing their pupil populations change dramatically. One Maryland county for example, "long the nearly exclusive domain of middle- and upper-class students," whose teachers were "used to teaching an upscale, homogeneous body of students," has seen "the proportion of students coming from low-income families...increase by almost 75 percent" in the 1990s. "A growing number of children entering kindergarten [are] without preschool experience, [and] the percentage of children with limited English proficiency has doubled."[4]

As a result of their experiences and circumstances, just sitting in a chair positioned at a table will be a novel experience for some schoolchildren. Attending to a teacher's words, gestures, and instructions will be foreign and initially intrusive. Abiding by rules intended to facilitate group processing will be aggressively refused. Reading and writing and the very act of acquiring new knowledge will seem to be without inherent purpose or payoff. Some children, it has been said, will come to school "without ever having seen printed words."[5] These children will be expected to coexist and cooperate with children at the other end of the continuum. Their general educators will be expected to teach them all.

Combine this diversity with general education's hesitancy to match curriculum to students who deviate a trifle from that curriculum's predetermined path, with the numbers of children being crowded into classrooms, with the varying stages of acceptance and implementation of the present "inclusion" movement, and the result is that the population of bright youngsters who will suffer measurable problems with reading, writing, and mathematics is considerable. Providing supportive services to these children only if they meet some arbitrary eligibility numbers will benefit few of these youngsters or those of us who live with them.

Children's Life Space

On some days, my desert school psychology and social worker colleagues would return to the office drawn and quartered by their day's school-related experiences. Their descriptions of the living conditions and support systems impacting the struggling children they had recently seen were bleak to the point of hurting. I had experienced the same despair after observing a class of difficult children and talking with their school's community representative about soliciting help from the children's parents. This tireless minister of social well-being would try, as she always promised. Today, the clear image remains of a beautiful little girl with soft brown eyes and a quiet, almost frightened voice, who would cry most every afternoon after school because she had to leave her teachers and their security. Her home conditions were deplorable, and the school was helpless to provide her with an escape. This little girl, a gentle wisp barely taller than her teacher's desk, would go home and with her sisters and mother, cower in the darkness of the evening while gunshots rang across her neighborhood.

The poverty, the lack of parental supervision and absence of support, the turmoil, the daily priorities more directed at survival than succeeding in the classroom, all affecting bright, capable children, all embedded within the American educational scene, all imposing enormous pressures on willing teachers, all coming to the classroom.   If we are driven obsessively to use the term disabled, let's paint the sign and nail it where it belongs.   The children, doing the best they can with what they've been given, are fine.   Something else isn't. Imagine the difficulties many parents face while attempting to provide suitable support for their children both at home and school.

Facts

Parental Support

[E]ach day in the United States, forty teenagers give birth to their third child; in Florida in 1985, 1,000 children were born to mothers under the age of 11.[6]

In 1990, 13 percent of all [U.S.] children were regularly hungry, 25 percent were born to unmarried parents, over 20 percent of all children under age 18 were poor, about 350,000 children were born to drug-addicted mothers.[7]

More children are living with single parents.   The number of single-parent situations rose from 3 million in 1970 to 10.5 million in 1992.[8]

Of children under 6 years of age living in families with a female householder (no husband present), 65.9 percent were poor.[9]

More than 60 percent of children live in a family in which both parents work or the single parent works.[10,11]

82 percent of all children (under age 18) now have working mothers and six of ten mothers of preschool-age children (under age 6) work outside the home at least part time.[12]

Leisure Time

Our children watch an average of 28 hours of television a week.   By high school graduation, most American teenagers will have spent more time watching television than going to school. [13]

Students—Top, Middle, and Bottom

The top 15% of America's students are world class on any set of indicators. The "forgotten middle" needs some work, but will graduate from high school and pay taxes.   America's lowest 35% (in terms of school attainment) is truly awful, due to factors that were present when they first knocked on the kindergarten door. (Factors such as poverty, out-of-wedlock birth, teen births, cocaine addiction at birth, shortness of food and housing, and premature birth are only a few.)[14]

DIVERSE CULTURES

Our country has been described as "one of history's first universal or world nations—people [of the United States] are a microcosm of humanity with biological, cultural, and social ties to all other parts of the earth."[15]   Children from this microcosm bring an enormous array of differences and distinctions with them as they enter school.

Ethnicity remains a vital force in this country, a major form of group identification, and a major determinant of our family patterns and belief systems. The premise of equality, on which our country was founded, required us to give primary allegiance to our national identity, fostering the myth of the "melting pot," the notion that group distinctions between people were unimportant. Yet, we have not melted....Second-, third-, and even fourth-generation Americans, as well as new immigrants, differ from the dominant culture in values, life-styles, and behavior.[16]

The differences and distinctions these culturally diverse children bring to school can easily challenge the limits of what some educators, given their own cultures, interpret as normal or appropriate. I was witness to such a circumstance while teaching at the university. An undergraduate student was being berated by his professor for failing to complete an assignment. As the professor raised his voice at the student, the young man stood silently, hands at his side, face down toward the floor. This demeanor apparently infuriated the professor. "Look at me when I speak. Do you have no respect?"

Respect was precisely what the student was showing. In his culture, looking into the eyes of an elder when being admonished was a clear sign of not only disrespect but brashness. The professor's interpretative error (not his onslaught) was understandable. The man had little working knowledge of the student's culture or the attitudes and actions that that culture promoted.   In our schools, cultural ignorance can lead any professional to inadvertently misinterpret what is being observed.   Culturally diverse, minority youngsters enrolled in a dominant-culture school, taught by dominant-culture teachers, evaluated by dominant-culture instruments are particular susceptible to such misinterpretation. To the culturally uninformed, diversity and disability can wear the same veneered coat.

Minorities

The minority children are here. Today, the term is outdated. Equally outdated are many of special education's assessment tools used to estimate the skills and achievements of these very able, diverse youngsters. My desert colleagues most often used the same dominant-culture tests, asking the same eligibility-qualifying questions to culturally different African Americans, Asians, Caucasians, Hispanics, and Native Americans.   While certainly convenient, such testing guarantees inaccurate interpretation of test data, producing a measurable number of special education identification errors. The testing also ensures a significant waste of professional time and district dollars. Special education's eligibility system promises a continuation of that waste.

Facts

Minority Numbers

In [the] California public school system 1 out of 6 students was born outside the United States...The Los Angeles school system now absorbs 30,000 new immigrant children each year.[17]

Before the turn of the century, 33 percent of children under the age of 17 will be minorities. Twenty years into the new century, about half of America's school children will likely be from diverse ethnic and cultural groups.[18]

Approximately 30 percent of elementary students are members of racial and ethnic minorities.[19]

Already 1 American in 4 defines himself or herself as Hispanic or nonwhite. If current trends in immigration and birth rates persist, the Hispanic population will have further increased an estimated 21%, the Asian presence about 22%, blacks almost 12% and whites a little more than 2% when the 20th Century ends. By 2020...the number of U.S. residents who are Hispanic or nonwhite will have more than doubled, to nearly 115 million, while the white population will not be increasing at all. By 2056...the "average" U.S. resident, as defined by Census statistics, will trace his or her descent to Africa, Asia, the Hispanic world, the Pacific Islands, Arabia—almost anywhere but white Europe.[20]

DIVERSE LANGUAGES

Many of these minority schoolchildren bring to the classroom a variety of diverse languages (see Table 10.1 and Table 10.2). These languages, of course, possess limitless concepts with uniquely defined attributes shaped by generations of relatives, friends, and experiences. What can happen if a sizable group of these diverse children are asked the same questions from a standardized test of intelligence? Wildly divergent (correct) answers that receive no points toward their IQ score are ensured, as is the misinterpretation of that score. For years, research studies have "repeatedly indicated that considerable bias (culture...linguistic...) may exist such that a...test administered to an individual may produce results which are significantly determined by factors other than actual achievement or ability."[21] Low scores on standardized tests resulting from language issues are reflective of the test's worth, not the capability of the child being assessed. When tests contain language that is obscure and confounding to a child, it is little wonder why confusing disability with diversity is such a likely prospect.

Table 10.1
Selected Languages of School Children with Increases of at Least 50% Since 1980[22]

Language	1980	1990	% Change
Asian	243,000	644,000	+164.8
Vietnamese	195,000	507,000	+160.6
Thai / Laotian	85,000	206,000	+142.8
Korean	266,000	626,000	+135.3
Chinese	631,000	1,319,000	+109.2
Filipino	474,000	899,000	+89.5
Farsi	107,000	202,000	+88.7
Arabic	218,000	355,000	+63.3
Spanish	11,116,000	17,340,000	+56.0

Facts

Varied Languages

In the California public school system, 1 in 3 students speaks a language other than English at home.[23]

Total enrollment in U.S. public schools rose only 4.2 percent between 1986 and 1991...while the number of students with little or no knowledge of English increased 50 percent, from 1.5 to 2.3 million.[24]

About 6.3 million, or 14 %, of students in grades K-12 speak languages other than English at home.[25]

The following school systems have students speaking more than 100 languages or dialects:[26]

Washington, D.C.
New York
Chicago
Los Angeles
Fairfax County, Virginia

Table 10.2
States with at Least 300,000 Home Speakers of Languages Other Than English

California	8,619,000	Michigan	570,000
Texas	3,970,000	Ohio	546,000
New York	3,909,000	New Mexico	494,000
Florida	2,098,000	Connecticut	466,000
Illinois	1,499,000	Virginia	419,000
New Jersey	1,406,000	Washington	403,000
Massachusetts	852,000	Maryland	395,000
Pennsylvania	807,000	Louisiana	392,000
Arizona	700,000	Colorado	321,000

Along with ethnic and racial diversity often comes linguistic diversity. Increasing numbers of children are entering school from minority language backgrounds and have little or no competence in the English language. While Spanish is the predominant first language of many children in the United States, an increasing number of students are entering the schools speaking Arabic, Chinese, Hmong, Khmer, Lao, Thai, and Vietnamese.[27]

Today, less than 5 percent of teacher education students in the United States claim fluency in a language other than English. [28]

CULTURALLY AND LINGUISTICALLY DIVERSE STUDENTS AND LEARNING DISABILITIES

> Since a person's language provides the symbols used to understand the world, children whose symbol systems differ from those of the dominant group are likely to see the world from a different perspective, to look for meaning in different ways, and to attribute different meanings to common objects and processes.[29]

The results of standardized paper and pencil tests used in special education's eligibility process, administered to culturally and linguistically diverse (CLD) students, are easily misconstrued. An intelligence test, for example, administered in English may not match the English skills a child brings to the testing arena or tap the cultural subtleties known only to the child being tested. This potential mismatch can hold true regardless of a child's birthplace or dominant language. Administering an intelligence test to a child whose present environment communicates in more than one language, where a child holds limited command of those languages, exacerbates assessment problems.

Results from these standardized tests may give an impression that a child is mentally disabled, when more accurately the scores reflect the child's language and conceptual diversity.

> When testers use tests developed in their own culture to test members of a different culture, testees often do not share the presuppositions about values, knowledge, and communication implicitly assumed by the test...When testing conventions themselves are not shared by participants in a new cultural context, the tester ends up measuring the participant's (deficient) knowledge of these conventions rather than measuring the intended ability.[30]

It is not surprising that many CLD students find themselves labeled "mildly mentally retarded" or "learning disabled" by schools districts that use traditional eligibility formulas. There is little question we are often "misinterpreting the lack of proficiency in English as a second language as a widespread intelligence deficit among CLD students."[31]

> The lack of valid and reliable assessment procedures for evaluating intelligence, achievement, and language proficiency in CLD students has resulted in the disproportionate representation in special education of students in the process of learning English as a second language[32]

So long as special education continues to use its standardized instruments that result in unsound assessment and misinterpretation, we should not be surprised at the excessive numbers of CLD children said to be disabled and placed in special education.

DIVERSITY AND CURRICULUM CASUALTIES

Educational methods designed to tutor individuals or to teach small groups of highly selected students are now being used to teach everyone in large groups.   A fourth-grade teacher could have students of the same chronological age whose achievement levels reach from kindergarten to eighth grade. [By grade 4 students already show a range of skills amounting to more than four grade levels, and this disparity may increase in the future.[33]] Yet all of these students are getting the same kind of instruction. It is as if all shoe stores sold only one size of shoe, and everyone was expected to wear that size. [34]

Diverse cultures and their accompanying rich and distinctive languages are not the only challenges facing today's educational system. Dramatically diverse academic entering skills common to today's public school students present even greater problems to the system that seems to have a most difficult time accommodating its different youngsters. It is not surprising that many children, possessing varying levels of academic strengths, facing general education's relatively fixed curriculum and who are performing poorly in classrooms, find themselves at special education's front door. Despite general education's efforts to excuse itself by finding the problem within the children, the youngsters do not produce the predicament in which they find themselves.

Curriculum Casualties: Time: 1950s, 25 Years Prior to PL 94-142

Recall that before Public Law 94-142 was instituted, and parent groups gained victories on behalf of all children, markedly diverse youngsters were kept a safe distance from general education's classrooms. Student exceptionality, as viewed as though it was a leper, was shunned and ignored. I cannot recall a single, unusually exceptional child being in any of my classes during my entire public school experience. Once in grade school we were taken on a field trip to see a child who had been struck down by polio. Lying forever on her back, the little girl was wedged within the tight circular confines of an iron lung that was housed in a semi-trailer truck body left standing in the middle of a beachside park. As we numbly filed past her, she watched us gawking at her by looking into a mirror aimed back at the moving line. Only the horrible (and very frightening) throaty sounds emanating from that metal breathing machine broke the pained silence. For the longest time, I had grown up thinking all kids were like us: pleasantly unexceptional. That naive belief was uprooted that day.

Academic Entering Skills

Nearly all of my school friends and classmates possessed academic entering skills that fit comfortably within our schools' modest, fixed academic curriculum. Most of us successfully played or studied our way through those warmly remembered days. There were a few student friends and acquaintances, of course, whose scholastic entering skills did not fit the school's curriculum. Despite the poor fit, those academically struggling students were required to journey through the same curriculum as everyone else. (I doubt any educator recognized a poor curriculum fit existed.) In most cases, students without entering skills necessary to satisfying their curriculum's requirements fell increasingly behind in their studies—a fixed curriculum that doesn't constantly match a student's uniqueness guarantees that end. Some of the students rejected their studies in favor of activities where success was more likely. Most of these students graduated from high school, steadied as young adults and did well in a variety of ways. No doubt many of them went on to exceed everyone's expectation. No doubt a few of the most able carried deep scars, incorrectly thinking themselves dumb.

I also had some friends whose advanced entering skills prepared them for work much more challenging than the schools' curriculum provided. Like those classmates who struggled academically, these advanced students also were forced to endure, although boredom was more their enemy than work that was too hard. Those advanced students who didn't reject their studies in favor of more exciting endeavors were most probably saved by a parent or cousin or forward-thinking teacher who answered their questions, teased them with more questions, and talked to them about everything from planets to pollen to protoplasm.

Yesterday: Fewer Curriculum Casualties

It seemed that during those comparatively quiet days of the 1950s we had only a few "curriculum casualties"[35] at our school: classmates who suffered academic misery because of instructional mismatches where their academic entering skills and their teachers' classroom curriculums were square pegs and round holes. Instead, the vast majority of my friends and classmates possessed the basic scholastic entering skills, budding curiosities, and family support systems to advance quite easily through our schools' curriculums. To be sure, our relative school success was a result of many factors. Two of those factors, however, stand out as most important as we now investigate the role diverse entering skills play in our frequent mistaking diversity for disability. Those two factors were our academic entering skills and our schools' curriculum requirements. During my school days, these two factors usually matched, making our classroom-lives much easier. My friends and I were very fortunate. *Sputnik* and America's cultural explosion, both lying on the near horizon, would soon make such good fortune scarce.

GRAPHIC DEPICTIONS OF CURRICULUM MISMATCHING

The current literature supports most teachers' observations that the range of academic entering skills found in the same classroom has certainly mushroomed. Unlike the 1950s, instructional mismatching and resulting curriculum casualties are increasingly common today. So, too, is the misinterpretation that accompanies them. As you will see, educational disabilities and curriculum mismatching are often inseparable.

Figure 10.1 will provide a visual representation of the relationship between academic entering skills, school curriculum, and curriculum mismatching and casualties. It depicts how a distribution of students experiencing virtually no curriculum mismatches and no curriculum casualties might appear. For the most part, Figure 10.1 is quite representative of my school days. Most of us were able to meet the schools' curriculum requirements without much difficulty.

The Ledger

From Figure 10.1, locate letters A through F. Beginning with the letter F, I will explain the figure's different components and purposes.

The bottom line, marked by the bold F with the numbers 1, 5, and 10 running across its length, represents students' entering skills and their general academic readiness for schoolwork. Imagine that we are talking about a pupil's skills with reading, writing, and mathematics. A youngster with reading, writing, and mathematics entering skills gauged at about the number 5 level would possess skills that would fit comfortably within a teacher's reading, writing, and mathematics curriculum. On the other hand, if the child's skills were closer to the number 1 level, at the far left of the depicted distribution, then the child's entering skills would be below what would be needed to succeed with the curriculum. Number 10, to the far right of the distribution, would represent entering skills beyond what would be needed to satisfy the curriculum's requirements. Critically, the closer a student was to the hypothetical 1, the less likely that student would be prepared for what the teacher was requiring and the more likely the student would lose touch with class assignments and become restless, inattentive, and bored. For this student, the classroom requirements, given the student's entering skills, would be too hard. Equally critically, the closer a student was to the hypothetical 10, the more likely the student would suffer the same fate: losing touch with class assignments and experiencing boredom. This student, needing more challenge, would find other ways to discover intellectual stimulation, perhaps with activities unrelated to class requirements. For this student, given his or her entering skills, the classroom requirements would be too easy.

The vertical line E, marked "number of kids," depicts the proportion of students whose entering skills matched or failed to match the teacher's curriculum. Note the bell-shaped curve to the right of the vertical line E. The highest part of that curve is above the number 5, indicating that most of the students I went to school with (and most of the pre-*Sputnik* kids I knew) possessed entering skills well-suited to their (not overly demanding) classrooms' requirements. Move in either direction away from the 5, and the portion of students with entering skills fitting within the curriculum lessens. As entering skills move farther away from the hypothetical 5, chances of curriculum mismatches and subsequent curriculum casualties increase.

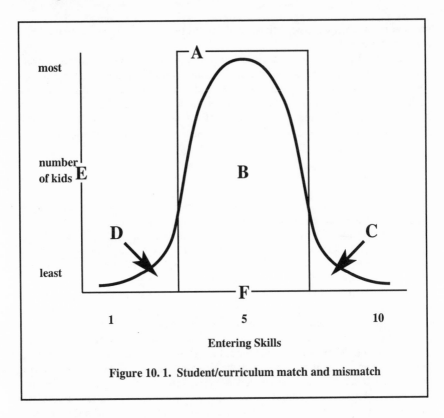

Figure 10. 1. Student/curriculum match and mismatch

The rectangle A symbolizes a school's curriculum. The walls are drawn with solid lines, signifying that, when I went to school, our curriculum, quite traditional in content and application, virtually was fixed. Our teachers knew what they were to teach and when they were to present their materials to their classes. Most teachers had their lesson plans developed months in advance—generally for the entire school year. Students were expected to fit within the curriculum, its content, pace, and schedule.

The tubular shaped curve B depicts the students who attended school with me. As indicated, most of the students had good quality entering skills. Educationally at least, my friends and I were very much alike. Almost all of us fit within rectangle A, the curriculum's represented boundaries. A satisfactory curriculum match existed between our entering skills and our school's predetermined curriculum requirements. Most important, this match practically guaranteed that even without the curriculum being adjusted in any fashion, we would most likely experience success with our class assignments. Our teachers could follow their curriculum guide and present the chosen materials with their own brand of enthusiasm and animation. Accommodation was unnecessary. We learned whatever we learned. For plain vanilla kids at least, school was a safe and fun place to be. (Thanks, Mrs. Proper, Mr. Coleman, Ms Austin, Tiger

Terry, and a double handful of other marvelous [and eccentric] teachers who were much admired.)

The letter C represents the students whose entering and readiness skills were advanced. Notice they are outside the rectangle's walls. Faced with a fixed curriculum, they experienced a curriculum mismatch: Their entering skills, attitudes, and needs, were beyond their classroom curriculum (some well-beyond). No big deal. At my school, their numbers were few, and I don't recall anyone screaming too loudly about the inequities. I doubt too many of them realized they were being shortchanged academically.

The letter D represents students whose entering and readiness skills were less than what was needed to find success within the school's curriculum. Notice that they too are outside the rectangle's walls. They too experienced a curriculum mismatch.

No one seemed to know what to do with these children whose entering skills fell below what was needed to succeed in school with relative ease. Excluding a teacher or two who understood the meaning of responsibility, no one thought about assessing the students' strengths and adjusting their curriculum. Instead, after they were painted their particular color ("slow learner" or "educationally retarded"), they were ignored. My recollection is quite clear: by any measure, they were neither slow nor retarded. Their work, perhaps its quality and/or quantity, was less than someone expected given the mismatched curriculum that was presented. Had their curriculum matched their entering skills, the students' work would have been better, both qualitatively and quantitatively. Again, those students were few, presenting neither political nor financial problems to the educational system. In the 1950s, no squeaky wheels were around to suggest that something within the educational system might be wrong.

TODAY'S ENTERING SKILLS: A DIFFERENT CURVE

Although Figures 10.1 and 10.2 are hypothetical, their radically different representations are more real than fictional. Despite the time-honored view that "the more things change, the more they are the same,"[36] today, almost everything in education has changed, leaving virtually nothing the same. The one exception is the fixed walls of education's curriculum. This one variable most in need of change has remained steadfastly inflexible. My drawn representations in Figures 10.1 and 10.2 depict that precise situation: The curriculum rectangle remains a pillar of rigidity. As you consider these figures, keep in mind that a curriculum that is not elastic, one that refuses to bend to match the scholastic entering skills of diverse youngsters, will not meet their educational needs. That curriculum will produce disabling learning conditions for those students regardless of their neurological or developmental footings.

Comparison of Entering Skills: Yesterday's and Today's

First, notice the shape of Figure 10.2's curve. Once tubular, as drawn in Figure 10.1, indicating most students had adequate scholastic entering skills that fit within the curriculum, Figure 10.2's curve is a great deal flatter suggesting

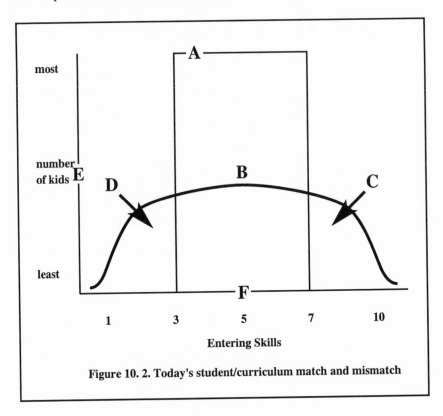

Figure 10. 2. Today's student/curriculum match and mismatch

that comparatively speaking fewer students today have entering or readiness skills matching their teachers' curriculum.

Second, notice the dispersion of students toward the edges of the curve in Figure 10.2, depicted outside today's curriculum rectangle A. I have added new data points, 3 and 7, along the line of entering skills to represent a greater diversity of students' scholastic readiness.

Third, notice the larger areas, letters D and C, outside rectangle A in Figure 10.2. Since so many students are outside the boundaries of the classroom curriculum, instructional mismatches are increasingly ensured. These mismatches begin in kindergarten. They can remain through the last days of high school.

Fourth, notice how far Figure 10.2's flatter curve extends beyond or outside the curriculum rectangle. Where there once were few curriculum mismatches and casualties, their numbers today are massive.

Fifth, most students depicted in Figure 10.1 experienced scholastic success with little to no adjustment to their curriculum. Today's students are not so fortunate. Without accommodations tied directly to students' specific, diverse entering skills in reading, writing, and mathematics, classroom success for a huge number of these youngsters hardly will be possible. Students D are particularly susceptible to mismatches and casualties. Speaking of these students, it has been said that "[t]heir one basic fault or problem, if it can be called that, is that their readiness levels or learning rates do not synchronize precisely with the instructional entry skill requirements and rates of introduction and review making up grade level programs."[37] Overlooked by special educators who cannot see past their eligibility formulas, many youngsters will be made exceptional by general education's failing to accommodate and by special education's failing to provide additional help as soon as it is needed. This fact has been clearly pointed out:

> [These low achieving children with inadequate entering skills]...are expected to proceed up the developmental curriculum ladder at the same rate as everyone else their age and to make the same uniform progress given the same amount of instruction and practice. Unable to adapt to instruction and a curriculum that moves too fast and demands too much in relation to their existing skills, they get further and further behind and become entrenched in a failure cycle. Basically, these are the forgotten, the "curriculum casualties" of school systems that sweep them aside through the use of programs and materials that follow grade level or normative instructional standards.[38]

WILL EDUCATION RECOGNIZE DIVERSITY IN TIME?

Social, economic, and political pressures are bringing more diverse children to our schools. Many of these children are bright and successful with activities of their choosing.   Because of their past educational experiences, their present entering skills and attitudes toward the value of education, and their manifold language differences, many will struggle with school assignments that bear little resemblance to what they have seen or enjoyed outside of school.

If special education maintains its stance that educational differences and disabilities are one and the same, the following outcomes are ensured:

1. Special education (and general education) will assume that a large portion of these diverse children suffer some intrinsic, neurologically based dysfunction.

2. Special education (and general education) will center its investigatory energies on labels and etiologies, and in the process will allow all culpable parties, other than the child, off the hook.

3. Special education (and general education) will look beyond its role of assisting the total educational system and, instead, continue to spend fortunes on tests and standardized assessments that provide impressive clinical terms while offering no instructional assistance to teacher or student.

4. Special education will convey to general education that it need not evaluate and diversify its curriculum.

5. Special education (and general education) will fail to use the talents of its own professionals to serve all school children effectively.

6. Both educational systems will gorge further the swollen river of youngsters said to be disabled.

Legal Fallout

7. Special education (and general education) will afford billboard lawyers new opportunities for destructive adjudications against schools, such as those in which parents are winning suits forcing public schools to pay for their children's private school education.

Tantalizing quantities of money have thicken the legal waters. Perhaps the present lawyer-initiated feeding frenzies will become so financially painful to special education that the field will rear its head and initiate radical changes across its educational board. By all accounts, if carefully considered changes aren't begun, one grievous end is likely to be forced: "the end of special education."[39]

A DIFFICULT FIRST STEP: RELINQUISHING THE CONCEPT OF LEARNING DISABILITIES

These [mildly "disabled"] children, who are in fact the curriculum casualties or curriculum handicapped, would not have acquired their various labels had the curriculum been adjusted to fit their individual needs, rather than having tried to force the children to achieve in the artificial but clerically simpler sequence of grades, calendar and materials that comprise the curricula.[40]

Samuel Kirk was right to move away from describing children as "educationally retarded." Most any term would have been an improvement. Learning disabilities was fine. It didn't say much other than children who seemed bright were having difficulty with reading and other subjects. It didn't remain so simple or casual, however. It became something to have, and, in some circles, prized. In the past, it served the purpose of opening eyes that previously had been closed to any type of educational diversity. Today, neither the categorical label nor the failed discrepancy model that is its buoy are necessary to help kids be more successful in school.

Is it difficult to identify children who are struggling with schoolwork? Only to those teachers who choose not to see. We've made the identification process so absurdly complex that we've become "child-blind" rather than "child-find." Children in need of our assistance are as easy to spot as a harvest moon. Knowing what needs to be done is no less obvious, particularly to school psychologists whose national organization's position is crystal clear: "[N]ecessary support services should be provided within general education, eliminating the need to classify children as handicapped in order to receive these services."[41] The National Association of School Psychologists' (NASP) wisdom draws a chorus of support from every corner.

A growing number of researchers, parents, and educators...believe that it is time to stop developing criteria for who does or does not belong in the mainstream, and turn the spotlight instead toward increasing the capabilities of the regular school environment...to meet the unique needs of all students.[42]

FOCUS: SUPPORTING DIVERSITY THROUGH MODIFIED CURRICULUMS

One major reason students are not successful in school is the failure to examine and diversify teaching methods.[43]...[A]n educational program must be prepared by a teacher in response to an individual student's educational need and behaviors, not in response to a diagnostic label or definition the student may or may not satisfy.[44]

Diverse entering skills and inflexible curriculums are not compatible. They are combatants without winners. They are as devastating for teachers as they are for students. Together they increase the number of pupils who appear, and who wrongly are said to be, learning disabled. Once more, look at today's hypothetical distribution of entering skills and the number of children depicted outside the limits of the curriculum, thus experiencing a curriculum mismatch (see Fig. 10.2). Imagine those diverse children in a classroom whose fixed, traditional instructional[45] curriculum has all the flexibility of near-set cement. Pay particular attention to the first three elements below.

1. Fixed instructional objectives for all learners

2. Fixed entry points into curriculum

3. Fixed time and pacing

4. Limited participation of learner in decision making

5. Large group intervention

6. Norm-referenced evaluation of learner [to determine how the student compares with other students or with a hypothetical average student][46]

No parent, teacher, principal, or psychologist would ever agree to such a mis-match, particularly if their youngster was forced into such a pugilistic arena. They would demand (with lawyer in tow) recognition of their child's diversity. They would demand a curriculum that would adjust to the ebb and flow of their child's achievements. They would seek out a flexible curriculum[47] capable of moving in all directions. Again, notice the first three elements.

1. Varied instructional objectives as a function of direct skill assessment

2. Variable entry points into curriculum

3.   Variable pacing

4.   Active participation of learner in decision making

5.   A variety of instructional arrangements as a function of task

6.   Criterion-referenced evaluation of learning[48] [to determine how the student compares with the curriculum rather than with classmates][49]

Safety Net Once Again

Where might such a flexible curriculum utopia for diverse youngsters be found? Of all places, in a classroom directly influenced by a skilled special education teacher who has been trained to accommodate student differences. How does one gain access to that classroom? Most often, a child must be found eligible before personalized instruction can be offered! If a child can be identified and labeled learning disabled, there's a good chance the child might find himself or herself with a special education teacher in a classroom where success, regardless of entering skills, is probable. Where

1.   There is an appropriate instructional match

2.   Goals are clear, expectations are explicitly communicated, and lessons are presented clearly

3.   Students receive good instructional support

4.   Sufficient time is allocated to instruction

5.   Teachers actively monitor student progress and understanding

6.   Student performance is evaluated appropriately and frequently[50]

Today, the special education teacher has taken over the regular education teacher's job. It is called accommodating diversity. Not much more. Special education's tools aren't significantly different from those available to regular education, and there's little difference among well-run classrooms, regardless of student diversity. We do not have "...two discrete sets of instructional methods— one set for use with 'special' students and another set for use with 'regular' students"[51]; "...[T]here is not one kind of instruction that works best in general education and another kind that works best in special education....[T]here are certain instructional factors that must be present and are appropriate for individual students' needs, regardless of setting [or exceptionality]."[52] [And] "while some methods need to be tailored to individual characteristics and needs, few, if any, can be clearly dichotomized into those applicable only for special students or for only regular students."[53]

Special education, rather than laying out its net for everyone who is different from those students whose entering skills are 5s, must take its talents into the regular classroom and help general educators adopt them. We have too many diverse students at the margins for special education to label them all exceptional and try to solve general education's problems on its own.

NOTES

1. McDaniel, E. (1994). *Understanding educational measurement.* Madison, WI: WCB Brown & Benchmark, p. vi.

2. Bateman, B. (1992). Learning disabilities: The changing landscape. *Journal of Learning Disabilities, 25,* 29-36.

3. Gonzalez, V., Brusca-Vega, R., & Yawkey, T. (1997). *Assessment and Instruction of Culturally and Linguistically Diverse Students With or At-Risk of Learning Problems.* Boston: Allyn and Bacon, p. 4.

4. Libit, H. (1997, May 18). After years of teaching children of privilege, schools grapple with needs of disadvantaged. *Baltimore Sun (in Carroll County)*, p. 11B.

5. Libit, H. (1997). After years of teaching children of privilege, schools grapple with needs of disadvantaged. *The Baltimore Sun (in Carroll County)*, p. 11B.

6. Cushner, K., McClelland, A., & Safford, P. (1996). *Human diversity in education: An integrative approach.* New York: McGraw-Hill Companies, Inc, p. 7.

7. Hodgkinson, H. L. (1993). *A demographic look at tomorrow.* Washington, DC: Center for Demographic Policy, Institute for Educational Leadership.

8. Rawlings, S. W. (1993). Household and family characteristics: March 1992. U.S. Bureau of the Census, Current Population Reports. *Washington, DC: U.S. Government Printing Office*, p. 20-467.

9. Rawlings, S. W. (1993).

10. Ysseldyke, J. E., & Algozzine, B. (1995). *Special education: A practical approach for teachers.* Boston: Houghton Mifflin Company.

11. Rawlings, S. W. (1993).

12. Hodgkinson, H. L. (1993).

13. Curran, Jr., J. J., Attorney General of Maryland, Executive Summary, September 9, 1996.

14. Hodgkinson, H. L. (1993).

15. "The Columbus Quincentenary Position Statement," National Council for the Social Studies (1982). In Monica McGoldrick, John K. Pearce, and Joseph Giordano (Eds.) . *Ethnicity and Family Therapy* (p.23) New York: Guilford.

16. Monica McGoldrick, John K. Pearce, and Joseph Giordano (Eds.) (1982), p. 3.

17. Gray, P. (1993, Fall). Teach your children well: But what to teach the newest arrivals in what language still vexes the nation's public schools. *Time*, p.69.

18. Hodgkinson, H. L. (1993).

19. Snyder, T. D. (1993). Trends in education. *Principal, 73* , 9-14.

20. Henry III, W. A. (1990, April 9). Beyond the melting pot. *Time* , p. 28.

21. Cushner, K., McClelland, A., & Safford, P. (1996). *Human diversity in education: An integrative approach.* New York: McGraw-Hill Companies, Inc, p. 313.

22. Waggoner, D. (1993). The growth of multilingualism and the need for bilingual education: What do we know so far, *Bilingual Research Journal, 17,* 1-12.

23. Gray, P. (1993).

24. Gray, P. (1993).

25. Gonzalez, V., Brusca-Vega, R., & Yawkey, T. (1997).

26. The new face of America: How immigrants are shaping the world's first multicultural society. (1993, Fall). *Time* .

27. Oxford-Carpenter, R., Pol, L., Gendell, M., & Peng, S. (1994). *Demographic Projections of Non-English-Background and Limited-English-Proficient Persons in the United States to the Year 2000 by State, Age, and Language Group*. Washington, DC: National Clearinghouse for Bilingual Education, InterAmerica Research Associates.

28. Cushner, K., McClelland, A., & Safford, P. (1996), p. 10.

29. Cushner, K., McClelland, A., & Safford, P. (1996), p. 9.

30. Greenfield, P. M. (1997). You can't take it with you: Why ability assessments don't cross cultures. *American Psychologist, 52*, 1115-1125.

31. Oller, J. W.,Jr. (1991). Language testing research: Lessons applied to LEP students and programs. In *Proceedings of the First Research Symposium on Limited English Proficient Students' Issues: Focus on Evaluation and Measurement*: Vol.2 (pp. 42-123). Washington DC: U.S. Department of Education, Office of Bilingual Education and Minority Languages Affairs.

32. Gonzalez, V., Brusca-Vega, R., & Yawkey, T. (1997), p. 61.

33. Ysseldyke, J. E., & Algozzine, B. (1995). (See also Biemiller, A. (1993). Lake Wobegon revisited: On diversity in education. *Educational Researcher*, *22*, 7-12.).

34. Detterman, D.K., & Thompson, L.A. (1997). What is so special about special education? *American Psychologist, 52*, 1082-1090.

35. Hargis, C. H. (1982). *Teaching reading to handicapped children*. Denver: Love Publishing.

36. Karr, Alphons. (1849). Plus ça change, plus c'est la même chose. *Les Guêpes Les Femmes*, Jan, vi.

37. Hargis, C. H. (1982). [Reported in Gickling, E. E., & Thompson, V. P. (1985). A personal view of curriculum-based assessment. *Exceptional Children*, *52*, 3, 205-218.]

38. Gickling, E. E., & Thompson, V. P. (1985). A personal view of curriculum-based assessment. *Exceptional Children*, *52*, 3, 205-218.

39. Staples, B. (1996, October 7). The end of special education: Private schools at public expense. *The New York Times*.

40. Hargis, C. H. (1982), p. 4.

41. National Association of School Psychologists/National Coalition of Advocates for Students. (1985). *Advocacy for appropriate educational services for all children*. Washington, DC: Author.

42. Stainback, S., & Stainback, W. (1989). Classroom organization for diversity among students. In D. Bilken, D. Ferguson, & A. Ford (Eds.), *Disability and society: Eighty-eighth yearbook of the National Society for the Study of Education* (pp. 195-207). Chicago: University of Chicago Press, p. 41-42.

43. Dettmer, P., Thurston, L. P., & Dyck, N. (1993). *Consultation, collaboration, and teamwork: For students with special needs*. Needham heights, MA: Allyn & Bacon.

44. Hammill, D. D., & Bartel, N. R. (1986). Meeting the special needs of children. In D. D. Hammill & N. R. Bartel, *Teaching students with learning and behavior problems* (4th ed.). Boston: Allyn & Bacon, p. 2.

45. Talmage, H. (1975). Instructional design for individualization. In H. Talmage (Ed.), *Systems of individualized education*. Berkeley, CA: McCutchan.

46. added as explanation

47. Talmage, H. (1975). Instructional design for individualization. In H. Talmage (Ed.), Systems of individualized education. Berkeley,CA: McCutchan.

48. Mercer, C. D., & Mercer, A. R. (1989). *Teaching students with learning problems*. Columbus: Merrill.

49. added as explanation

50. Christenson, S. L., Ysseldyke, J. E., & Thurlow, M. L. (1989). Critical instructional factors for students with mild handicaps: An integrative review. *Remedial and Special Education, 10,* 21-31.

51. Stainback, W., & Stainback, S. (1984). A rationale for the merger of special and regular education. *Exceptional Children, 51,* 102-111.

52. Ysseldyke, J. E., & Christenson, S. L. (1987). Evaluating students' instructional environments. *Remedial and Special Education, 8,* 17-24. (See also Christenson, S. L., Ysseldyke, J. E., & Thurlow, M. L. (1989). Critical instructional factors for students with mild handicaps: An integrative review. *Remedial and Special Education, 10,* 21-31.)

53. Stainback, W., & Stainback, S. (1984), p. 103.

11

Entering Skills at the Margins

The more a youngster's entering skills differ from the regular classroom's curriculum, the greater the likelihood of curriculum mismatches, curriculum casualties, and ultimately a special education eligibility hearing that rarely points at the curriculum mismatch as culprit. That aside, what happens to a youngster once eligibility has been granted is of particular interest. After countless, time-consuming meetings where educational plans are determined and scheduled, the exceptional child's team responsible for the youngster's individual educational plan will finally and carefully assess the child's entering skills. Why will the special education team assess the child's entering skills? The teams wants to be certain the child's skills match the new curriculum. The special education team wants to avoid asking the student to work on material that is too easy or too difficult.

As so often happens, once curriculum and skills are matched closely, academic progress is achieved. While it is appealing to conclude that the special education label and placement were responsible for progress, the more plausible explanation for the child's growth was the fact that the curriculum was assigned only after his or her entering skills were determined. Had general education immersed itself in the child's education from the moment he or she first entered school, the matching of those two components could have occurred long before special education was asked to spread its safety net.

STUDENTS AT THE MARGINS

Students at the academic margins are easily recognizable by their classroom work and their differing entering skills (see Fig. 11.1). Because their reading, writing, and arithmetic achievements differ from teachers' expectations, and because their achievements fail to fit with their classroom's established lesson plans, these students can experience a mismatch with all or part of their regular classrooms' curriculum. This mismatch can occur any time during a school year, beginning as earlier as a school year's first bell. If the students' work does not

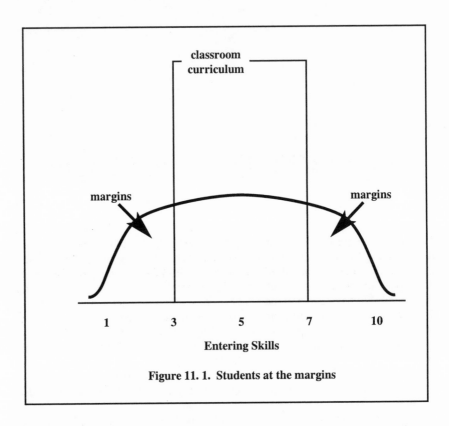

Figure 11. 1. Students at the margins

change, if the discrepancy between their work and their classroom curriculum continues or worsens sufficiently, they will be seen as exceptional. To gain extra school services and professional support, many of these mismatched students will be labeled exceptional through either a formal eligibility hearing or extensive standardized testing. At opposite ends of the students' distribution, one group may well be tested, labeled, and thought of as "mildly mentally retarded" (MMR), the other group labeled and thought of as "gifted and talented" (G/T).

Intellectual Potential: One More Time Around

The formal hearings, extensive standardized testing, and resulting labeling have always been unnecessary prerequisites to providing school children with good quality education, no matter their diverse entering skills. Without permission from anyone, general educators could have accommodated their classroom curriculum to match their students' unique entering skills as soon as any disparity in classwork was observed by the classroom teacher. In actual practice, incredibly, such classwork accommodation, if it ever does occur, must often wait until special education has attempted to accomplish the impossible: to quantify intellectual potential. Despite their known and acknowledged inadequacies, tests of intelligence and their purported ability to measure intellectual potential continue to play a key role in labeling children MMR or G/T. Remarkably, special education obsessively persists in believing IQ tests reveal a student's present competence and future possibilities. They don't. Once more, they don't measure intellectual potential[1,2,3] or abilities.[4] They do not measure innate intelligence or capacity. They only sample an individual's repertoire of cognitive skills and knowledge at a given point in time.[5,6] They need not play any part in identifying which students need assistance, or determining what that assistance should be. This holds true for youngsters whose entering skills are at the margins.

MILD MENTAL RETARDATION OR LOW ENTERING SKILLS

Mental retardation, like "learning disabilities," is another broker term that standing by itself says virtually nothing. The population the term references varies so much within itself that it tells us nothing of worth about any individual member. The term "mental retardation" does little but provide a basis on which to draw wrong impressions about an individual's reachable sky.

As worthless as is the term "mental retardation," its variation, "mildly mentally retarded," constituting some 75% of the retarded population,[7] is a far worse descriptive term. Within its ranks are schoolchildren who certainly are bright and capable. Such gross errors in judgment occur when professionals mistakenly choose (or are required by school districts) to use intelligence tests to estimate students' intellectual potential and to equate low scores with retardation.

School Confusion Caused by IQ Scores

"Since MMR does not convey a precise description of the people being discussed,"[8] there is little wonder why confusion continues to exist around its designation. IQ numbers, the determination some public schools use to classify a child MMR, provide a false sense of discernibility given that MMR (like learning disabilities) is not something to have,[9] not something within the youngster that is detectable,[10] but a social construct, arbitrarily defined through scores on a paper and pencil test. They are arbitrary enough that if a youngster with an IQ score of 85 happened to catch the right historically significant weekend, the child would have been retarded when leaving school on Friday, but not retarded when returning to school on Monday: Awhile back, it was common for practitioners to use a cutoff score of 85 on an IQ test as an indication of mental retardation. This cutoff score was endorsed by the AAMR [American Association of Mental

Retardation] until the mid-1970s, when they made it more difficult for people to be identified as retarded by establishing a cutoff score of 70-75.[11,12]

Instructional Relevance of MMR and IQ

The term retardation is so arbitrary that it "is possible for a person to be classified as mentally retarded at some time...but not at others."[13] It is possible that a rural youngster not classified as retarded may have that classification reversed upon taking up residence in a major city.[14,15] It is possible that a child might be referred to as retarded while in school but not at home.[16] If the relative nature of the term mentally retarded wasn't enough to render it virtually useless, consider that the term MMR possesses absolutely no instructional relevance. Neither the awarded label nor its associated IQ number shed any light on what the exceptional child knows, what classroom exercises and experiences he needs, what best ways are required to teach him, or what entering skills are available for curriculum matching (see Fig. 11.2).

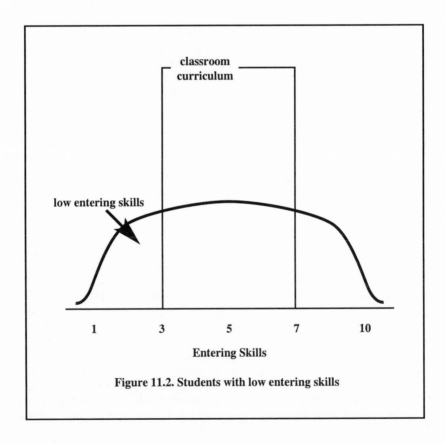

Figure 11.2. Students with low entering skills

Deleterious Side Effects of MMR Label

Our persistence in using MMR as a special education designation carries with it two significant and serious side effects. First, MMR, when assigned to a child, gives permission for the naive to believe that the child has a condition intrinsic to himself, a condition that is unalterable. Second, MMR provides regular education permission to excuse itself from having any part in the child's academic difficulties.

In the present educational atmosphere, the label MMR is both obsolete and detrimental. It possesses nothing that is detectable or relevant. An observant regular education teacher will notice immediately when a student is struggling with assigned classwork or when that student's entering skills are well below the curriculum being used in the classroom. Accommodation, built on those entering skills, must become the focus of that teacher and of special education. Amazing things can then happen: "A person's level of mental functioning does not necessarily remain stable; this is particularly true for those individuals who are mildly retarded. With intensive educational programming, some persons can improve to the point that they are no longer retarded."[17]

LD and ADHD: Disorders of Choice

Interestingly, MMR classifications "have fallen from favor as a diagnostic category."[18] Their reduced use, however, should not be interpreted as a sign that special education has grown any wiser to the limited value of the classification. Instead, MMR has been usurped by other deficit-oriented, ill-defined, exceptional categories: "LD and ADHD [attention deficit hyperactive disorder] are becoming the 'disorders of choice' for children manifesting mild learning or behavior problems."[19] Recent popularity aside, unless one uses IQ numbers as means of artificially differentiating MMR from LD, distinguishing between children from the two obscure categories is a time-wasting exercise. All we know for certain is that both sets of highly heterogeneous children share the same problem: The children are struggling with their classroom assignments and perhaps themselves. Whether a child having difficulty with schoolwork is described as MMR or LD fails to convey anything about the child's entering skills, the curriculum the child needs, the teaching techniques to use, or the upper scholastic limits the child might attain. Succinctly, the terms have no educational or instructional value. As discouraging, both terms communicate to the naive listener that something is wrong with the student rather than the system that is charged with the responsibility to provide the student with supportive services and academic success.

The term mild mental retardation, like learning disabilities, does not belong in schools as a category of exceptionality. In place of arguing the suitability of one label over another, our educational concerns should center on identifying students' entering skills and matching curriculum to those skills, not on which label to use to inadequately describe what the children can do.

GIFTED/TALENTED OR ADVANCED ENTERING SKILLS

Moving to the opposite end of the entering skill continuum does not lessen the problems that were visited with the label MMR (see Fig. 11.3). The construct "gifted" is equally noninstructive: "Defining gifted and talented is...a complicated matter. There is no one definition. Common usage of the terms even by experts is ambiguous and inconsistent, ranging from gifted to profoundly gifted...extremely gifted...low-incidence gifted...[even] 'severely' gifted."[20] The truth is that "giftedness is whatever we choose to make it."[21] "Someone can be gifted...one day and not the next, simply because an arbitrary definition has changed."[22]

Since the concept of gifted is so culturally relative, it was removed from federal reports in 1993 and replaced by the term "talented."[23] That decision was probably influenced by the editor of *The Gifted Child Quarterly*, John Feldhusen, who advised that "there is no psychological, genetic, or neurological justification for a diagnostic category called 'gifted'." Editor Feldhusen, suggested insightfully that

Schools should abandon efforts to identify gifted students as though they were a biologically distinct category of human beings and concentrate our efforts instead on: (1) searching for talent or strengths in all children, and ...(3) seeking to provide the best instruction possible to help youth develop their talents to the fullest. [24]

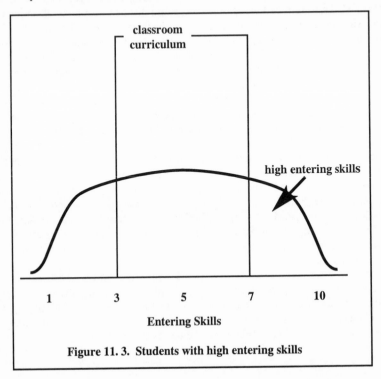

Figure 11. 3. Students with high entering skills

Beyond definition issues, the term and the system that produces it create other concerns that magnify problems associated with the term gifted. Authors Judy Eby and Joan Smutny explain.

> We believe that children themselves do not understand [gifted] and are often confused by it. Children who are labeled gifted may feel set apart from their peers; they may feel guilt and fear when they don't live up to the label. While their parents may relish the label at first, they may find it difficult to explain to other children in the family. Such a label also causes enormous difficulties in school programs when either a child's performance or the criteria for selection change and the child's eligibility for the program changes. It is difficult to explain to parents why a child who was labeled gifted in an earlier grade or in a different district isn't gifted anymore.
> [I]n our view, one effect of labeling a small minority of children gifted is that we are also unwittingly labeling the remaining children in the family or school nongifted.[25]

School Confusion Caused by IQ Scores

As was the case with MMR, identification problems surrounding giftedness are very troublesome. We act as though being gifted is a detectable entity, gleaned from a score on a test of intelligence. Once again, an IQ score is interpreted wrongly as a measure of intellectual potential.

Once the IQ score is given the power to separate supposed gifted from nongifted youngsters, arbitrary cutoff scores and confusion over identification are inevitable. Although we give lip service to knowing better, we persist in thinking that an IQ number is as real, solid, and forever as the Washington Monument. We establish eligibility cutoffs where one IQ point is given the power to mark a child gifted or indirectly brand another not gifted.[26] "[S]eemingly irrational [identification] procedures persist....A major sin is enforcing a rigid IQ cutoff score—a student with an IQ of 130 is gifted, but one (who may be more creative and energetic) with an IQ of 129 is not gifted and is excluded from the program."[27]

How smart is such a one point program exclusion? Not very. Despite what we know about the limited worth of intelligence tests scores in general, and specifically the worthlessness of their single point variations, myopic program administrators continue to establish narrow IQ cutoff scores that are used to determine which children will be eligible and ineligible for accelerated or especially challenging (and exciting) school programs. These administrators choose to ignore that any score from a test of intelligence carries within itself considerable error, reducing further its already limited value. As an example, some gifted program administrators use a cutoff IQ score of 140 as an entrance requirement. In those programs, a child who receives a score of 138 is considered ineligible for that program. This practice continues even though it is clearly recognized that the standard error of measurement inherent in IQ testing means that the score of 138 has a literal meaning somewhere between 134 and 142.[28] In other words, preventing a child from experiencing the benefits of an exciting, challenging classroom because an IQ score was a few points below an arbitrary cutoff is invalid and an open invitation to acrimonious litigation.

Call a Lawyer

In fact, if I were an unemployed ambulance-chasing lawyer, I would search out a family with a verbally competent, energetic youngster who was kept from a school's accelerated (read "gifted") classroom because his or her IQ score was one point (or ten points!) below the school's or district's established cutoff. Then, because the youngster was prevented from entering the school's best program, I'd sue the pantaloons off the district for misidentification, infringement of civil rights, and exceeding the legal amount of ignorance a school district is allowed to exhibit. Once again, some of our school administrators (and school psychologists) act as though special education's psychoeducational tests used to qualify children for special programs are surgically precise instruments. They aren't.

> Tests are only relatively crude measurements of very complex human traits. Test developers recognize that there are many possible factors that can cause inaccurate estimates. The SEM [standard error of measurement] is calculated to account for such factors as fatigue, difference in examiners, time of day, and health of the individual being tested. Most IQ tests have SEMs of approximately 4 to 5 points. This means that the actual intelligence quotient [IQ score] of a child is the reported score plus or minus 4 points. [29]

Instructional Relevance of Gifted and IQ

Well beyond the sizable error inherent in IQ scores, from a few to ten or twelve points (assuming the psychologist administering the test hasn't dabbled too much with accommodating instructions, interpreting answers, and playing with scoring), the awarded label possess no instructional relevance. The term gifted, and its accompanying IQ number, fail to shed any light on what the exceptional child knows, what classroom exercises and experiences are needed, what strategies are required to most successfully teach the youngster, or what entering skills are available for curriculum matching. If an IQ score is the major determinant for identifying children with special talents, significant curriculum mismatching is a certainty.

Advocates for youngsters with advanced entering skills have known for years that curriculum mismatching in public schools has been outrageously rampant. This mismatch between the entering skills of talented youth and the discordant curriculum they are required to study has been described as being "nothing short of an American tragedy. The human waste in terms of both student and faculty time is inestimable, and this waste can be found in both rich schools and poor." [30] These same advocates have known for years that general education consistently has failed to accommodate curriculum to support the children's advanced entering skills. Evidence shows that few regular classroom teachers make any provisions for talented students' special curricular needs. These youngsters, it has been noted, spend most of their time working on grade-level assignments given to the entire class.[31,32]

Why have these children's advanced academic needs been so thoroughly ignored? I would argue that had advocates for advanced students been less concerned with waving their gifted flags and touting their children's IQs, had they closed ranks and joined forces with spokespersons advocating for other children with highly diverse entering skills, they might have forced general education to assume more responsibility for its predictably diverse population. But advocates for these advanced children did not pressure general education, and the results are sad:

> [T]alented elementary school students have mastered from 35 to 50 percent of the curriculum to be offered in five basic subjects before they begin the school year.[33]

> A 1979 study by the Educational Products Information Institute showed that 80% mastery of subject matter was attained by 60% of a group of fourth graders when they were tested in September on the material they would be studying throughout the year.[34]

Had general education been required to accommodate curriculum to meet all pupils' academic needs, and had special education focused on assessing entering skills and learning strengths rather than exceptional categories and academic deficits, we wouldn't have a situation where tens of thousands of...[35]children and adolescents are sitting in their classrooms—their abilities unrecognized, their needs unmet. Some are bored, patiently waiting for peers to learn skills and concepts that they had mastered two years earlier. Some find school intolerable...Some feel pressured to hide their...skills...Some give up on school entirely.[36]

Entering Skills, Not Labels

A youngster's academic entering skills, what classroom achievements he or she can presently accomplish at or near 100% mastery, tell us significantly more than either a categorical label, a fabricated estimate of intellectual potential, or a score from a standardized achievement test's limited questions. Entering skills make it easier for interested educators to match curriculum and ensure student growth, a goal sought after by all of us. The attempted identification of MMR or G/T by means of an intelligence test is a needless step toward that goal.

If we would forgo eligibility as a prerequisite for classroom assistance, we could provide supportive services to all students and their general educators on an as-needed basis. The field could take all children with their personal, ever changing entering skills, embrace the children's diversities, identify their strengths, accommodate both content and pacing of their curriculums, and relish the results. Special education could do all this whenever it chose to.

FOCUS: THERE'S A FLY IN THE OINTMENT

There's a hitch, however, and a mighty big one. Assuring success in the classroom for all students regardless of entering skills will require more than special education's change in attitude and paradigm. Indeed, special education alone can accomplish very little. Yes, the field can admit that its present categorical model does not adequately differentiate students' strengths or needs. It can disavow the discrepancy model, declaring it a failure and flawed beyond repair. It can chose a noncategorical and nonpathological format. It can help the federal government develop new funding schemes for financially supporting education in the absence of special education categories. It can convince dubious parents, thoroughly entrenched in the categorical system, that eligibility testing has given way to a new manner of achievement testing, one in which each child's strengths will be clearly delineated and accommodated. It can hire a cadre of special education teachers and trained assistants who, rather than administer standardized achievement tests that provide little assistance to anyone, can help regular classroom teachers develop and implement individualized academic programs for all students. It can direct its school psychologists to forgo intelligence testing, allowing them the opportunity to exercise the enormity of their acquired skills by providing counseling and therapeutic interventions directly to all children while initiating systemic changes that will favorably impact and reverse the students' emotional and academic difficulties. Special education can do all of the above and more and still not experience much success. Alone, special education can do very little. It is going to need an ally. It is going to need The Rudder.

NOTES

1. Aiken, L. R. (1987). *Assessment of intellectual functioning.* Boston: Allyn and Bacon.
2. Reschly, D. (1979). Nonbiased assessment. In G. Phye & D. Reschly (Eds.), *School psychology: Perspectives and issues.* (p. 24) New York: Academic Press.
3. McLoughlin, J. A., & Lewis, R. B. (1994). *Assessing special students.* New York: Merrill.
4. Zigler, E., Balla, D., & Hodapp, R. (1984). On the definition and classification of mental retardation. *American Journal of Mental Deficiency, 89,* 215-230.
5. Sattler, J. M. (1988)). *Assessment of children.* San Diego: Jerome Sattler Publishing.
6. Taylor, R. L. (1989). *Assessment of exceptional students: Educational and psychological procedures.* Englewood Cliffs, NJ: Prentice-Hall .
7. Grossman, H. J., & Tarjan, G. (Eds.). (1987). *AMA handbook on mental retardation.* Chicago: American Medical Association.
8. Macmillan, D. L., Siperstein, G. N., & Gresham, F. M. (1996). A challenge to the viability of mild mental retardation as a diagnostic category. *Exceptional Children, 62,* 4, 356-371.

9. Luckasson, R. (Ed.). (1992). *Mental retardation: Definition, classification, and systems of support.* Washington, DC: American Association on Mental Retardation.

10. Macmillan, D. L., Siperstein, G. N., & Gresham, F. M. (1996).

11. Hallahan, D. P., & Kauffman, J.M. (1997). *Exceptional Learners: Introduction to special education* (7th ed.) Boston: Allyn & Bacon, p. 123.

12. See Grossman, H. J. (Ed.). (1983). *Manual on terminology and classification in mental retardation* (rev.ed.). Washington, DC: American Association on Mental Deficiency.

13. See Heber, R. (1961). Modifications in the manual on terminology and classification in mental retardation. *American Journal of Mental Deficiency*, 65, 499-500.

14. Macmillan, D. L., Siperstein, G. N., & Gresham, F. M. (1996).

15. Gottlieb, J., Alter, M., Gottlieb, B. W., & Wishner, J. (1994). Special education in urban America: It's not justifiable for many. *The Journal of Special Education*, *27*, 453-465.

16. From 1970 report of the President's Committee on Mental Retardation. See also: Mercer, J. (1970). Sociological perspectives on mild mental retardation. In H. C. Haywood (Ed.), *Social-culture aspects of mental retardation* (pp.378-391). New York: Appleton-Century-Crofts.

17. Hallahan, D. P., & Kauffman, J. M. (1997), p. 121.

18. Macmillan, D. L., Siperstein, G. N., & Gresham, F. M. (1996).

19. Macmillan, D. L., Siperstein, G. N., & Gresham, F. M. (1996), p. 367.

20. Davis, G. A., & Rimm, S. B. (1994). *Education of the gifted and talented.* Boston: Allyn and Bacon, p.17 (See also Milgram, R.M. (1989). Teaching gifted and talented children in regular classrooms: An impossible dream or a full-time solution for a full-time problem. In R. M Milgram, (Ed.), *Teaching gifted and talented learners in regular classrooms.* Springfield,IL : Thomas.)

21. Hallahan, D. P., & Kauffman, J. M. (1997).

22. Howley, C. B., Howley, A., & Pendarvis, E. D. (1995). *Out of our minds: Anti-intellectualism and talent development in American schooling .* New York: Teachers College Press.

23. Piirto, J. (1994). *Talented children and adults: Their development and education.* New York: Merrill.

24. Feldhusen, J. (1992). *Talent identification and development in education (TIDE).* Sarasota, FL: Center for Creative Living.

25. Eby, J. W., & Smutny, J. F. (1990). *A thoughtful overview of gifted education.* New York: Longman.

26. Stankowski, W. M. (1978). Definition. In R. E. Clasen and B. Robinson (Eds.), *Simple gifts.* Madison, WI: University of Wisconsin-Extension.

27. Davis, G. A., & Rimm, S. B. (1994). *Education of the Gifted and Talented.* Boston: Allyn and Bacon.

28. Davis, G. A., & Rimm, S. B. (1994).

29. Eby J. W., & Smutny, J. F. (1990), p. 64.

30. Renzulli, J. S. (1991). The National Research Center on the Gifted and Talented: The dream, the design, and the destination. *Gifted Child Quarterly, 35*, 73-80.

31. Ross, P. (1993). *National excellence: The case for developing America's talent.* Washington, DC: U.S. Department of Education.

32. Gallagher, J. J., & Gallagher, S. A. (1994). *Teaching the gifted child.* Boston: Allyn and Bacon, p.71.

33. Ross, P. (1993). (See also Gallagher, J. J., & Gallagher, S. A. (1994). *Teaching the gifted child*. Boston: Allyn and Bacon.)

34. Piirto, J. (1994).

35. The phrase "gifted and talented" was purposely removed from the sentence. Their removal does not alter the statement's impact.

36. Davis, G. A., & Rimm, S. B. (1994), p. 1.

12

The Rudder

My father-in-law is an old salt. As a 16-year-old enlistee in the Navy during World War II, he sailed the high seas serving his cherished country. The sea rolled its way into his mind and bones, and he's been sailing ever since. His waters, now calmer and warmer are in the Gulf Stream off sunny Florida. His ship, infinitely more personal, is a beautiful single masted 30-footer.

I knew where I was going with this brief, pivotal chapter, but verification from a ship's captain settled my course. "Gus," I asked one fresh morning before sitting down at the computer, "suppose you were out there in the middle of your blue-green ocean and your boat's rudder fell off. What would you do?" I couldn't see his face (he was docked some 1,500 miles south), but I could easily imagine his boyish smile. "Grab my life preserver, my radio, and start swimmin,'" he answered laconically.

Rather remarkable, I thought to myself. A sleek 30-foot sailboat, weighing some 10,000 pounds, packed to the gills with sophisticated, life-preserving electronic equipment, designed and built to be capable of riding waves peaking higher than my two-story house, this magnificent vessel left to flounder helplessly by an absent, dinky piece of composite (or wood), weighing less than 1% of the ship's total weight. One failing part exercising such influence over the entire ship's operation. Remarkable, indeed.

THE PRINCIPAL: A SCHOOL'S RUDDER

In many ways the school principal is the most important and influential individual in any school...It is his [or her] leadership that sets the tone of the school, the climate for learning...If a school is a vibrant, innovative, child-centered place; if it has a reputation for excellence in teaching; if students are performing to the best of their ability, one can almost always point to the principal's leadership as the key to success.[1]

[T]here is clear evidence that effective principals influence the instructional programs of their schools by almost every act they perform.[2]

Of the many beneficial lessons I learned during my recent position with the Arizona school district, the most striking was that of a principal's influence over his or her assigned school. I met and worked with a dozen indefatigable leaders, captains, if you will, of their own vessels, professionals who knew where they wanted their schools to go and what was needed to reach (and surpass) their educational goals. They walked through their schools, shunning the isolation of their offices whenever possible. They were not afraid of hard work: A new day's beginning often touched the shadow of the day just past. Neither were they hesitant to implore their staff to squeeze yet another ounce of energy on behalf of a needy student. They wore their attitude high on their chests: being liked was less important than being effective. These principals were mirror images of those described in the professional literature two decades earlier: "Good principals tend to rock the boat. They forsake the desire to be loved for the hard task of monitoring students' progress. They set achievement goals for their students, and they judge their teachers and themselves by them."[3]

Some Were Less Effective

I met a few professionals who, while wearing the title "principal," bore no resemblance to that position. There weren't many, fortunately, but one is all that is necessary to witness the disastrous effects. One principal particularly ruffled my feathers. He chose to hide behind a closed door and a protective desk. He attended (and then only under duress) a scarce number of meetings where his students' instructional approaches were discussed or where their futures were debated. He left the business of the students' behaviors and academics to others. His attitude, different from his more admirable administrative colleagues, read: Someone else will take care of the problem. He offered his staff neither structure nor support, neither vision nor mission. The result was predictable, and is aptly described by scholar Roland Barth: "[W]ithout a vision,...our behavior [as principals] becomes reflexive, inconsistent, and shortsighted as we seek the action that will most quickly put out the fire so we can get on with putting out the next one."[4]

This irresponsible principal's fires were numerous and thoroughly disruptive to student and teacher alike. Most distressing, he possessed little knowledge of his school's curriculum, his teachers' strengths and weaknesses, or his students' uniqueness, who they really were and what they needed. It is sad but fair to say that his school and many of its teachers floundered. In retrospect, suggesting that a principal is the equivalent of a ship's rudder appears not an overly outrageous leap.

CHANGE WILL REQUIRE LEADERSHIP

I have argued that many of the problems limiting a school's ability to serve all its youngsters are identifiable and changeable. I have suggested that our evolving, highly diverse school population, with its multiple entering skills and multicultural faces, make educational system changes a priority.

Experience tells us that whatever changes are adopted to provide services to all children enrolled in a school will necessitate full, enthusiastic support of its principal. No matter what plan is ultimately fashioned, it will be contentious and thus contended. Without the endorsement of a school's principal, the plan, regardless of merit or promise, will fall flatter than a French crepe. Indeed, without the open arms of the principal, the plan will not be heard, much less implemented.

I watched as schools in the Arizona desert were given opportunities to consider an experimental program that promised to provide cost-effective augmentative services to children without the need of formal special education eligibility. The plan accomplished several goals, most notably providing students and teachers the help they needed and requested almost immediately. The plan was radical because it was different; too radical for some who feared what was unfamiliar. Fortunately, a dozen or more principals stood forth and gambled that a better system for providing services to their kids was possible. These principals were rudders and rockers.

Leery of Popular Explanations

These principals were also a touch skeptical when exceptionalities such as learning disabilities and attention-deficit were offered reflexively to explain a student's academic and behavioral difficulties. The principals understood clearly the concept of individual differences with respect to students' entering skills and attitudes, and how those differences, when exhibited by a room filled with diverse children, could make a teacher's job exceedingly demanding. When yet another troubling or academically delayed child appeared, these principal-leaders were not immediately sympathetic to an offered opinion that the child's troubles emanated from some physiological problem existing within the student. Intuitively or by training, these principals understood the lure of exceptionality, specifically how it could be used by general educators to avoid maintaining responsibility for a child's legitimate academic difficulties. These principals understood how unscrupulous it was to have in-hand a convenient excuse to do nothing to assist a struggling child, instead invoking some categorical or expert-driven excuse to lay blame on the youngster. Some years past, Benjamin Bloom, a noted educator, provided such a pretext when he confidently advised, "[F]rom conception to age 4, the individual develops 50% of his mature intelligence; from ages 4 to 8 he develops another 30%; and from ages 8 to 17, the remaining 20%. We would expect the variations in the environments to have relatively little effect on the IQ after age 8."[5] Reviewing Benjamin Bloom's authoritative nonsense, author-scholar Thomas J. Sergiovanni observed that during the 1970s, a time when school-related exceptionality experienced its greatest growth, "Some principals and teachers welcomed [Bloom's opinion], seeing within it a legitimate excuse for their own [poor] results. After all, they reasoned, the research shows clearly that poor student performance is linked to conditions beyond control of the school."[6]

The leader-principals I met in Tucson did not roll over and play that game. They focused instead on their students' entering skills, not on some valueless supposition of an individual's irreversible IQ (score) that somehow rendered school personnel impotent. To these principals, all children were exceptional. To these principals, all children could learn. Authoritatively imposed limitations on children's futures were unwelcome. Cyril Burt and his abhorrent lid were never invited to their parties.

Dedicated as they were, these principals faced serious problems providing assistance to many of their needy students. They recognized that special education's vehicle for providing services to these children, the discrepancy-eligibility model, was an expensive, time-consuming, and grossly ineffective process. They watched special education teachers and school psychologists spend hours trying to adhere to federal and state guidelines that had little bearing on the child they were assessing. They witnessed the deplorable situation in which a child was allowed to slip further behind in his studies in order have a large enough discrepancy so that future services might be assured. They saw special educators do whatever was necessary to get a child help, including documenting the presence of a disability even though none could ever be found. They observed special education and regular education split into isolated camps, straining sometimes toward an us and them mentality. They learned that money, rather than need, was the fulcrum upon which eligibility-decisions rested.

These principals were ripe for change. When they were informed that a noncategorical, nonpathological, nondiscrepancy model existed, that it had successfully passed a brief trial run, that it was theirs if they were interested, they greeted the news with great enthusiasm. That enthusiasm waned not a ripple when they were advised that the model, by federal standards, bordered on being a tad illegal. Nor were they daunted by an understanding that some of their own schools' teachers and psychologists would find the model disturbing, perhaps offensive, for it required the shedding of old skin and the growth of new roles and skills. The principals, nevertheless, remained steadfast in their support. They were willing to challenge an educational system they believed was no longer acceptably serving its students.

FOCUS: CHALLENGE

It was a dynamic Denver principal who set this experimental, nondiscrepancy model's wheels into motion. At a summertime lunch near the foothills of the beautiful Rocky Mountains, some 3 years prior to my working for the desert school district, the experimental program's developing components were described to her. She understood that the model did not have its own energy system, that it was not like a pill that once swallowed required its recipient only to rest quietly while the magic compound worked its cure.   There was nothing quiet about the program. Since the education of ever-changing, diverse children was its focus, it required constant action and energy, constant redrafting and re-vamping. It demanded an active leader who was manager, teacher, and cheerleader, the rudder my father-in-law said was essential to keeping a vessel on course. That remarkable Colorado principal, Susan H., heard what she wanted. Before the meal ended, she offered her school and personal commitment.

NOTES

1. Sergiovanni, T. J. (1995). *The principalship: A reflective practice perspective*. Boston: Allyn and Bacon.
2. Behling, Jr., H. E. (1984). *The effective school.* Monograph #10, The Maryland Association of Teacher Educators, p. 13.
3. Brundage, D. (1979). *The journalism research fellows report: What makes an effective school?* Washington, DC: George Washington University.
4. Barth, R. (1990). *Improving schools from within.* San Franciso: Jossey-Bass, p. 211.
5. Bloom, B. S. (1964). *Stability and change in human characteristics.* New York: John Wiley, p. 64.
6. Sergiovanni, T. J. (1995), p. 145-6.

13

BRKTHRU

We can whenever and wherever we choose successfully teach all
children whose schooling is of interest to us. We already know
more than we need in order to do this. Whether we do it must finally depend on how we feel about the fact that we haven't so far.[1]

The project originally named BRKTHRU took its germinal step on a schoolday
in the mid-1980s, not long after a kindergarten teacher quite comfortably referred
more than half of her class for special education eligibility evaluation.
Apparently the children's writing skills were viewed by their regular classroom
teacher as underdeveloped. Rumor had it that the school's principal, on hearing
of the multi-referrals to special education, went totally ballistic. Reverberations
from her punctuated words, like an air-borne tsunami, rumbled all the way to the
doors of the State Department of Special Education. Reacting to the dynamic
principal's insistence that the referral system was a gorilla out of control, the
state's assistant director met with the State Association of School Psychologists
prior to their national meeting in Chicago, challenging them to develop over the
next 12 months a system different from the traditional discrepancy-eligibility
formula for determining which children would be served by special education.
As that planning year came to a close, the assistant director called a status
meeting attended by the initiating principal, several school psychologists, a
small number of school district administrators, and a special education colleague
and friend of mine from the University of Denver. My role at the meeting was
that of an invited guest rather than participant. That changed, however, once the
principal and I began to exchange ideas about using assessment for instruction
rather than for eligibility. Before long, the determined woman and I were having

lunch near the foothills of the Rocky Mountains where quite confidently she planned what I would be doing for the next six months.

BRKTHRU'S PLANKS

A few days after that lunch, the principal and I met with her school's full-time and part-time special education staff to describe the project's basic goals and foundations. Not unexpectedly, their reactions to what they heard varied, but this principal had nurtured such a thoroughly trusting relationship with her faculty that once most of her staff realized their concerns would be heard, they listened intently as she and I introduced a list of unpolished components. Productive problem solving quickly replaced the staff's initial skepticism. By the conclusion of our second meeting, we had agreed that the project named BRKTHRU would accomplish the following:

1. Provide immediate help to as many enrolled students as possible with whatever classroom work was creating difficulties

2. Provide immediate assistance to all regular education teachers who were experiencing difficulties with their students' academic assignments and classroom behaviors

3. Make available many professional people within a school to offer immediate, direct support to both students and their teachers

4. Accomplish the above without the use of an ability-achievement discrepancy model, a formula-driven eligibility model, or categorical labels

Further, we determined the following objectives:

5. The project was to be a regular education program, available to all students regardless of their entering skills or academic needs. A student's enrollment in school would be the only prerequisite needed to receive additional educational services offered by school personnel. The project was *not* a special education program designed only for special education students;

6. The project's etiological stance was nonpathological and noncategorical. A student's academic difficulties would not be assigned to or explained through his or her neurology. Such constructs as learning disabled, mild mentally retarded, and gifted and talented, would not be used to describe or group students;

7. The project held that school curricula and classroom strategies were culpable and modifiable. Causes for academic problems would not be placed within a child or on the shoulders of the child's teachers;

8. The project's staff would be problem directed and solution oriented.

SUPPORT NEEDED

We recognized quickly that our efforts alone would not produce the ends we sought. Support from a number of sources would be critical, not just to the program's success but to affording it a beginning. In truth, obtaining the needed support from the following sources seemed a daunting task.

Support of the School District's Special Education Director

The project was an instructional, rather than a referral, program. Therefore, during the school's academic year, no new referrals to special education were anticipated. Since eligibility was not a prerequisite to special education services, a formal referral process was unnecessary. At the same time, the more traditional special education referral process would be available for needed exceptions:

1. Youngsters whose parents chose not to participate in the program

2. Youngsters transferring from other schools with an individual educational plan (IEP) the parents wanted maintained

3. Youngsters whose parents insisted on a formal eligibility hearing when an academic difficulty arose

The program's departure from traditional guidelines governing which children could be seen by special education personnel, as well as the anticipated absence of new special education referrals, would necessitate approval from the district's special education director.

Support of the State's Division of Special Education

Since it was likely that no new special education referrals would be made during the school year, the school district would suffer a loss of revenue from the state, money intended to help the district with its special education costs. Less money could translate into fewer special education positions at the school, severely reducing the number of support personnel available to the children and regular education teachers. Since support personnel were an essential key to the program's success, reduction of state monies could doom the program before it started. State support was mandatory. (The State of Colorado did support the program. It generously provided a waiver to the participating school district for the experimental school year, thereby postponing the very real problem that fewer special education children referred would lead to fewer special education staff. State support was one thing, of course. Everyone involved in the project recognized that special education funding rules at the federal level would need immediate changing. Continued insistence on tying together dollars and numbers of identified special education children was not programmatically sound or cost-effective.)

Support from General Education Teachers

It was clearly recognized that not all general education staff would welcome the program enthusiastically. Initial involvement in BRKTHRU would be voluntary. Those who wished to participate would assume responsibility for the education of all their assigned children regardless of entering skills. The general teacher would initiate, accommodate, and oversee educational interventions for his or her pupils. If assistance with a youngster was desired, the general teacher needed only to ask. General teachers had their principal's assurance that they would receive immediate help devising, accommodating, and evaluating programs from an array of professionals.

In place of referring children for eligibility assessment, as if special education was a distant rehabilitative summer camp to which difficult children were sent, general teachers were expected to request program assistance from BRKTHRU's resource team. Special education no longer allowed itself to fall into a position of providing regular education respite care or a safety net.

Every effort would be made to help all regular teachers embrace the new service delivery system. However, if a general teacher felt uncomfortable with the new format, it was expected the teacher would find a position elsewhere in the district come the following school year.

Support from the School's Principal

The principal (and assistant principal if one were available) was expected to spend significant time in each participating teacher's classroom, evaluating the teacher's efforts and noting what additional supports the teacher might need to further enhance the students' growth. The principal would need to inform the students' parents of the program, allay whatever fears they might hold, interpret their concerns, answer their questions, and ultimately seek their full cooperation. The principal would be expected to provide the same clarification for the district's other principals, assistant superintendents, and administrators who expressed curiosity or apprehension about BRKTHRU's principles and purposes.

Support of Students' Parents

Parental cooperation and consent were critical to the project's success. The school's entire staff would need to help parents understand the benefits their children would gain from the "service as needed" program. Several evening meetings would be required to explain the project's format and to answer the parents' expressed concerns and questions. It would be made perfectly clear that the traditional referral/eligibility process would be available to any parent who preferred those means of obtaining special education assistance. The project's format was such that any parent could choose to sit on the sidelines and watch everything unfold before making any decision about their child's participation.

Support of Special Education and Other Professional Staff

Special education staff, including teachers, psychologists, social workers, counselors, and accompanying therapists, would need to commit themselves to the program. Realistically, there was no program without them. Most special education personnel would find the project's theoretics familiar and comfortable. Inservices would be presented to explain the program's rationale and benefits. It was expected that all special education staff at the school would fully endorse the project and work earnestly to bring about its success. If the program was not to their liking, special education personnel would be assisted immediately in finding a non-BRKTHRU school within which to work.

ASSESSMENT FOR INSTRUCTION

Once the program's planks were fashioned, our attention turned to the question of instructing, or inservicing the school's educational staff. We met together and discussed the type of assistance teachers would receive and how that assistance was to be obtained. We spoke of the role and rights of parents: Did they need to agree to have their children part of the program? How would a child with an IEP be handled? Each time we presented an inservice to the teachers, we learned how to present better. But of all the many inservices provided to the teaching staff of that first experimental school, the most critical explained the project's basis for educational assessment. In the early days, as today, assessment was the project's major focus. Its purpose was simple and straightforward. It was used for instruction and subject-area accommodation. It was assessment directly tied to classroom curriculum, specifically targeting reading, writing, and mathematics. The bulk of the curriculum-based assessment[2] was to be initiated, directed, and most often administered by regular classroom teachers. Assessment, the gathered teachers were informed, was used to determine precisely the difficulty level of reading, writing, or mathematics students had reasonably mastered . The school's teachers were provided with the term "present performance level."[3] This present performance level (PPL), they were told, represented what a student seemed able (and willing) to accomplish at or near 100% accuracy at the time of assessment. The PPL would pinpoint students' instructional levels in mathematics, reading, and writing. Most importantly, the PPL measurement would lessen the chances of a curriculum mismatch, of asking too much or too little of the students.[4] The PPL, the teachers learned, represented a student's academic entering skills, a measure significantly more valuable to them than a student's age, grade level, or intelligence quotient. Among the experimental staff, those who were already committed to providing assistance to all students on an as-needed basis appeared comfortable with the new assessment position. (A note of interest and appreciation: The experimental school's Ph.D. school psychologist, knowing his responsibilities were to change dramatically from speculating on IQs to assessing something meaningful, spent the program's first summer at the local university boning up on the direct assessment of

students' reading skills. His commitment and dedication offered us all added assurance that the program would succeed.)

REFERRAL PHILOSOPHY

Even when the program first began in Colorado, few of BRKTHRU's tenets
were ever original. "The importance of attempting alternative interventions in
regular classrooms with students who [were] experiencing mild behavioral and/or
learning problems [had] been widely acknowledged."[5] Connecticut's State
Department of Education was already administering a similar program called
"Early Intervention Project: Alternatives to Referral." Authors John Salvia and
James Ysseldyke provided the following explanation of the Connecticut project:[6]
"Connecticut has a special project called the Early Intervention Project:
Alternatives to Referral, initiated in 1985, to address the misclassification of stu-
dents as disabled...The project is designed to assist teachers in intervening early
when students experience difficulty, in an effort to alleviate problems."

Q: What is the Early Intervention Project: Alternatives to Referral?

A: The Early Intervention Project (EIP) is an innovative effort initiated by
    the Connecticut State Department of Education in 1985 to address the
    misclassification of students as disabled. Since 1985, five urban dis-
    tricts and participated...Nonurban districts have also joined the project
    over the past several years....Ten additional school districts partici-
    pated beginning with the 1991 to 1992 school year. Since 1988, the
    EIP has been administered by the Special Education Resource center
    (sic) (SERC)....Participation is voluntary based on cooperation be-
    tween the local district and SERC. The project primarily addresses two
    emerging issues in special education : (1) the apparent overrepresenta-
    tion of minority students in certain categories of special education and
    (2) the increasing numbers of children being inappropriately diagnosed
    as disabled and placed in special education. The project also represents
    an initiative to more effectively integrate programs and services be-
    tween general and special education.

Q: What is the purpose of the Early Intervention Project: Alternatives to
    Referral?

A: The Early Intervention Project is designed to provide classroom-based
    services for at-risk students, primarily minority students, experiencing
    academic or social/behavioral problems. These classroom-based ser-
    vices are provided prior to...referral to the Planning and Placement
    Team for possible placement in special education. It provides early re-
    ferral and intervention that focus support in the regular education class-
    room.

Q: What outcomes can districts anticipate from participation in the
    Project?

A: Through long-term training and ongoing technical assistance provided by SERC, districts involved in the Project will

develop a systematic intervention process to be initiated by the regular classroom teacher or others seeking assistance for students experiencing academic or social/behavioral problems;

establish a non-special education building team specifically trained to assist classroom teachers in designing alternative strategies within the least restrictive environment of the regular classroom;

develop least biased, nonstandardized assessment techniques that provide information about the student's performance in the specific curriculum and within the specific classroom placement.

As a point of interest, other states have developed programs that mirror BRKTHRU and Connecticut's models and philosophies. The following is an excellent posting from the Internet.

An Iowa Experience

Iowa is in the midst of trying to rework the way we go about special education. Each AEA (Area Education Agency, intermediate service provider) and each school district has been given permission to develop their own special education plans. As long as they met certain criteria, there is fairly wide latitude. Because of this, many of the AEAs operate at least somewhat differently. I can describe my current situation, but the details may differ elsewhere in the state.

In a nutshell, we are using a functional assessment process to arrive at a noncategorical diagnosis. The details get fuzzy and frustrating, but the concept is delightful. Pre-referral interventions are all but mandated. Each school building is assigned a "building representative" from the support team (psych, social worker, sped consultant, speech/language pathologist). That person is expected to attend and participate in the child study meetings. Parent involvement is strongly encouraged from the beginning. As schools find out that most parents don't bite, we are beginning to see more success with home/school interventions.

If interventions are not successful, or circumstances indicate that immediate referral is needed, a referral is generated, but only through the child study process. The referral is supposed to focus on questions that lead to interventions. The evaluation team divides up the questions and each member does what ever they need to [do] to gather the information to answer the questions. This requires good team communication, and softening of cross-discipline boundaries.

Rather than do the old WISC/Woodcock-Johnson dance by the numbers ["Ability-Achievement" discrepancy formula], the assessments are authentic, performance based, and real world in nature. We always interview teachers and parents, and usually students. We collect current performance data from the teacher, including grades, review of permanent products, and curricular assessments. Standardized testing is conducted if needed, not just because there is a referral. I have only found the need to use an IQ test about ten times this year. Standardized academic assessment is usually done. If schools have CBM [Curriculum Based Measurement] norms we use that data as well. Reports and staffings tend to focus more on student needs and interventions and less on scores and qualifying.

For the most part I think the change has been very positive. I find myself much more focused on understanding the student's learning processes and less on rules and disability identification. The down side is, it's all new and pretty confusing. Recall, if you will, the first year on the job, and the bewildered feelings trying to get a gasp on all of the rules and procedures. At least there were others around who had experience with the same system. In this instance, everyone has been learning at the same time. It has been hard to break habits and old ways of thinking. It has been even harder to develop new ones. At least with the old way I knew I needed to observe and schedule an IQ. Now, there are times that the only data I gather is through teacher interviews and mining the teachers' gradebooks. The tasks of each evaluation are more variable, and I have to do more thinking and planning than before. (Honestly, how much thinking is necessary for: IQ + WJR/discrepancy formula = qualify.)[7]

As with the Connecticut and Iowa models, BRKTHRU's insistence was that assessment be for classroom instructional purposes, and that a close match exist between teachers' classroom curriculum and students' academic entering skills. These were principles already embraced by scholars throughout psychology and special education.[8,9,10,11] And the professional literature had long been filled with numerous calls and thoughtful rationale for using direct interventions in regular classrooms prior to formal eligibility assessment for special education.[12,13] The goals of this *prereferral* process, in part, were to reduce unnecessary referrals to special education, and to guard against misidentifying students as having disabilities.[14, 15, 16]

The Flaw With Prereferral

From its beginning, however, BRKTHRU rejected the logic and implementation of a prereferral process, as if that process represented a conspicuous rung on a ladder of options for school personnel. The term "prereferral" implied the availability of an A team (most likely a prized special education resource teacher), waiting in a back room of a school, ready to venture forth if a first wave of cavalry failed with their mission to help a struggling child and his or her teacher. It was as though the big gun could be called on if first, second, and third tutorial efforts proved futile. Sort of a safety net to a safety net.

Eligibility as Prerequisite to the A Team

The obvious goals for prereferral were appealing: reduce unnecessary special education evaluations and misidentifications. A less obvious but more important goal for the prereferral process was to help regular classroom teachers maintain responsibility for a struggling student with learning or behavior problems. If a prereferral team helped both student and teacher to succeed in the classroom, everyone benefited. If, however, the consulting team's prereferral efforts proved unsuccessful, the team and its school were provided an alternative, identifiably different option: conduct time-consuming and expensive eligibility testing so special education services could be sought.[17] The eligibility testing, of course, would not provide any instructional value, but that was not its purpose. Why was access to special education pursued after the prereferral team's efforts proved unsuccessful? Presumably, special education was seen as having the expertise to provide solutions to the student's (and teacher's) problems. If that is the case, the fair question gnaws: Why wait to use it? Why offer a student and his teacher access to the A team only if prereferral consultation fails?

Non-Eligibility

Since eligibility for special education was not an issue for BRKTHRU schools, prereferral and ability-achievement testing associated with eligibility were without purpose or value. BRKTHRU's referral team was its school's entire staff, including certainly its highly trained special education personnel. Every teacher and student had immediate access to the school's A team the moment a classroom problem was observed. BRKTHRU schools had no back rooms where talented professionals were called on only when a prereferral team's efforts proved inadequate—often because the prereferral team, no matter how motivated, lacked effective treatment skills.[18] Instead, all of BRKTHRU's professionals, including but not limited to school psychologists, school counselors, social workers, itinerant and full-time therapists, principals, assistant principals, curriculum specialists, librarians, diagnosticians, psychometricians, dietitians, and special education resource people, were always "on call." For BRKTHRU, prereferral as an intermediate often obligatory step to special education was unnecessary.

BRKTHRU'S EARLY OUTCOMES

Thanks to many hardworking, optimistic people—regular educators and special educators—BRKTHRU's initial efforts at the principal's school were successful. Said somewhat differently, the program survived and even experienced a bit of flourish. A second decisive principal from an unusually arranged integrated city school, serving some 300 kindergarten, third, fourth, and fifth-grade youngsters, heard of the program during an evening university lecture. Frustrated and angered by failed efforts to secure special education assistance for many of her students whose reading and math skills were dreadfully below grade level, she jumped at the opportunity to introduce a noncategorical, noneligibility system to her school. (It seemed many of her students' IQ scores were quite low. The district concluded ignorantly that the children were accomplishing as much as their potential allowed, therefore additional help for the children—and their teachers—would be fruitless. Cyril Burt's lid-business and all that rot.)

Unfortunately, the majority of the K, 3-4-5 regular staff balked at assuming more responsibility for assessing and accommodating their students' strengths. The principal, thankfully, was blessed with a truly outstanding special education teacher whose tiny resource room, already filled to the rafters with children who wanted to learn, was now made available to endless rows of needy kids. Additionally, her assistant principal, nothing less than pure cream, rose to the top of the adopted project and carried most of the administrative part on her diminutive shoulders. The principal, who weeks earlier had seriously threatened an assistant superintendent with her sabered finger if he failed to support her efforts on behalf of her kids, took comfort in knowing that her small school, after only one year of the "service-as-needed" program, was one of the very few city schools that did not show a decrease on citywide administered standardized tests. It was a small victory, at best.

While other schools in the area knew of the program, most, for their own considered reasons, looked away. A school north of the city, however, grabbed BRKTHRU's essence. The school's principal saw the benefits and adopted a variation of the program, despite receiving less than enthusiastic support from his special education director. This principal, with a zest and personality that were unignorable, closed his office for some 90 minutes (daily, I believe) to teach math to his fifth and sixth graders. With his very cooperative regular staff, he saw to it that all his students were challenged successfully at their individual entering skills. You walked from his school knowing his students' education was in good hands.

PRINCIPAL POWER

It should not go unnoticed that all three schools mentioned above, quite different in size, geographic location, and student demographics, shared the same bright beacon that lit up all manner of opportunities for staff and students. Each had the Rudder, the dynamic, intrepid leader, willing to journey upstream. Those principals were very much appreciated by all of us who believed BRKTHRU was worth the fight.

ABSENCE OF CONTROLLED DEPENDENT VARIABLES

During the early days of BRKTHRU, no thought was given to formalizing the dependent variables that would ultimately be needed to assess BRKTHRU's success. Instead, we choose indices we thought important, even if they did not lend themselves to experimental control. With some license, therefore, we considered our initial efforts to be successful. Our findings included the following:

1. Enormous numbers of diverse children with a wide variety of entering skills were contacted by and received assistance from their schools' BRKTHRU teams. Prior to the program's inception, only 5% to 10% of a school's population might have benefited from extra assistance with math, reading, or writing difficulties—those numbers fixed by special education's eligibility formula. Once BRKTHRU was adopted, the number of children assisted by the school's referral team rose above 60%. Under BRKTHRU, the number of children assisted is limited only by the amount of staff available to serve on the BRKTHRU teams.

2. Many regular teachers received assistance with children almost immediately after requesting such. Prior to BRKTHRU, a regular teacher might have waited months before receiving assistance with a particular child—assuming the child was found eligible for assistance.

3. Many regular teachers acquired or reacquired assessment skills, allowing them to assume more responsibility for their struggling students. Prior to BRKTHRU, many general teachers continued to hold the notion that special education would come to save them. With BRKTHRU, the net was available, but not as a respite. Now it was instructional.

4. Under- and over-identification and false positives and negatives, became obsolete. Those oft-mentioned educational cracks, if not closed, were at least narrowed to where the edges just about touched.

5. There was less negative talk about kids. More time was spent discussing strategies rather than speculating (or concluding) that a child's academic struggles were due to some intrinsic, neurological disability.

The Colorado experience, brief as it was, had provided an opportunity for BRKTHRU's launching. It appeared as though everyone had survived its entrance into the educational waters. The inevitable uncertainty common to beginning programs everywhere had come and gone without fractures, bruises, or anything requiring an apology. Those of us who had lived with BRKTHRU for the longest time learned that if everything necessary coalesced, BRKTHRU would work: It would provide children and teachers with classroom assistance, almost immediately. It would do so without cumbersome formulas or poorly fashioned eligibility models. Planned and unplanned staff changes, a factor of enormous proportions to any education program, influenced the Colorado school's course. Regardless of the experimental school's chosen direction, much had been learned. The experience ensured BRKTHRU's enduring spirit. A year or so after I left Colorado for Arizona, the project surfaced again in the desert Southwest. Once more a dynamic principal brought it to life.

CACTUS FLOWER

The desert's school system's efforts at helping its struggling schoolchildren and its dedicated general education teachers were hardly different from other school districts where strict eligibility formulas and ability-achievement discrepancy models blindly ruled decision making. The district's river of referrals (with its inevitable false positives and negatives) was as contentious and overflowing as most any school district found throughout the United States. Few psychologists, social workers, and diagnosticians I worked with in my new position in the desert appeared satisfied with special education's formal (flawed) referral system. Most, however, seem resigned to its existence in perpetuity .

It is remarkable though, how easily forever can change. BRKTHRU reemerged under circumstances similar to those that gave it birth in Colorado. An Arizona elementary school principal I was meeting with one morning was bemoaning the steady, growing stream of students being referred by general education to special education, as well as the numbers of stumbling students being refused services because they failed to qualify under special education's strict, arbitrary formulas. The principal's frustrations flashed and hissed like an angry cobra. I had seen such rage and exasperation before. "If you're interested in a different approach to providing services to your students, let me know," I said mainly out of habit, casually walking toward the door of her office. Her furious words, like a recoiling cowboy's lasso, headed me back to the edge of her desk. Her interest was pointed; her concerns urgent. I did not contain my excitement. With the help of sympathetic colleagues, I began to develop a working paper that described the project. BRKTHRU, a close cousin to the Colorado model, came to her school within the month.

BRKTHRU: CIRCA 1992-1993

Between my conversations with interested principals throughout the desert district and an active professional underground communication network, other school staffs became aware of the experimental program. They discovered that it was strongly supported by the district's director of Exceptional Education and that a school that adopted its format could provide services to schoolchildren without using traditional special education eligibility or categorical labeling. If little else, BRKTHRU stimulated a flurry of reactions to some of its more pronounced, identifiable features:

1 . Special education eligibility was not a prerequisite to students receiving assistance from special education resource personnel.

2 . Children were described and accommodated on the basis of their academic entering skills, not special education labels.

3 . Assessing students' academic strengths took precedence over assessing weaknesses. Classroom curriculum was to match what students could

do. Success was not defined by the achievement of a standardized, grade level goal established for an entire class of very diverse children. Success for a particular student was defined as growth beyond that student's present performance levels.

4. The model expected and was prepared to accommodate intrasubject variability (e.g., an individual student having vastly different present performance levels: PPL in reading—third grade; PPL in mathematics—first grade).

5. The model expected and was prepared to accommodate intersubject variability (e.g., many students in the same grade level class with different PPLs).

6. Grade-level retention was unnecessary. A student's curriculum was based on assessed PPLs, not on the students assigned grade level; matching curriculum to entering skills followed the student to the next class placement.

7. Children were not compared academically. Each child was compared against his or her own entering skills or PPLs. Differing classroom achievements among students were expected. Different pacing of curriculum for students was also expected.

8. Present performance level probes and academic accommodation began in kindergarten. Prevention was critical.

9. Professional job roles changed to meet classroom needs of students. Additional training with assessment methods was provided. All professionals were expected to provide direct services to students and general education teachers.

10. General education teachers were expected to assume responsibility for assessing students' strengths and accommodating their classroom curriculum to match those strengths.

11. Cross-grade and cross-age remediation throughout a school was expected. Students moved to different locations in the school (or within a classroom) where their PPLs were matched and challenged by curriculum. No student stayed in a classroom that provided no discernible benefit.

12. Student errors were considered invaluable and were documented and analyzed carefully by general education teachers and their special education consultants. Continual error analysis allowed those teachers access to their students' mechanical, conceptual, or motivational errors. Student errors indicated what curriculum accommodations were necessary for continued academic growth.

13. The model was emphatically nonpathological. Academic errors were due to curriculum mismatch and motivational issues, not to neurological dysfunction.

BRKTHRU IN OPERATION

The program's announced (and rumored) components raised many questions about its very implementation and acceptance both from parents and professionals accustomed to the more traditional special education delivery system. To help answer some of these questions, the developed working draft of BRKTHRU was disseminated to those Arizona district principals who requested further information. Principals were requested to discuss the contents of the working draft with their school staff and to develop questions and concerns that would later be addressed during a series of introductory inservices.

As was the case in Colorado, the draft met with decidedly mixed reviews. The materials were intended to stir the sediment of complacency with special education's eligibility system and general education's lackluster support for accommodating different learners. The materials accomplished this end.

• • • • •

BRKTHRU

A Program To Help Teachers and Students

WORKING DRAFT   WORKING DRAFT[19]

JUSTIFICATION

With large class sizes and diverse student entering skills, teachers' roles have become increasingly demanding and difficult. More students are presenting problems, and more of their problems require collaborative interventions. A system drawing on the combined strengths and resources of regular and special education is needed to provide the classroom teacher with easily accessible help for all students who might benefit from additional assistance. The present mandated eligibility system, which often requires a teacher to wait many weeks to learn whether special education help will be forthcoming, needs revising.

PROGRAM'S PURPOSE

BRKTHRU represents a collaborative effort between regular and special education to advance student competencies. The project has been designed as an instrument to provide immediate, direct services to all students and teachers who are experiencing difficulties succeeding at their classroom assignments. Specifically, any student whose educational growth is perceived unsatisfactory will receive instructional support and guidance from personnel within the student's school. BRKTHRU is designed to serve all students, at all levels of entering skills.

ELIGIBILITY REQUIREMENTS

No eligibility requirements other than being officially enrolled in a BRKTHRU school will serve as prerequisites to receiving assistance.   BRKTHRU is an error-driven, rather than a label-driven program: It will be a student's persistent difficulties with assigned classroom work, rather than an awarded exceptional label, that will initiate assistance.   Entering skill assessments (i.e., measuring a student's present performance levels in mathematics, reading, and writing), will take the place of traditional categorical assessment and "process-deficit" testing. In the proposed model, intelligence testing will be unnecessary.   Exceptions to this noncategorical assessment policy will be available on an as-needed, selective basis.

DIRECTING THE STUDENT'S ASSISTANCE PROGRAM

A student's regular classroom teacher, along with other designated school personnel, will direct and supervise efforts to assist the student.   The assistance can include whatever the school's collaborative team decides is needed for a particular student, including skill acquisition, concept formation, integration, and generalization. Academic competencies and difficulties, not age, grade level or developmental similarity with age-peers, will govern the type of assistance made available to the student.   A school's collaborative team, with major input from the regular education teacher, will decide

1. what specific classroom work in reading, mathematics, or writing warrants remediation;

2. what teaching methods will be used to provide assistance;

3. the location where the assistance will be provided;

4. the times during the school day when the assistance will be provided;

5. who will provide the assistance;

6. projected duration of assistance;

7. when applicable, which resource individual will work with a teacher's classroom while the teacher works individually with the student;

8. what data-gathering system will be used to evaluate the effectiveness of the employed teaching strategies.

SCHOOLWIDE CURRICULAR PROBES

BRKTHRU requires that school personnel have an accurate measure of all students' mastery levels in reading, mathematics, and writing.   This mastery level is referred to as a student's present performance level (PPL).   Students' PPLs will be measured by schoolwide criterion-referenced probes developed by various sources including classroom teachers, resource personnel, and curriculum specialists from the district.   Curricular probes can be conducted early in the school year prior to the beginning of formal instruction, or they can be initiated on an individual student basis when a student demonstrates difficulty with class assignments. Classroom teachers can conduct the probes or they can request assistance from the school's BRKTHRU resource team. (A probe-training packet will be made available to all school personnel.)

Probes will occur throughout the school year, on a schedule determined by the classroom teachers and support team members. They will be used to assess a student's progress and curriculum-fit. Probes will provide teachers with a clear indication of their instructional adequacy.

SUPPORT PERSONNEL

Not all district schools have equal numbers of available support personnel within their ranks. A school's principal will assume responsibility for assigning school personnel to serve on BRKTHRU's support team. All professionals assigned to the school, full-time and/or part-time, will be expected to become active members of the resource team to lend their expertise. These include all exceptional education teachers, psychologists, diagnosticians, social workers, speech therapists, librarians, counselors, integration specialists, physical and occupational therapists, vision and hearing itinerant professionals, and other specialized teachers and personnel assigned to the school (e.g., Chapter One, ESL, Reading Recovery, African-American Studies, Bilingual Program). To their ranks must come professional and paraprofessional support personnel from the school, including teacher assistants, monitors, art and music instructors, lab technicians, curriculum specialists, and administrators who will also be expected to provide direct assistance to classroom teachers and their identified students. BRKTHRU schools will need to be very creative in identifying their support personnel.

SPECIAL EDUCATION SUPPORT

A school's collaborative team will determine how best to use their special education support personnel. Special education professionals will offer a variety of services including consulting with classroom teachers, working with groups of multi-aged students, and providing direct interventions with specific students. Special education teachers and school psychologists may be asked to assume responsibility for an entire class, for brief periods of time, while the regular teacher conducts probes and explores new strategies with individual students. When requested, BRKTHRU staff will assist the school's teachers with developing alternative strategies for their students, as well as evaluating the effectiveness of the approaches they have chosen.

CROSS-GRADE/AGE ASSISTANCE PROGRAMS

Schools will be expected to make available cross-grade, multi-age assistance programs for its students. Throughout any given day, and for any length of time (both parameters to be decided by the collaborative team), students will benefit from content-specific and/or integrated thematic units presented by regular teachers in classrooms other than their own. These experiences will be offered to any student when regular education teachers have determined that a particular youngster might benefit from a second teacher's materials or exercises. This approach, found in multi-age and multi-grade classes, provides the needed flexibility to accommodate for an individual student's intrasubject, academic variability. As with many aspects of the BRKTHRU project, a school will need to evaluate its scheduling of course-content classes to accommodate for its students, particularly for those who are experiencing difficulties in its subject areas.

ASSIGNED SPECIAL EDUCATION PERSONNEL TO SCHOOLS

Several formulas are being considered for determining the total number of support personnel available to each school under the BRKTHRU project. The traditional formula has used a school's enrolled number of special education students in conjunction with consensus caps to determine the assignment of special education professionals to that school. Since BRKTHRU employs a noncategorical, nondeficit model foundation, a new formula is needed to determine an adequate representation of special education support personnel. During this upcoming experimental year, numbers of support personnel for a coming year will be the same as the number of support personnel assigned to the school during the preceding year. Exceptions to this formula, due to a school's special programs, special populations, or special needs, will be noted. An increase in the numbers of resource personnel made available to all regular classroom teachers in each of the district's BRKTHRU schools will be aggressively sought.

DATA COLLECTION

The following variables will be closely monitored during the school year. Not only will the obtained information be helpful to teachers and their students, it will provide state and federal regulators with data needed to evaluate the effectiveness of BRKTHRU.

1.   Percent of students attending school assessed through PPL probes

2.   Number of students receiving intervention by resource team

3.   Number of teachers receiving intervention by resource team

4.   Time elapsing between teachers requesting and receiving assistance

5.   Amount of time interventions were implemented, both for students and teachers

6.   Subject areas receiving assistance

7.   Growth over time (academic progress) of selected students

"EXIT" CRITERIA

BRKTHRU does not constitute a program which students attend. From that viewpoint, there is no formal entrance or exit criteria that governs students' movements. As indicated earlier, by the very nature of being enrolled in school, a given student is eligible to receive assistance. This assistance begins only after a classroom teacher, once observing the student having consistent difficulties with particular classroom assignments, requests additional help for that student. Support services, provided by the collaborative team, continues until the student's errors or difficulties have either been completely resolved or until they have decreased to a point where the regular education teacher believes further direct assistance is no longer necessary. For many students, this assistance will be short-lived, perhaps commanding no more than a total of a few minutes on a given day, repeated over several days (i.e., "space-trial learning") to facilitate remembering what was learned. For other students, assistance may be required for extended periods of time, perhaps for an entire school year. These last issues need further clarifying.

1. As soon as a teacher observes a student's reliable errors (e.g., a similar or exact error to the same question or exercise that occurs repeatedly), an immediate probe is taken to evaluate the student's PPL as it pertains to the material that appears to be creating difficulty. If the teacher requests assistance through BRKTHRU, assistance focuses on the student's identified errors. Successful remediation serves two purposes: a) the student learns the material that was conceptually difficult or confusing; b) the student's PPL changes, i.e., the student's entering skills improve. Unless the teacher chooses otherwise, the student no longer receives assistance under BRKTHRU until additional, reliable errors are once more exhibited.

2. A student may be served in his or her regular classroom with direct instruction provided by the classroom teacher; the student may be served in the classroom with direct instruction provided by a resource professional; the student may visit another teacher's class to receive instruction; the student may be served in a quiet site away from class, including a resource room, library, conference room, and so on. The collaborative team will determine which of the above options will best serve a particular student. Whichever option (or their combination) is chosen, supportive assistance provided to the student by personnel other than the regular teacher most often occupies a small percentage of a student's total school day.

TRACKING ISSUES

1. A BRKTHRU school may choose to provide assistance to a group of students who share very similar PPLs and who reliably commit the same academic errors.

2. A BRKTHRU school may choose to group together several students whose PPLs and academic error patterns are quite different from each other.

Such homogeneous and heterogeneous groupings may meet briefly or for extended periods of time for instructional purposes. Homogeneous groupings warrant additional discussion.

1. A student would remain in a homogeneous group only as long as his or her PPL matches the group's PPL.

2. The duration and frequency of homogeneous groupings is a school policy determined by its principal and teachers.

The following question has been raised by parents and teachers: "Might BRKTHRU create a homogeneous grouping of 'low achieving' students that would receive instruction together for an entire school year? Isn't this the same as tracking where 'ability' groups were always kept in the same room or program?"

While all of a group's students might have similar PPLs and commit basically the same type of errors, they only would remain together for brief periods of time during any schoolday. Most importantly, the vast majority of these students would "exit" the group as soon as their PPLs improved to the satisfaction of those professionals who provided assistance. If one student failed to exit the group, a reevaluation of the instructional methods being used by the team would be undertaken. Beyond the above, BRKTHRU would never use the term "low achieving" to describe students. Students are discussed in terms of their strengths, their ever-changing present performance levels or entering skills. Tracking, in the traditional sense, a product of intelligence testing, would be nonexistent under BRKTHRU.

PARENT COMPONENT

Every effort will be made to include parents in the BRKTHRU project. BRKTHRU's components will be clearly explained to all parents whose children attend the BRKTHRU school. Parents will be shown the value of the noncategorical, nondeficit model. They will be introduced to academic probes and error analysis. They will have the option of receiving frequent feedback from their child's teacher regarding their child's school performance. Further, if they choose, parents will be shown how to use probes and error analyses with their child's homework assignments.

STUDENTS WITH CURRENT OR REQUESTED IEP'S

The issues of IEPs and the BRKTHRU project have been raised by the following pertinent questions.[20]

Question A: What happens to a special education student enrolled in a BRKTHRU school?

Parents of students with IEPs attending a BRKTHRU school will meet with the school's collaborative team to learn of the advantages of the BRKTHRU project. (Private meetings will be arranged if parents request such.) The team will explain that for mildly involved students, special education in a traditional sense is not essential. The children will receive more services through BRKTHRU than through the traditional system. Further, the parents will learn that their youngsters' IEPs can be altered to "Supplemental Aids and Services" status. This change will accomplish several items:

1. It will allow documentation of consultation with a resource teacher.

2. It will allow the children to maintain their IEP.

3. It will allow the collaborative team to provide services not previously written on the document.

When a child leaves a BRKTHRU school, the IEP would go with the student to the new school. If that new school is not part of the BRKTHRU model, the school would change the IEP to reflect a change of services back the level of "resource."

On an individual basis, and with approval by the collaborative team, the school's psychologist will explain to the parents that while attending a BRKTHRU school, a child can be dropped completely from special education rolls without suffering any loss of school services.

Question B: What happens to a student enrolled in a BRKTHRU school who has not been evaluated for eligibility, who receives supportive services while attending the BRKTHRU school, and who subsequently moves to another school that is not part of the BRKTHRU project?

Every student seen by the BRKTHRU team will be provided with a folder or portfolio in which his or her work will be stored. The folder will consist of present performance-level information, examples of academic errors, repeated probes, successes and difficulties, along with a description of the BRKTHRU model. If a student leaves a BRKTHRU school to attend a non-BRKTHRU school, the following is envisioned: The student will carry the folder to the new school, providing the receiving regular education staff with invaluable information regarding the student's successes. Further, the folder will contain examples of methodologies tried at the BRKTHRU school, with evaluations of their success. When the student arrives at the new school, the regular staff can begin to provide assistance to the student on the basis of the accompanying PPL data. If the new school personnel choose to evaluate the student for special education services, they will have data from which to draw while awaiting the results of a traditional psychoeducational evaluation. The student's folder would contain information that would alert the receiving team of the amount of academic support the student received through BRKTHRU.

Question C: What happens if parents of a student who attends a BRKTHRU school wish to have a traditional psychoeducational evaluation of their child?

While the BRKTHRU staff will explain to the parents that a formal psychoeducational evaluation (e.g., WISC/Woodcock-Johnson) and determined categorical label (e.g., LD) do not tell the staff what general or specific curriculum assistance the student needs, the parents can request that formal psychoeducational testing be completed for their child. However, the parents will be reminded that by virtue of being enrolled in the BRKTHRU school, their child will be eligible for services without any psychoeducational testing. If the parents are uncertain as to the best choice for their child, they can decide to try the BRKTHRU system for a period of time to see if its results are satisfactory.

INSERVICES

[Note to the reader: Because the project's working draft contained many new (and potentially inflammatory) issues, a series of inservices were developed and presented to staff interested in the BRKTHRU program. The detailed explanations provided an effective forum for understanding how BRKTHRU could be refined and tailored to fit different student population needs. The topics included:

1.   Probes and Error Analysis

2.   What to Probe

3.   Yield to Results: What and When to Post-Test

4.   Obtaining Assistance

5.   Growth-Over-Time Charting

6.   Shaping Your School's BRKTHRU Program

7.   Scheduling Your Opening Week

8.   Levels of Commitment

Most often, a school's entire staff gathered for 3-hour blocks of time to listen and discuss the material presented. On occasions, smaller groups of teachers and special education personnel met together to discuss various BRKTHRU components, specifically their rationale and implementation in classrooms. Handouts, such as the following under the heading of Definitions, were provided to the staff during the presentations. The participants were asked to keep the materials from the inservices for reference and future discussions. The presentations were similar to the following.]

Topic: Curricular Probes and Error Analysis

Definitions

Probes are brief, specific assessment tests, written or oral, administered to your students. Probes are developed primarily from the curriculum you use in your classroom. For BRKTHRU's purpose, your curriculum probes are used to assess a student's present proficiency in reading, mathematics, and writing. Most often, your probes are administered with paper and pencil; they can be administered in large groups or with individual students. Probes will tell you what your students can do. Since

BRKTHRU is a nondeficit model, determining what a student can do is significantly more important than noting what he or she isn't doing.

Error analysis represents a method to determine the types of errors made by students as well as what curriculum factors most likely are responsible for their persistent occurrence. Most frequent errors are mechanical (those requiring only practice to overcome), conceptual and motivational. The term "miscue analysis" is a term often used in place of "error analysis."

Purpose

Curricular probes will help you identify your students' proficiency levels in reading, mathematics, or writing. This level is most often referred to as a student's present performance level (PPL). It is also commonly referred to as a student's mastery level or a student's level of entering skills. It is the level at which a student succeeds at or near 100% accuracy.

Curricular probes will help you determine the point at which your student's successful academic behavior in reading, mathematics, or writing begins to produce consistent errors.

Your probes will show you which skills and proficiencies your students bring to the classroom. Probes will also allow you to see what learning strategies a student uses to arrive at his or her correct or incorrect answer. Repeated probes will tell you how well your student is doing with your curriculum. They will tell you whether you need to revamp your curriculum for a particular student.

The Development of Probes

There are no hard, fast rules governing the development of probes. A piece of paper with a few strategically chosen math problems can be a very effective probe. Having a student decode a line or two from a paragraph can provide important information regarding the student's decoding proficiency. Asking the same student a few comprehension questions, calling for literal or inferential interpretations, can be equally helpful. Every time you request a student to write a sentence or two, you have conducted a writing probe.

So long as your academic probes assess your students' competencies (or PPLs), they will serve their purposes. Some schools have developed schoolwide probes for reading, writing, and mathematics that are to be used by all the school's teachers at the beginning of the year and throughout the school year on a schedule decided by the staff. Other schools have opted to have teachers develop their own probes to be used during the first few days of the school year. In some instances, schools have requested that their special education team develop probes for regular teachers to use. Other schools have considered using preprinted, standardized tests for probing basic readiness skills.

Who Administers Probes?

You and your colleagues will decide who will be responsible for administering the subject area probes. Eventually, classroom teachers will do the majority of the probing since they have the most up-to-date, accurate knowledge of their students' academic successes and difficulties. At any time, you can request assistance with probing from your school's resource team. In fact, your school may decide that various members of the resource team will assume responsibility for probing all the students. Deciding who administers the probes may depend on your school's decision as to when the probes will be administered.

When Are Probes Administered?

Probes generally are administered in one of two ways. The first option is to administered them schoolwide (or gradewide) during the first few weeks of the school year. This approach is the most effective for accurately matching your students to your curriculum. A second option is to administer probes at any time throughout the school year when students exhibits consistent errors or difficulties with classroom assignments.

If a school chooses to administer probes at the beginning of the school year, classroom teachers will administer most of the probes inside their individual classrooms during the first few days of school—with, of course, help from the collaborative or resource team if it is requested. If your school decides not to collect schoolwide probes, but opts to have probes administered when students begin to make consistent errors with class assignments, you and your BRKTHRU resource team will decide how that probing will be accomplished.

How Often Are Probes Administered?

Your school staff must decide what type of information they wish to gain from their probes, how they intend to use that information, and how they wish to share the findings among themselves and interested parents. Once those decisions are made, the frequency of administration can better be determined. Once PPL testing has been momentarily completed, probes are used to measure student progress, or "growth over time." You may wish to measure your students' growth daily or weekly through short classroom quizzes or exercises, written or oral. Some of the best probes occur as you are walking alongside a student in the hallway. Asking a youngster to identify a letter, number, color or concept printed clearly on a hallway poster can serve as a quick, fun probe of what you have been teaching. You can choose to probe selected students in your classroom either because they are struggling with their assignments or because you believe their entering skills are strong enough to warrant additional challenges.   A handy piece of paper and pencil will help you keep track of your student's response, both its content and the ease with which it was offered. An incorrect response, equally valuable, will tell you that more practice (or a better explanation) is needed.

Where Are Probes Administered?

General education teachers most often administer their probes inside their classrooms. With BRKTHRU, they can request assistance with this effort. If so, the probe can be conducted in the classroom or any other location within the school that is made available for such purpose. If resource people are requested to execute probes, a decision will need to be made as to where those probes will take place. Possible locations include a resource room, a corner of the school's library, or outside under a tree.

Error Analysis

Jean Piaget can be thanked for much that is good about education. Arguably, his most important contribution was his interest in and resulting research on the cognitive processes students use to arrive at their answers, both correct and incorrect. He believed we can learn most about the child (and thus how best to help) by investigating the basis for the child's responses and conclusions.

Probes lend themselves to immediate (and very easy) analysis of a student's errors. Asking one of your students to share how she arrived at her answer may provide you with what you need to develop innovative ways of helping the student work through some confusing academic requirements. Questions such as: "How did you arrive at your answer?" "What were you thinking about when completing the problem?" "Show me what steps you used to answer the question." can illuminate what skills and concepts a student possesses and has yet to acquire. Error analysis is pure fun, not to mention highly illuminating.

What to Probe

You should probe any activity, skill, or proficiency that you have introduced through your curriculum. You should probe any student's school-related effort you believe either needs improving or challenging. Probes of the following activities have been administered at schools using programs similar to BRKTHRU:

1. Mathematical calculations, conceptualizations, and functional generalizations

2. Reading, including decoding, comprehension, main idea identification, structural analysis, deriving meaning from context cues

3. Writing: word production, spelling, syntax, variety of words, punctuation, independent work

4. Clarinet playing

5. Reading maps

6. Shooting basketballs

7. Comparing and contrasting concepts

8. Identifying and writing letters and numbers

9. Identifying colors

10. Attention to and identification of detail

11. Sound discrimination

The list, quite literally, is endless. Any time you see a student exhibiting consistent difficulty with any subject area, a probe is in order. Think of what activity, skill, or proficiency you believe is impeding the student's progress. Note questions or assignments for which the student has no answers, or questions or assignments that produce consistently wrong answers. Your probe will offer some notion of how much of that missing component the student has acquired, as well as what experiences are needed.

While probing can be schoolwide, covering all basic subjects, it does not have to be such an extensive procedure. A single question, such as asking the student to explain how he or she arrived at an incorrect answer, may be a most fruitful probe. A request to write one sentence, to pronounce two similar (or dissimilar) words, to spell a few carefully selected words, to solve a couple of math problems involving only words, words and numbers, or only numbers can provide important information regarding a student's strengths and academic needs.

Yield to Results: What and When to Posttest

It is essential to posttest whatever you have probed. Your posttest will help you determine if your student has learned what you have intended. By analyzing the posttest, you will know if your methods are effective. Yielding to the results of your probe will reduce the chances of a poor strategy being repeated.[21] Frequently, the posttest probe will be identical to your original. Sometimes you will develop a slight variation. What your post-test measures (and what your post-test looks like) will depend on what you want to investigate. Did the student learn the concept that was confusing? Can she or he use it? Can she or he explain what previously was not understood? Can the student solve the problem, recognize the letter, word, number, or color, read the sentence, write the sentence, use a period, upper case letter, quotation mark, and so on?

You can posttest as often or as infrequently as best fits your needs. Ideally, you'll want to posttest soon after you've presented your student with a lesson (or exercise) intended to help with the troubling skill or concept. You will want to posttest again after some time has passed to see if the learning has been maintained.

You can, of course, do class-wide posttests on any subject or exercise at anytime. These probes can serve as "screening" tools for further inquiries.

Yield to Results: Change Curriculum

Once more, probes will provide you with an estimate of the effectiveness of your teaching strategies. Probing that reveals limited or less than expected scholastic progress is an indication to evaluate and perhaps alter teaching methods. BRKTHRU is an accountable program that relies on its ability and willingness to mend itself. If a student fails to progress, the cause is always the curriculum, never the child solely, and never the teacher solely. Accommodation is BRKTHRU's cornerstone. "Yield to results" is BRKTHRU's flag.

CLASSROOM ASSISTANCE

[Note to the reader: After the above information was discussed with the participants, the school's principal stood in front of the general education teachers and assured them they would receive direct assistance from a coordinated resource team composed of their colleagues almost immediately on its request. After being reminded of the frustration inherent in the traditional eligibility system, the teachers were shown how BRKTHRU would significantly reduce the down-time between their seeking and receiving assistance from the BRKTHRU team. The teachers were reminded that BRKTHRU was a schoolwide project utilizing the expertise of all the school's staff, that assistance would be on-going and readily available, nearly on a daily basis. The following specifics related to obtaining assistance with challenging children were presented:

1. *Receiving assistance.* A sign-up sheet with suitable space for dates, teachers' names, students' initials or developed identification codes, and brief, broad descriptions of problems (e.g., math difficulty) was posted in a prescribed location near the principal's office. Space on the sheet was available for teachers to indicate the best days and times for support personnel visits and observations.

2. *When to seek assistance.* A teacher could request help any time a concern arose. A student exhibiting and repeating the same or similar academic or conceptual error was sufficient justification for using the sign-up sheet.

3. *What to expect when assistance is requested.* The school had in place a team of staff personnel drawn from within the school's ranks who would provide a variety of services to its regular teachers. Within 48 hours of a request for assistance, a member of the support team would contact the requesting teacher to obtain specifics.

4. *What services could be provided.* BRKTHRU's intent was to place full responsibility for a student's scholastic program on the shoulders of the regular classroom teacher. With consultation and collaboration, the regular teacher would assume responsibility for determining the nature of services to be provided by BRKTHRU's team. Several options were available to the teacher who was experiencing difficulty with a student:

    1. With the student alongside, the regular teacher might choose to have the BRKTHRU team demonstrate the use of probes, including implementation and interpretation, in order for the teacher to improve his or her probing skills.

    2. The teacher might ask the team to take the youngster from the room and complete the probing process, returning with suggestions for curriculum accommodation. Eventually, the regular teacher would assume those responsibilities.

    3. The teacher, more as observer than participant, might choose to have the team work with the student in the classroom. Eventually, the regular teacher would change roles and become full participant.

    4. The teacher, having assumed full responsibility for assessing and matching curriculum, might choose to have the team directly observe teaching methods, offering advice as to their improvement.

Once the participating teachers understood they governed the type of assistance the team provided, they were reintroduced to the concepts of yielding to the results of their teaching efforts and to the importance of keeping a sharp watch for needed revisions in their classroom strategies if student achievement was less than the teachers hoped for. To that end, they were introduced to a charting system that would provide them with data necessary for evaluating student progress. The charts were called growth-over-time charts. The teachers were assisted with their possible use.]

Growth-Over-Time Charts

School_____   School Year_____

Student's Name	Month/Day	Subject Area/PPL	
			DATE (D) SCORE (S)
DATE (D) SCORE (S)	D S	D S	D S

Charting

The provided chart will enable you to monitor your student's growth over time with respect to the academic subject areas you are targeting. The chart has several boxes that should make data collection somewhat easier. Enter into the first box your student's name. Next write the present day and month. The third box will contain the subject area you are working on, specifically described (e.g., double-digit addition with regrouping, identification of lower case letters, use of periods and question marks). Enter your student's present performance level (PPL) with respect to the above skill. (This PPL measure is very important; it impacts how you will use the provided "Date/Score" posttest boxes. It would be best if the Subject/PPL box contained numbers representing your student's proficiency—number correct, reading level, percent correct, frequency of errors.) The final boxes will contain the date and score of your subsequent posttest probes. These data will represent your student's growth over time. The team will show you how to transfer data to a line graph. The number of data boxes used will depend on how long you work on an objective and how many times you probe your student's progress.

SHAPING A SCHOOL'S PROGRAM

[Note to the reader: It did not take long for school staff to understand they could fashion BRKTHRU to fit their school's needs and philosophies. They realized quickly they could begin BRKTHRU on a very small scale, perhaps limiting their initial efforts to kindergarten through second or third grade. To help them determine the direction they wished to take, the following information was provided.]

Developing the Program

You are a part of the experimental project titled BRKTHRU. While a few principles and guidelines will cut across all schools adopting the BRKTHRU philosophy regarding eligibility for additional academic services, each school has the option of tailoring its program to fit comfortably with its staffs' preferences and its students' needs. You and your colleagues will need several blocks of time to meet and decide how you wish BRKTHRU to work at your school. There are many different approaches you can use to organize these meetings.

1. You can meet in one large group to discuss your school's priorities, to keep a record of what decisions are made, and to decide, as a group, how BRKTHRU will be implemented on a daily basis,

2. You can identify which of the issues and questions presented below are important to you, and you can assign several of your faculty to meet in small groups to propose answers and present them at a later date to the faculty,

3. You can appoint a small, core group of faculty to assume responsibility for developing the BRKTHRU components that will be adopted by your school's faculty.

Questions and Issues To Consider

The following questions are intended as "advanced organizers" to help you and your colleagues with your group decision-making process. You might consider briefly discussing whichever of the following issues you believe to be important to your school. As you proceed, keep in mind BRKTHRU's major purpose: To provide immediate assistance to as many of your students as possible.

1. Do you want a specific role in developing BRKTHRU for your school, or do you want a core group of personnel to assemble the program and present options to you?
   COMMENTS AND PREFERENCES (C/P) _____
   _____

2. Do you want present performance level (PPL) testing administered schoolwide at the beginning of the school year? Do you want PPL assessment at grade level only? Would you prefer the assessment procedure to be administered by you, only for your students?
   (C/P) _____

3. Who will be included on your schoolwide resource team? Is membership voluntary or appointed? If appointed, who should assume responsibility for assigning roles?
(C/P)_____

4. Do you want the resource team, after consulting with each of you, to develop the probes to be used schoolwide or grade-level-wide? Do you want to develop the probes yourself?
(C/P)_____

5. Do you want to identify and/or prioritize your students in terms of academic needs at some time during the first few weeks (days) of school so that additional probes can be administered by the resource team (or yourself) as quickly as possible?
(C/P)_____

6. Do you want brief, flexibly scheduled, cross-grade groupings (based on PPLs and common errors) for math and/or reading and/or writing to be available to you and your students throughout the school year?
(C/P)_____

7. How do you want to communicate with your resource team? How do you want to ask for help for a particular student?
(C/P)_____

8. How would you like to schedule your resource team? Would you like them to decide, for example, that 3 days a week will be devoted to working with children in classrooms, leaving 2 days a week for programs to be held in resource room or other locations?
(C/P)_____

9. After one of your youngsters has been seen by a resource team member, what information would you like communicated to you by the resource personnel?
(C/P)_____

10. Would you like to reduce the number of children in your room at times during a week by sending advanced students to centers throughout the school covering a variety of challenging topics, allowing you time to work with students who need extra assistance with classwork already mastered by the advanced students?
(C/P)_____

11. If feasible, do you want one appointed resource team member to be permanently assigned to one or two grade levels (e.g., first and second grades, third and fourth grades)?
(C/P)_____

12. Would you like your staff inserviced on probes and error analysis procedures?
(C/P)_____

13. Would you consider having multi-age groupings in your classroom for purposes of presenting similar materials that would benefit different-aged children with similar entering skills? Do you have a preference for days and times?
   (C/P)_____

14. Would you like the resource team (and other school personnel) to offer study groups for multi-age students with similar PPLs, targeting specific topics (e.g., regrouping, main-idea, punctuation, spelling) that are selected on the basis of the frequency of academic errors as reported by you and fellow teachers? Are any days and times best for these brief study groups?
   (C/P)_____

15. Please identify any of your own particular academic (and nonacademic) talents that you would share with students other than those already enrolled in your own classroom.
   (C/P)_____

16. Would you like subject areas taught throughout the school at prescribed times during the day (e.g., reading at 9:00 A.M. daily)? If so, would you like to have multi-age/grade level groups formed on the basis of PPLs and common errors that would temporarily meet together during those prescribed times?
   (C/P)_____

17. What can you do to help the resource team see as many students as possible?
   (C/P)_____

18. What BRKTHRU information—program, progress, errors, PPLs, and so on—do you want communicated to your students' parents?
   (C/P)_____

19. If you have one, how do you want to use your child-study team? Will they be your resource team? Your BRKTHRU team? Who else will you add to that team? What will be their duties?
   (C/P)_____

20. Would you mind a suggestion and/or complaint communication box for information to be forwarded to BRKTHRU personnel?
   (C/P)_____

Scheduling Opening Week

Participating staff were then directed toward a series of options that would help them with the above school-shaping process. The options were intended to stimulate discussion centered around their collective commitment to BRKTHRU or to any programmatic change within their school that might require they alter their professional roles. The exercise proved very revealing: Many of the teachers and resource staff appeared quite comfortable, vocally siding one way or another with the project's tenets.

First Weeks

As with most components of BRKTHRU, you can tailor your opening weeks to fit your preferences. To provide you with some ideas to consider during your planning phases, several participation options are listed below:

Options

A. You can begin your school year as in the past. As an option, suppose you decide not to become involved in any gradewide or classwide academic probing during the first week or so of school. That decision makes BRKTHRU a purely error driven system. In other words, BRKTHRU would begin only after you have noticed one of your students having difficulty with whatever you are introducing in class. Having observed your student's errors or confusion, you can choose to enter your name on the "request for assistance" sheet. If so, a member of your resource team will be in touch with you as soon as possible, hopefully within 48 hours. You can decide if you want the resource personnel to provide services for the identified student within your classroom or at a different location. The above can be the extent of your involvement in BRKTHRU.
    C/P_____

B. A second option exists that also requires minimal involvement with BRKTHRU. On your own, you can administer individual probes in your classroom. You can decide if you want resource personnel to help you develop (or refine) your in-class probes to assess some of your more difficult students. You can prioritize and categorize your students in terms of needs, errors, and PPLs. You can decide in class which students need immediate help from resource personnel. You can decide whether you want help offered inside and/or outside your class. You can also decide that you would prefer no help from your school's resource personnel. Your commitment to BRKTHRU need not extend beyond the above.
    C/P_____

C. Your school may choose to have schoolwide probes completed by the end of the first week of school. If you wish to commit yourself to BRKTHRU, you can administer the probes in your class. (The probes probably will be developed through a joint effort of regular education and resource personnel.) You can send the raw data from the probes to the resource personnel for evaluating. At the first school-wide meeting, your resource personnel will report their observations and suggestions. (They will have a good idea of the numbers of children whose entering skills are at, below, or above grade level vis-a-vis reading, math, and writing.) You and your colleagues can then develop a school-wide plan to serve these children immediately. At a group meeting, your staff will need to discuss various options: employing multi-age groupings at times during the day or week; using brief homogeneous remedial sessions based on PPLs and common errors, and deciding, in general, which children will be seen first by the resource personnel. As a preventative measure, you can request your resource personnel to see as many of the children that you have identified as needy as soon as possible, perhaps in groups based on PPLs and common errors.

C/P _____

D. Grade level teachers can form their own groups. (Perhaps kindergarten and first grades will work together.) The groups will administer gradewide PPL probes in common subject areas. The groups can decide if they want multi-grade groupings, based on PPLs and common errors, during parts of the school day for each subject area. The teachers can ask the resource personnel for assistance in developing materials suitable for diverse PPLs in math, reading, and writing. You can decide which of your students' PPLs are sufficiently divergent to warrant additional assistance from resource personnel.

C/P _____

E. A Nonparticipation Option: Suppose none of the above options seem appealing. While you would not turn down assistance from your school's resource personnel, you would prefer not to be involved with BRKTHRU to any great degree. If your school is going to adopt the program, you would prefer that the major portion of the responsibility for its operations fall on the shoulders of the resource personnel, along with other regular education professionals. That option, similar to the first one presented, would likely appear as follows:

After spending the first few days of school developing their schedules, deciding how they will provide services to previously identified IEPed students, and determining who will be available to support regular teachers, your resource personnel will send out their schedules indicating the times, days, and locations assistance will be available to all teachers. Forms for referrals to the resource team will be attached. You will be notified which resource personnel have been assigned to specific grade levels. If you choose, you can prioritize your children in terms of needs and requests for help. Probes with your students will be conducted immediately by the resource team, after which your students will be assisted.

C/P _____

COMMITMENT

[Note to the reader: The participants recognized that BRKTHRU's success was tied to a school's level of commitment. The project had no magic, only potential. Commitment, therefore, was essential. To help the general (and special) education staff verbalize their positions, commitment options were without any gray areas. Every effort was made to support a teacher's right to refuse participation in the program. Extensive discussions centered around the staffs' willingness to be an integral part of the program.]

The following information is intended to clarify different levels of professional involvement, which regular education personnel may choose to assume while associated with a BRKTHRU school. At present, two levels of commitment exist:

I.   Observer/Participant—Regular classroom teacher primarily requests and receives assistance from resource team with little active participation in the process.

II. Collaborator/Initiator—Regular classroom teacher assumes major responsibility for probing, evaluating and accommodating for each student in class; uses resource team members as consultants.

Level I Commitment: Observer/Participant

1. Request assistance from resource team for a referred student

2. Request resource team to assess referred student's present performance levels through probes

3. Request resource team to analyze referred student's errors

4. Request resource team to develop action plans for referred student

5. Request resource team to provide direct services to referred student

Level II Commitment: Collaborator/Initiator

1. During the first week of school, assess all students' entering skills in mathematics, reading, and writing through present performance level (PPL) probes

2. Develop individualized curriculum on the basis of students' PPLs to accommodate significant differences in entering skills

3. Log student errors on a daily basis to determine academic progress

4. Execute in-depth error analyses on student errors that occur consistently

5. Request collaboration with resource team for purposes of:

    a. evaluating error analysis

    b. suggesting academic exercises

    c. assisting with direct services

       d. generalizing material learned if "pull-out" is used

       e. keeping growth-over-time data

6. Continue repeated PPL assessment and, when necessary, accompanying error analysis and academic accommodation

EARLY RESULTS

[Note to the reader: BRKTHRU's early results (real and hoped for) were predictable. On some days, BRKTHRU was a Swiss watch. On other days the project's pieces seemed covered in thick glue. On some days everything clicked. Other days, "clacked" was more accurate. BRKTHRU never achieved all that was intended. Drawing boards and playing fields contain a different number of dimensions. Despite its own inevitable system-variability, kids, tons of them, were seen and assisted by professional staff. Their exploratory and tutorial meetings were easily established without a paper trail clogging the machine. Pull-outs, as in permanent respite, were absent. As hoped, assessment most often was direct, functional, and applicable to the classroom curriculum. Cyril Burt's lid was dead. When the system clicked, IQ test kits remained on shelves, closed tightly. Likewise, standardized achievement tests were rarely administered. When they were, the standardized component intended to allow someone to compare children's performances were not used. When all was right, teachers used simple, easily administered probes to assess student achievement with curriculum, past, present, and future; statements made about children's entering skills and subsequent classroom achievements were more accurate, more reliable, more useful to teachers and the children's parents. Comparing children against their own progress became a priority. More general teachers took charge of their classes, seeking assistance but never a net. With some nudging from principals and supportive colleagues, wary teachers took important first steps. Those teachers who couldn't handle the fire left the kitchen.

Not everyone liked BRKTHRU, true, but not everyone likes chocolate ice cream either. Some days the towel seemed on the verge of being tossed in. Change for most of us is difficult.

BREAKTHRU: 1993 TO PRESENT

In addition to a change in spelling, Breakthru, during the latter part of 1993, came under the able guidance and mentorship of Rick Burch. Dr. Burch is a practicing school psychologist with a long and successful history of generating and implementing creative programs serving (often very difficult) school youngsters. While the mechanics of Breakthru remained basically unchanged, Dr. Burch's influence brought a vision and instruction that took the project to a higher level of meaning and potential. The following are his thoughts on Breakthru:[22]]

Visionary

Breakthru is one among a growing number of proposals which challenges educators to find more effective means of serving students and families. Breakthru emphasizes linking instruction with assessment, identifying effective teaching strategies, and maximizing school resources available for students. The recommendations offered by Breakthru can be used in a wide variety of educational settings and are not specific to any particular educational philosophy. Furthermore, Breakthru is compatible with many of the reforms being introduced throughout many schools. Breakthru is also sensitive to the ever growing demands placed on public schools. The ideas which follow are based on the assumptions that class sizes will remain large, student competencies will remain diverse, and schools will be expected to educate an increasingly heterogeneous population of students.

Instructive

Current practices in education involve the use of "valuative" assessment. Within a valuative assessment mode, students are tested periodically for the purpose of measuring group gains and judging multi-school performance. While these data provide some interesting information about groups of students, they are of little help in developing effective classroom instruction. Teachers need assessment information that helps them with the daily education of their students. Specifically, teachers need to be aware of what their students know and which educational methods are productive for which students.

Breakthru uses ongoing assessment as a part of each student's regular education program. Assessment assists teaching by assuring that instruction is timely and effective. Timely instruction ensures that students are academically ready to benefit from the material being presented.

By assessing a student's entering skills prior to instruction, and assessing learning on a regular basis during instruction, teachers can be certain that teaching begins and continues at the student's present performance levels.

Assessment also serves to evaluate the effectiveness of a particular instructional approach for an individual student. Since all teaching methods are not equally effective with all students, it is important to know when to change the strategies being used for a particular student.

Breakthru offers alternatives and/or additions to pull-out programs which can fail through the message they send classroom teachers. By identifying students as remedial, gifted, disabled, or slow and removing them from classrooms for part of the school day teachers are given the message that they do not possess the knowledge or resources needed to work effectively with students so identified.

Challenging/Alerting

It is expected that eventually, all teachers in Breakthru schools will be committed at Level II [Collaborator/Initiator—the classroom teacher assumes major responsibility for probing, evaluating and accommodating for each student]. Time must be set aside for the development of Level II collaboration in schools with mixed levels of teacher commitment. Left unchecked, Level I services [Observer/Participant—with little active involvement on the part of the regular teacher] will consume large amounts of available resources, leaving little time for effective collaboration.

> Note that it is expected that all teachers will comfortably embrace a Level-II commitment by the beginning of a Breakthru school's 3rd year of operation.

Materials

[Note to the reader: Mindful of the need for structuring Breakthru's components, Dr. Burch and his colleagues developed additional materials to make Breakthru schools more successful. Dr. Burch explains how, under the heading of "Opening Day," participants were offered guidelines.]

Opening Day

The first days of school will be filled with probing special education students, probing students in regular classes, and developing an effective communication system within your building. It is essential, however, that the following activities take place during the first week of school.

Day 1

> Send home parent consent form for each student registered in school. These forms are to be gathered by the school principal. Parents who do not return forms to school giving permission for their child to participate in Breakthru are to be contacted by the school principal or designated staff member for purposes of explaining the program to parents and requesting that the form be returned to school. Lists of parents granting and not granting permission are to be provided to classroom teachers as soon as possible. Note: Classroom teachers are still to notify parents verbally whenever they are requesting Breakthru assistance.

Day 1 through 3

> Parents of special education students are to be notified of a group meeting to explain Breakthru. The meeting should be held at a time convenient for parents. At least one evening meeting is recommended. The principal, special education resource teachers, school social worker, and school psychologist should attend the meetings.

Day 1 through 5

> Begin and complete probing special education students in goal areas on IEP.

Day 1 through 5

Begin and complete probing all students for curriculum fit.

Explanations of Forms

The following explanations are provided to assist you in developing specific forms you should consider using when initiating Breakthru in your school. The actual forms should be customized by your team to fit your school's populations and preferences. (I have provided an example of a parent consent form Dr. Burch used to gain parental permission.)

Student Referral

This simple form is to be competed by classroom teachers whenever they wish Breakthru assistance for a student in their classroom. It is imperative that parents be notified of this action at the same time the request is made. This notification is in addition to the Parent Consent obtained at the beginning of the school year. This form should include student's and teacher's names, grade level, subject area of concern (e.g., reading, writing, math, speech/language, motor, behavior), observations made, student's PPL in particular area, recommendations, if any, made by referring teacher, a signature line for parental notification of action, and a signature line with date for referring teacher.

Student Roster

This form is to be maintained by Breakthru support members (resource teachers, social worker, school psychologist, diagnostician, etc.) to document their responses to Breakthru referrals. This form essentially helps to keep track of the numbers of students seen by Breakthru staff, dates students were seen, and dates students were judged improved enough to no longer warrant Breakthru assistance.

Student Probe Record: Growth-Over-Time Chart

This form is to be maintained for each student receiving Breakthru academic assistance. This growth-over-time chart should keep a running record of PPL probes, specifically dates of the probes and their results. The results will essentially represent a student's new PPL.

Report Card Addendum

This form is to be completed by Breakthru support members and included with each quarterly report card sent home with the student. This form allows school staff to provide parents with valuable information regarding their student's progress.

Notification of Academic Assistance

This form is to be completed for each student withdrawing from school and is to be added to the student's cumulative file before being forwarded to the new school. The form provides staff with an opportunity to share with a child's new school what services, progress, and special accommodations were made while the student attended a Breakthru school. Most critically, this form can provide the new school with usable information that will immediately assist the school in creating a positive educational experience for the transferring student.

Letter to Parents

Parental consent and participation in Breakthru was an essential element from the project's beginning in Colorado. The full understanding of Breakthru's role as it pertained to their children had to be ensured. Nearly all the parents I spoke with over the past 10 years enthusiastically approved of Breakthru's purposes and methods. They were very willing to have their children become a part of the project. Dr. Burch sought their permission through the following letter:

Dear Parents,

We have been selected as one of several demonstration schools...to implement a new educational model (Project Breakthru) for students who need supplemental assistance at school. The new model combines the efforts of classroom teachers, special program teachers, support staff, parent volunteers, and administration to ensure all students receive the best education possible.

The new model is all-inclusive and provides specialized instruction for special education and regular education students. No standardized testing or special education labeling will be necessary in order for your child to receive help. This model will better serve children who are currently enrolled in special education and enable all students to participate in the program.

Classroom teachers, teacher's assistants, and volunteers will take part in this program to maximize each child's learning experience. You might see that your child is working within his or her regular classroom, with another teacher at that grade level, with a tutor, or with one of the special program teachers in the classroom. Children will also be attending classes in the learning center. Support staff including the school counselor, social worker, and school psychologist will be an integral part of the model and will work with the teachers, students, and parents to ensure that each child has the best year possible.

Your support is important and you are encouraged to become involved. In order for your child to be included in the program, please check one of the boxes below, sign, and return this form to school as soon as possible.

Sincerely,

Principal

_____   Yes, I approve of my child's participation.
_____   No, I do not wish my child to be included.

_____   _____   _____ _____

Parent signature   Student name   Date   Teacher

Parent Comments: _____

• • • • •

CONCLUSIONS

Assuming no glitches, the general education teacher who requested assistance for the student would be visited by a member of the Breakthru team quickly, without need for artificial justification, manipulated formulas, categorical labels, suggestions of pathology, or excruciating weeks of waiting. What a relief! For this writer, the project, even with its identifiable weaknesses, has always carried that ring from those early days when my fellow graduate students and later my professional practitioners and I were problem directed, solution oriented, and child focused.

While far from the utopia that scholar Wong[23] spoke of earlier, a "place" she feared was impossible, Breakthru succeeds in providing a service-as-needed option for all schoolchildren, their schools, and their parents. Its mechanics and heart are on the table.

NOTES

1. Edmonds, R. (1979). Some schools work and more can. *Social Policy, 9,* 28-32.

2. See James A. Tucker. (Ed.) (1985). Curriculum-based assessment: An introduction. *Exceptional Children, 52,* 199-204.

3. Macht, J. (1975). *Teacher/teachim: The toughest game in town.* New York: John Wiley & Sons.

4. Macht, J. (1975).

5. Will, M. C. (1986). Educating children with learning problems: A shared responsibility. *Exceptional Children, 52,* 411-416.

6. Salvia, J., & Ysseldyke, J. E. (1995). *Assessment.* Boston: Houghton Mifflin.

7. Hood, Connor. (1997, February 7). *An Iowa Story.* naspfor-L@uncg.edu, 13:11:28 -0600.

8. Marston, D., & Magnusson, D. (1988). Curriculum based measurement: District level implementation. In J. L. Graden, J. E. Zins, & M. J. Curtis (eds.), *Alternative educational delivery systems: Enhancing instructional options for all students* (pp. 137-172). Washington, DC: National Association of School Psychologists.

9. Reschly, D. J. (1987). Learning characteristics of mildly handicapped students: Implications for classification, placement, and programming. In M. C.

Wang, M. C. Reynolds, & H. J. Walberg (eds.), *The handbook of special education: Research and practice* (Vol. I) (pp.35-38). Oxford, England: Pergamon Press.

10. Reschly, D. J. (1990). Adaptive behavior. In A. Thomas & J. Grimes (eds.), *Best practices in school psychology* (2nd ed.). Washington, DC: National Association of School Psychologists.

11. Shinn, M. R., Tindal, G. A., & Stein, S. (1988). Curriculum based measurement and the identification of mildly handicapped students. *Professional School Psychology, 3*, 69-85.

12. Graden, J. L., Casey, A., & Christenson, S. L. (1985). Implementing a prereferral intervention system Part 1: The model. *Exceptional Children, 51*, 377-384.

13. Zins, J. E., Curtis, M. J., Graden, J. L., & Ponti, C. R. (1988). *Helping students succeed in regular classrooms: A guide to developing intervention assistance programs.* San Francisco, CA: Jossey-Bass.

14. Turnbull, A. P., Turnbull III, H. R., Shank, M., & Leal, D. (1995). *Exceptional lives: Special education in today's schools.* Englewood Cliffs, NJ/Columbus, Ohio: Merrill/Prentice Hall.

15. Ponti, C. R., Zins, J. E., & Graden, J. L. (1988). Implementing a consultation-based service delivery system to decrease referrals for special education: a case study of organization considerations. *School Psychology Review, 17*, 89-100.

16. Nelson, J. R., Smith, D. J., Taylor, L., Dodd, J.M., & Reavis, K. (1991). Prereferral intervention: A review of the research. *Education and Treatment of Children, 14*, 243-253.

17. Gutkin, T. B., Henning-Stout, M., & Piersel, W. C. (1988). Impact of a district-wide behavioral consultation prereferral intervention service on patterns of school psychological service delivery. *Professional School Psychology, 3* , 301-308.

18. Reschly, D. J., Robinson, G. A., & Ward, S. (1990). *Evaluation of the Iowa renewed service delivery system: Research report #1.* Des Moines, IA: Bureau of Special Education, Iowa Department of Education.

19. These materials were co-produced by many psychologists and special educators, most notably, Dr. Rick Burch, Tucson Unified School District.

20. Thanks to Dr. Betsy Bounds, Exceptional Education Director, (and Rick Burch) for assistance with this section.

21. King-Sears, M. E. (1994). *Curriculum-based assessment in special education.* San Diego, CA: Singular.

22. personal communication

23. Wong, B. Y. L. (1989). Concluding comments on the special series on the place of IQ in defining learning disabilities. *Journal of Learning Disabilities, 22*, p. 519.

Index

About the Author

JOEL MACHT currently co-coordinates certification and graduate programs in special education at Western Maryland College. He frequently consults in areas of direct student assessment, accommodation of curriculum, and special education services.

ISBN 0-89789-589-4

HARDCOVER BAR CODE